The World of Anne Frank:
A Complete Resource Guide

Betty Merti

J. WESTON
WALCH
PUBLISHER

Portland, Maine

User's Guide
to
Walch Reproducible Books

As part of our general effort to provide educational materials which are as practical and economical as possible, we have designated this publication a "reproducible book." The designation means that purchase of the book includes purchase of the right to limited reproduction of all pages on which this symbol appears:

Here is the basic Walch policy: We grant to individual purchasers of this book the right to make sufficient copies of reproducible pages for use by all students of a single teacher. This permission is limited to a single teacher, and does not apply to entire schools or school systems, so institutions purchasing the book should pass the permission on to a single teacher. Copying of the book or its parts for resale is prohibited.

Any questions regarding this policy or requests to purchase further reproduction rights should be addressed to:

Permissions Editor
J. Weston Walch, Publisher
321 Valley Street • P. O. Box 658
Portland, Maine 04104-0658

1   2   3   4   5   6   7   8   9   10

ISBN 0-8251-3736-5

Copyright © 1984, 1998
J. Weston Walch, Publisher
P. O. Box 658 • Portland, Maine 04104-0658

Printed in the United States of America

Contents

Acknowledgments .... *vii*

Foreword .... *viii*

Introduction .... *ix*

Author's Introduction .... *ix*

To the Teacher .... *x*

To the Student .... *xiii*

Reproducible Student Readings

The World of a Jewish Girl Named Anne Frank 2

Chapter 1: The Franks Suffer Persecution in Germany 4

Chapter 2: Nazi Terror Moves to Holland 7

Chapter 3: The Franks Go into Hiding 13

Chapter 4: Who Are the People in the Secret Annexe? 20

Chapter 5: The Secret Annexe Residents Live and Die in Nazi Prisons 26

Chapter 6: Mr. Frank and Anne's Diary Testify Against
            Nazi War Criminals 34

Chapter 7: Anne Frank Lives On in the World 37

Chapter 8: Time for Reflection: Anne's Message of Peace Through the
            Perspective of Holocaust Experience 49

Student Activities

Suggestions for Using the Student Activities 55

Activities for Chapter 1: The Franks Suffer Persecution in Germany 56

Vocabulary 56

Reproducible Reading Comprehension Quiz 58

Discussion Questions 59

Word Derivations 59

Short Essays 60

Answers to Reading Comprehension Quiz 61

Answers to Discussion Questions 61

Possible Topics for Research Reports 62

Activities for Chapter 2: Nazi Terror Moves to Holland 63

Vocabulary 63

Reproducible Reading Comprehension Quiz 66

Discussion Questions 68

Short Essay 68

Answers to Reading Comprehension Quiz 69
Answers to Discussion Questions 69
Possible Topics for Research Reports 70

Activities for Chapter 3:   The Franks Go into Hiding **71**
Vocabulary 71
Reproducible Reading Comprehension Quiz 73
Discussion Questions 75
Short Essays 75
Answers to Reading Comprehension Quiz 76
Answers to Discussion Questions 76
Possible Topics for Research Reports 77

Activities for Chapter 4: Who Are the People in the Secret Annexe? **78**
Vocabulary 78
Reproducible Reading Comprehension Quiz 80
Discussion Questions 81
Short Essays 81
Answers to Reading Comprehension Quiz 82
Answers to Discussion Questions 82
Possible Topics for Research Reports 83

**Activities for Chapter 5:   The Secret Annexe Residents Live and Die
in Nazi Prisons** **84**
Vocabulary 84
Reproducible Reading Comprehension Quiz 86
Discussion Questions 89
Short Essays 89
Answers to Reading Comprehension Quiz 91
Answers to Discussion Questions 91
Possible Topics for Research Reports 92

**Activities for Chapter 6:   Mr. Frank and Anne's Diary Testify
Against Nazi War Criminals** **94**
Vocabulary 94
Reproducible Reading Comprehension Quiz 95
Discussion Questions 97
Short Essays 97
Answers to Reading Comprehension Quiz 98
Answers to Discussion Questions 98
Possible Topics for Research Reports 99

Activities for Chapter 7: Anne Frank Lives On in the World **100**
Vocabulary 100
Reproducible Reading Comprehension Quiz 103
Discussion Questions 105
Short Essays 105
Answers to Reading Comprehension Quiz 106
Answers to Discussion Questions 106
Possible Topics for Research Reports 107

Activities for Chapter 8: Time for Reflection: Anne's Message of Peace Through the Perspective of Holocaust Experience **109**

Vocabulary 109

Reproducible Reading Comprehension Quiz 116

Answers to Reading Comprehension Quiz 118

Possible Topics for Research Reports 119

Suggestions for Discussion Topics 119

Cooperative Learning Activities

**Activity 1: Extending Research and Reflection:
An Overview of Human Experiences in the Holocaust** **121**

Reproducible List of Research Topics 122

**Activity 2: Using the Crime of the Holocaust
As a Model of Racism-in-Action** **124**

Extending Student Interest

Putting on a Play With a Holocaust Theme 129

Suggested Resources for Student Research and Reports 130

Audiovisual Materials for the Classroom 134

Bibliography

Photographs

Dedication

I dedicate this book to Anne Frank and the millions
of other Jewish children the Nazis destroyed.
And, as my way of giving life to Anne Frank's wish,
"to work in the world and for mankind,"
I dedicate all the proceeds from royalties
earned from the sale of this book and another book,
Understanding the Holocaust (1995), to purchase food and shelter for the
hungriest, neediest, and poorest of the poor souls, from all religious and cultural
denominations, that I can identify in the world. I believe this gesture to be in
harmony with the spirit of love in this girl who touches us with such a compassion
for humanness, she must shame us all into righteousness, or else we are truly lost.

Acknowledgments

My thanks to the following authors and the publishers of their works for permission to reprint copyrighted material:

Excerpts from *Anne Frank: The Diary of a Young Girl* by Anne Frank. Copyright 1952 by Otto Frank. Reprinted by permission of Doubleday and Company, Inc.

Excerpts from *A Tribute to Anne Frank* edited by Anna Steenmeijer. Translation copyright 1970 by Doubleday and Company, Inc. Copyright 1970 by Otto Frank. Reprinted by permission of Doubleday and Company, Inc.

For events of the Franks' capture, Miep's reaction to their arrest, the fate of the Franks and their helpers, and Anne's behavior in Nazi prisons, credit must to go Ernst Schnabel, author of *Anne Frank: A Portrait in Courage,* published by Harcourt, Brace, and World, New York, 1958. Permission to paraphrase this copyrighted material granted by Harcourt Brace Jovanovich.

To Lore Cowan, author of *Children of the Resistance,* published by Hawthorne Books, Inc., New York, 1969, credit for the carnation-wearing incident staged by the Nazi-defying children of Holland. Permission to paraphrase this incident granted Elsevier/Nelson Books, New York, New York.

Credit goes to Nora Levin, author of *The Holocaust: The Destruction of European Jewry, 1933–1945,* published by Harper and Row Publishers, Inc., New York, 1971, for the resistance of the Dutch to the Nazi occupation. Permission to paraphrase this material granted by Harper and Row, Publishers, Inc.

My thanks also to Bauco van der Wal, executive director of the Anne Frank Center and the Anne Frank Foundation in Amsterdam, Holland, for their permission to reprint all the photographs in this book. I am also grateful to Mr. van der Wal for an interview conducted at the Anne Frank House in Amsterdam, Holland, in August 1980.

I am grateful to Rabbi Mordecai Haalman, Sam and Leah Gottesman, and Freida S., all Holocaust survivors who consented to have their testimony included in this text. Thanks also to Willemina Ratnavale, who lived through the Nazi occupation of Holland and provided valuable background information in my research.

I extend my appreciation to Ernest Nives, president of The American Friends of Anne Frank, for providing materials during my earlier research of this book.

Above all, the major credit for my personal motivation to write two schoolbooks on the Holocaust include: Anne Frank's undiminished faith in the goodness of people; my students' sincere investment in the study of the subject; my wonderful and supportive husband and family; my old friends; and the strongest influence of all on my own ideals and undertakings: a number one priority based on the words of Jesus Christ, "Love one another as I have loved you" (Jn 15:12). Back in 1970, the person of Anne Frank, through her gift of writing and the vibrant spirit of goodness she projected in her hope for people to incline the world toward righteousness and rightfulness, moved me to present her story to my literature students. Their eagerness and sensitivity toward Anne's circumstances produced a classroom inquiry and scholarship, compelling us all to research the Holocaust (a subject not routinely discussed back then) and preparing me for my next journey with this young Jewish girl. Once the formal writing project took shape in 1980, my husband Edward, daughter Valerie, and son Greg provided the key ingredients for such a task: much love, critical home support, and patience. And in the scheme of this whole experience between Anne Frank and me and my concurrence with her faith in God, I give ultimate credit to my own deep trust in divine intervention, in having goodness eventually come to fruition, for all of the above, and more.

Foreword

Since I am of the generation of Anne Frank and a survivor of Auschwitz, it would be very difficult for me to write a purely objective text. But the subjectiveness of my text will only serve to underline the importance that Anne has played both with the people who have gone through the Holocaust and those who have not. The true essence of her writing is its simplicity even when she expresses her deepest feelings, hopes, and ideals. In the most perceptive, mature way she described the events that took place in this hiding place. She renders a personal account of the emotions of a young girl thrown suddenly from a happy, free teenager to one that has to face suddenly the bitterness of life and the fears of adult persecution as a Jew. As was the case in my own life, when I was 13 and Hitler came to Austria, so in Anne's life there was no easy transition. It was a sudden, terrible shock to become a hunted animal, pursued by the very same people, neighbors, and friends we lived with or grew up with. Anne describes these fears and her puzzlement in her own way, yet throughout, her deep faith in humanity shines through her writing.

It is because of the effectiveness of her writing that her diary has now become a masterpiece of literature of our time. Yet, this tragic personal account of a young girl should remind the world forever that such cruel events should not happen again. We speak of the millions that were put to death during the Holocaust; yet, this simple story of this young, frail-looking girl, the dark, childlike eyes that have become so famous, the voice that could not be stilled and killed by the Nazis, should serve as an inspiration to all of us and reaffirm our beliefs in humanity and civilization. We should remember that, despite all the horrors and cruelties, despite man's evil—rigorously organized to commit mass murder on a scale heretofore unknown, despite the world's fears and repressions, despite Anne's tragic death . . . her voice survived and her ideas are still with us.

That is the greatness of humankind, of the human mind. As a survivor, this positiveness makes it worth-while living. The faith in humankind should be perpetuated through the reading of *The Diary of Anne Frank*, yet remain as a warning that when blind prejudice gains the upper hand, events and results far beyond those foreseen at the beginning may happen.

It is incumbent upon us to perpetuate Anne Frank's legacy and to transmit it to future generations. One way this can be done is the way we are doing it. I, of the generation of Anne Frank, was entrusted by Otto Frank, her father, to form an organization called The American Friends of the Anne Frank Center, Inc. I was honored to be approached by Ms. Merti as president of this organization to write this foreword. It is the next generation, such as Ms. Merti, who will bring this legacy to the younger generation. The most effective means to do so, is through the reading in class of the *Diary,* coupled with the teaching of the historic context in schools. There is no better tool than this book for teachers and instructors to make the reading of the *Diary* a vivid and emotional experience for youngsters. We also stand ready to assist you with the additional visual materials, cassette recordings of passages from the *Diary* read by actresses, etc. Please feel free to contact us any time. We hope that you all will play your part in perpetuating The American Friends of the Anne Frank Center, Inc.

I am not sure I can capture alone the meaning and the essence of Anne Frank. But what better way than to quote the words of Otto Frank, which he sent to our organization as a message during our commemoration of her 50th birthday on June 12, 1979.

"We also continue to strive for the ideals of Anne Frank and all of you who may assist us in doing so, are most welcome among our friends."

Ernest Nives
The Anne Frank Center, USA
200 West 57th Street, Suite 1206
New York, NY 10019
(212) 431-7993

Introduction

The Diary of Anne Frank is one of the most well-known books in the world. It has been translated into more than 50 languages and tens of millions of people all over the world have read it.

Why is this diary of a young girl from Amsterdam so universally understood? The answer is quite simple: her feelings, problems, and emotions are experienced by people all over the world.

Anne Frank was only exceptional because she could write and express things that are common, yet so important, to all of us. Reading the intimacy of a diary and recognizing it means understanding that you are not alone. But there is more to the *Diary.*

After reading the *Diary,* people will wonder what happened to Anne Frank and when they hear about the senseless destruction they will ask: *can it happen again and can it happen here?*

Yes, it can happen again. World War II or the Holocaust will never be repeated in the same way, but anti-Semitism, racism, fascism, and oppression do exist today and in our own countries. We must not deny these things but reveal and fight them.

—*Bauco van der Wal*
Executive Director
Anne Frank Center
212-431-1648

Author's Introduction

Martin Luther King, Jr. once said, "Our goal is to create a beloved community and this will require a qualitative change in our souls as well as a quantitative change in our lives."

The World of Anne Frank works toward this requirement for community formation. Anne Frank is presented here as one of the world's most authentic leaders who calls for peaceful coexistence among people of differences. We can use Anne's diary as a powerful leadership tool for this purpose. Her voice has risen above and beyond her own tragedy to touch the consciousness of readers in nearly every nation on earth. That this legendary figure has stirred the souls of millions toward higher levels of human behavior is a matter of record.

This book is written to encourage Anne Frank's spirit of peace. The text leads to the understanding of how both good and evil can take root from just a single person and grow to influence the entire world. On one hand, Adolf Hitler's mania mushrooms into wrecked lives and world disorder. On the other, Anne Frank's voice and her hope in the "goodness

of man to make things turn out right" continues to live on and serve as a motivator for peaceful human interactions for generations to come.

The goal here is to activate Anne's beliefs so that they are most accessible to students. The teaching and learning objectives are to inform and to effect positive interaction and interactivity involving students and others in the school and outside world who need help. This text challenges the students, saying, "Now, *you,* as one individual, can make a difference, too. How can *you* make the world a better place? Please take the first step. Make a 'quantitative change in your life' to cause a qualitative change in the life and soul of another person less fortunate than you. Just one small gesture can enrich someone else's life, will make you feel good about helping others, can encourage more people to follow your lead, and may fulfill the desirable goal Martin Luther King Jr. proposes above. Such a formation of "beloved community" is at the very heart of Anne Frank's message to everyone in the world today.

To the Teacher

Twenty-five years in public education has taught me one important thing about teenagers. Their indifference and lukewarm attitudes are only a facade. Though sometimes buried down deep, that burning curiosity and excitement gleaned from learning new and challenging topics are still very much a part of the young adults who once faced me every day. How do we teachers bring these qualities to the surface? The motivation is thought-provoking materials plus our own interest in our subjects. Presenting *The Diary of Anne Frank* for 13 years to students in my English classroom proved that to me more than anything.

This text is the result of research done by me and at least 1,375 of my 13- and 14-year-old students at Dorseyville Junior High School in suburban Pittsburgh, Pennsylvania. (I also wrote another text entitled *Understanding the Holocaust,* published by J. Weston Walch, Publisher, in the spring of 1995.) This search for answers began in 1970 when I exposed my English classes to Anne Frank's diary for the first time. My students dug into books about the subject every year after that.

Why is there a need for researching Anne Frank's situation? Only a partial story, Anne's diary—her account of 25 months of hiding from the Nazis during World War II—covers only a bit more than one seventh of her short lifespan. After students read the diary, they want to know more. Their typical questions are: What happened to her? Why did she have to die? How could Hitler have gotten away with killing so many Jews? What did he have against them in the first place?

When I began this unit, those same questions baffled me. Not being Jewish myself, I lacked the cultural background to provide the necessary answers about European Jewish history, a subject so intricately tied to the 20th-century crime of the Holocaust. That phase of World War II history had not been a real part of my past high school or college education, either, for teachers and professors and textbooks had barely touched the surface—if at all.

So our investigation for answers began back then, and it grew by leaps and bounds over the years. Not one school year started without several new students entering my classroom in September asking, "When do we get to do the Anne Frank unit, Mrs. Merti?" Nor did many years pass without former students sending me materials related to the Holocaust and Anne Frank. It has become a mutual involvement, a real sharing of material that my pupils and I know we learned together.

Try this text with your class. Do you have to use it in conjunction with Anne Frank's diary? Not really. You may use *The World of Anne Frank* independently, for it is a complete teaching tool within itself. However, this book is but a mere response to Anne's dilemma. The true impact of the tragedy of Anne Frank can be felt only through Anne's personal testimony, through her eyes, and with her own haunting words.

Therefore, I encourage you to use *The World of Anne Frank* as a supplement to Anne's personal story. By doing so, you will enable students to gain:

1. a richer insight into Anne's goodness and character,

2. a deeper appreciation of the humanness of other personalities involved,

3. added empathy toward the Jews' struggle to carry on a semblance of routine daily life in the midst of fearful surroundings,

4. more intimate exposure to the evil, harsh realities surrounding all Jewish victims of the Nazi Holocaust, and

5. an increased awareness of the need to fulfill Anne's hope that goodness in people will eventually form true community in the world.

Several available resources reveal Anne's firsthand testimony. Anne's handwritten diary, left behind in the Secret Annexe after her capture, is in two forms: an ongoing original diary written in several books during her entire two-year hiding period and an edited copy of the original she rewrote on loose sheets during her last year in hiding.

In published form, Anne's diary appears in three different editions in the English language (different translations appear in other languages). Listed here are my personal recommendations for appropriate reading audiences. The first edition, read by millions around the world, is *Anne Frank: the Diary of a Young Girl* (1952, edited by Otto Frank). This version is particularly suitable for high school or middle school classroom use. Its contents maintain the integrity of the primary educational goal: teaching the important lessons of the Nazi Holocaust through the poignant experiences of Anne Frank and her family and friends.

A second version, *Anne Frank, 1929–1945, The Diary of Anne Frank: The Critical Edition* (1989), includes Anne's original diary in two forms and the one edited by Otto Frank and published in 1952. *The Critical Edition,* first published by the Netherlands State Institute for War Documentation in Amsterdam, responded to doubts of some disbelievers about the diary's legitimacy. *The Critical Edition* establishes without a doubt the authenticity of Anne's work and is geared more for scholars and research. (Diary quotations used in this text are taken from *The Critical Edition.*)

The most recent translation of Anne's diary is *Anne Frank, The Diary of a Young Girl: The Definitive Edition*, edited by Otto Frank and Mirjam Pressler (1995). Coming 15 years after Otto Frank's death, the book uses his 1952 edited version as a basis but includes 30 percent more of Anne's original text. Some inclusions, revealing Anne's personal and innermost thoughts about sexuality and adult/parent behaviors, are those which Otto Frank, on the advice of publishing consultants, thought better to leave out of the 1952 edition. In American school circles, such passages, included in the more recent *Definitive Edition,* may provoke controversies unrelated to Holocaust issues and subsequently may cloud the real purpose of including Anne Frank's story in the academic curriculum. For this reason, *The Definitive Edition* is more appropriate for adult readers.

In addition, two other excellent resources for Anne Frank study, besides the earlier book edited by Anne's father, add the dimensions of visual and auditory dramatizations to Anne's diary passages. They are the Pulitzer Prize winning Broadway play based on the diary: *The Diary of Anne Frank*, adapted by playwrights Frances Goodrich and Albert Hackett (1955) and the 20th Century-Fox award winning film, *The Diary of Anne Frank* (1958). All students in my classes have read the play with great interest and sensitivity. Many have also read and used Anne's diary for classroom reports and projects. Finally, showing students the Hollywood film was a perfect follow-up to the entire unit.

You may wish to follow the way I taught my entire Anne Frank unit:

1. For background information about the Holocaust and time period before the Franks go into hiding, have students read the Background and Chapters 1, 2, and 3.

2. Then, have all students read orally and discuss the play, *The Diary of Anne Frank,* by Goodrich and Hackett, as a classroom activity.

3. Return to *The World of Anne Frank*, Chapters 4, 5, 6, 7, and 8 for character study, details of the capture of the Jews in hiding, details of their fate in Nazi prisons, examples of Anne's influence in the world, and reflection on Anne Frank in the context of Holocaust experience.

4. Heighten student interest in all phases of this unit by incorporating ideas from the Student Activities section of *The World of Anne Frank*—the Cooperative Learning Activities after Chapter 8 are especially valuable for extended research and student reflection on the entire unit of study.

I recommend four bibliographic resources, in particular, for teachers who wish to examine the diary for its literary merit or as a tool for analyzing Anne Frank's personality. For a critical literary analysis of the Diary as both an extraordinary art form and a narrative of personal growth and development, without parallel, consult "Writing Herself Against History: Anne Frank's Self-Portrait as a Young Artist" by Rachel Feldhay Brenner (*Modern Judaism,* 1996) and "The Development of Anne Frank" in *The Freedom of the Poet* by John Berryman (1980).

Another excellent resource is a scientific psychological analysis of Anne's personality as a persecuted victim in the extreme situation of hiding for two years during the Holocaust. The author, Dr. Henry J. C. Piszkalski, a psychology professor and Polish priest, is a former Nazi concentration camp prisoner himself. Fluent in Dutch, he used the original version of the Diary in writing his thesis, *The Personality of Anne Frank in the Light of Karl Jasper's Theory of Extreme Situations.* Piszkalski's study shows evidence that Anne's prime source of inner strength as a persecuted person was her deep religious faith. It also explains why the *Diary of Anne Frank* and other adolescent journals, written during long periods of duress, can be used as authentic psychological records for scientific studies.

In the fourth key study, "Authenticity: From Philosophic Concept to Literary Character," Robert Leahy presents the attribute of human authenticity as an ethical paradigm built on democratic principles, integrating reason and emotion, commitment to human rights, meaningful dialogue, and the ethic of caring (Educational Theory, 1994). Leahy develops this concept of authenticity through an analysis of the behaviors of several well-known literary characters. Though Anne Frank is not mentioned, teachers of literature can use Leahy's paradigm for presenting Anne Frank as a moral person who continually demonstrates the highest levels of authenticity, despite increasing anxiety and personal suffering over the two year hiding period.

You may wish to contact the Holocaust Center of the United Jewish Federation, which has offices in many major U.S. cities, and The Center for Holocaust Studies of the Anti-Defamation League of B'nai B'rith in New York City, for a wide array of classroom teaching aids for the Holocaust and Anne's Diary.

As a final, culminating activity you may also wish to have students view the 20th Century Fox movie *The Diary of Anne Frank* and/or invite a Holocaust survivor to your classroom to speak to students.

My unit on Anne Frank spanned about five weeks in the classroom. This book, *The World of Anne Frank: A Complete Resource Guide*, is based on that unit and will provide many avenues for learning about Anne and other Holocaust victims, especially when used in conjunction with the play and Anne's diary. The suggested learning tasks focus on many communication skills to enhance classroom interactivity and enrich learning: reading, researching, interviewing, participating in cooperative learning activities, creative writing, giving oral presentations, note-taking and summarizing, analyzing human behavior, building and applying vocabulary, applying listening skills, creating three-dimensional projects, and encouraging students themselves to be community builders through creation of positive relationships.

In conclusion, no matter what classroom strategies you use in teaching Anne Frank literature, my personal classroom experience makes me bold enough to offer you a guarantee: your students will never forget Anne Frank and will ever carry her message of peace, conveyed in the midst of unimaginable torture to the human spirit.

—Betty Merti

To the Student

Reading *The World of Anne Frank* will teach you about the real world and the two sides of human nature. Here, in dealing with a real life tragedy of this Jewish girl, you swing between the two extremes. You learn about the savage mindset of Nazi racism and tyranny. And you encounter the destruction of one of the most authentic human beings you will ever meet in a lifetime, a young Jewish girl named Anne Frank, who eventually dies in a Nazi prison camp. You will shake your head in disbelief at learning facts about the Jewish Holocaust. Nazi brutality will fill you with disgust and outrage. And becoming acquainted with Anne Frank and her family and friends will touch your heart in a way usually reserved only for your own family members.

This is because Anne Frank emerges from her diary as a legend—bigger than life. Her words stay with you, and will echo in your mind. You will discover Anne as a special person with such good sense and high-leveled integrity and dignity, you won't help but want to be more like her. And strange as it seems, you, too, will be moved to place more stock in the goodness of people, even though Nazi behavior belies this probability. You will want to prove Anne right. And like many readers, you will undoubtedly feel prompted to do something humane and worthy for others.

This text calls on you in this prompting to do something special to help others in need. Anne Frank envisioned a future where goodness in people makes evil wrongdoing take a backseat. If her story moves *you* to help just one needy person, you will have fulfilled Anne Frank's hope in *you* and the main teaching goal of this text. Most important, your positive interactions with others will mean at least some good has resulted from student learning about the nightmare of the Jewish Holocaust.

Reproducible
Student
Readings

The World of a Jewish Girl Named Anne Frank

What Is the Holocaust?

IT HAS been said that because one man lived, 55 million people died. That man was Adolf Hitler, leader of the Nazi party and dictator of Germany from 1933 to 1945. An evil person with an unquenchable thirst for power, Hitler led his country and the world into a second global war that was a nightmare beyond comparison. No other war ever caused so much destruction and death.

Hitler waged war for two reasons: to rule the world and to make all conquered peoples the slaves of the "master German race." He came very close to accomplishing both of those goals.

Most of the 55 million people who died in the war were soldiers, prisoners of war, and civilians living in combat zones. All these war-related deaths are called *casualties*. However, the Nazis killed one group of people not because they were the enemy, but because they were Jews. This was deliberate murder.

People had tried to destroy one another in wars before, but Hitler's crime against the Jewish people was unique in scope, force, and organization. In fact, his crime provided our dictionaries with a new word, *genocide*. It means "the planned killing of an entire racial or cultural group of people."

Why did Hitler have Jews murdered? His hatred of this minority group cannot be explained. It consumed his mind like a dreadful disease. For seven years after he came to power, he sent his men to harass Jews, steal their possessions, force them into slavery, and starve them. But slavery, he decided, was too good an existence for Jews.

In 1941 Hitler's mania progressed: he decided Jews were even unfit for life. He ordered his Nazis to systematically kill every last Jew in Europe. He almost accomplished that goal, too.

The Allies brought the German armies to defeat just four years after Hitler's order to kill. By then, six of the nine million Jewish men, women, and chil-dren of continental Europe were dead. One and a half million of the children had been under the age of 14. All the victims had been starved, tortured, shot, gassed, or burned to death.

After the war, the Allies captured and punished many Nazi war criminals for this terrible crime.

The word *holocaust* means "a fire that causes total destruction." Because this mass killing of Jews was like a great fire burning everything and every-one in its path, the term Holocaust is used to describe it.

Were Jews the only ones to suffer? No, brutal Nazi murders had extended to at least five million other innocents. Victims included Russians, Poles, Czechs, Slavs, Gypsies, and others whom the Nazis called "inferior races." Gypsies were especially targeted for mass killings. The Hitlerites killed between 270,000 and 500,000 Gypsies of all ages seemingly without any pangs of conscience. Some historians estimate the loss of Gypsies living in Europe to be as great as 80 percent.

However, of all the 11 million victims, Jews alone were slated for annihilation. Hitler's goal was to make the world *Judenrein*, or free of Jews. So, just for them, his killers formed searching parties. Only for Jews was a specific railway system orga-nized to remove them from every European country under Nazi control. And especially for Jews were death camps in Poland designed with equipment to handle mass murder on a grand scale.

Was the Jewish slaughter solely a German crime? No; it was a Nazi crime. All Germans were not Nazis. Nor were all Nazis Germans. Many Euro-peans besides Germans joined the Nazi party. Others who held prejudices against Jews collaborated with Nazi Jew hunters and turned in their Jewish neigh-bors. And still others in Europe and the free world who were in a position to help the victims stood by and did nothing. So the responsibility of the Holo-caust crosses nationality lines and reaches beyond the actual perpetrators of the crime.

Who Is Anne Frank?

Anne Frank was a German-Jewish girl who fled from Germany when Hitler came to power in 1933. *(See photo 1.)* She and her family took refuge in Amsterdam, Holland. Unfortunately, they had not run far enough. In 1940 Hitler's armies invaded and captured the Netherlands.

Soon afterward, the Nazis began their roundup of Jewish families. That was when the Franks and four other Jewish refugees decided to go into hiding. Desperately hoping to avoid capture, they hid from the Nazis like trapped animals in fear of hunters. For over two years, they remained shut in a hidden Amsterdam apartment they called the Secret Annexe.

When her family went into hiding, Anne Frank was 13 years old. She kept a diary of everything that happened during those two years of secret living.

That her diary survived the war is almost a miracle. To hide their crimes against the Jewish people, the Nazis tried to destroy all records of their terrible deeds. A Gestapo sergeant actually held Anne's diary right in his hands. Had he known what it was, he'd have destroyed it in a minute. Luckily, he overlooked it.

Over 200 other diaries written by Jews during the Nazi persecution have also survived the war. All are moving accounts of this period. However, none has become as famous as Anne Frank's book. Nor has any writer of those other logs touched the hearts of so many people around the world. Over 25 million readers in 55 nations have pored over Anne's pages of memories. Her story has also reached audiences from television, movie screens, and stages everywhere. Anne Frank has truly become a legend.

Why do millions find *The Diary of a Young Girl* by Anne Frank so fascinating? No doubt there are many reasons, but two stand out: her readers get a firsthand look at how evil people are and how good people are. Hitler and his Nazis were, without question, cruel and evil. On the other hand, many good, unselfish people helped Jews to hide and risked their own lives in doing so. And when we speak of goodness in people, there is Anne Frank herself.

At the end of two years of hiding indoors, Anne desperately missed breathing the fresh outside air. She missed it so much that she used to try to sniff it through a crack in a closed window of the Annexe. Even though she and the others endured hardships like that, she wrote at the end of her diary, "In spite of everything, I still believe that people are really good at heart."

Isn't that comment alone a broad statement of who Anne Frank was?

Chapter 1:

The Franks Suffer Persecution in Germany

The Franks Are an Old German-Jewish Family

OTTO FRANK, Anne's father, came from an old German-**Jewish** family whose ancestors had lived in Germany for hundreds of years. Like the rest of their Jewish compatriots, the Franks believed they were true Germans. Germany was the only home they had ever known. The Franks, in fact, did not even emphasize their Jewish religion or heritage. Neither Otto nor any of his brothers attended Jewish schools to study Hebrew or the Jewish religion and culture. On the other hand, Anne's mother Edith and her family had stronger ties to **Judaism** and attended the local Reform **synagogue**.

As children growing up, both Otto and Edith were used to the finer things in life because their families were prosperous. However, after a time, the lifestyles of both families dramatically changed. **World War I** dragged Germany's progress to a standstill. And after the war ended in 1918, hard times affected the lives of all German citizens.

1919–1924—Turmoil in Germany Follows the War

For a number of reasons, the morale of the Germans sank to an all-time low after World War I. Not only had the once proud and mighty German nation lost the war, but also the world was blaming Germany for having caused the conflict in the first place. And now the war-ravaged countries were insisting that Germans pay for all the war damages.

The German people lost all faith in their government.

To make matters worse, the German economy had been shattered by the cost of maintaining a four-year war. Burdened now by the war debts, the economic system suffered a new setback. Runaway inflation made prices so high that a huge bank account could not even buy a pound of sugar or a bunch of carrots! As their lifetime savings quickly slipped away, the German people became desperate. Laborers went on strike for higher wages, companies closed, and workers lost their jobs.

Five years of turmoil followed the war. Dozens of political parties claiming a solution to Germany's problems sprang up. Two of these parties called for extreme measures: the Communists and the **Nazis.**

The Communists were mainly German workers who took orders and received support from Moscow. They wanted Germany to become a satellite nation of Russia. To cure their country's many economic ills and vast unemployment, they wanted all property and business to be taken from the hands of a few private owners and to become state-controlled. All workers could share in the wealth.

Under the direction of **Adolf Hitler,** the Nazis also claimed a cure to each and every problem in Germany. Hitler promised to stop payment on the war debts and to give every worker a job and bread on the table.

Hitler also promised to restore the world prestige and military supremacy which Germany had enjoyed before World War I. To do this, he called for the creation of two things: a master race of "pure

Aryans" or "pure Germans" and a new **Third Reich,** or state composed of all German-speaking people, that would rule the world. Hitler wanted to rid Germany of all its Jewish citizens, for Jews, he said, were not only "non-German" but also an inferior race. He and his Nazis began to preach their hatred of Jews.

The Nazis and the Communists shared one common goal: they planned to overthrow the existing German government, which was a democracy.

1924–1929—Prosperity Returns; Anne Frank Is Born

Then America and other foreign countries came to the rescue of the suffering Germans. They began to pour money into the country. The German economy improved. As a result, people went back to work and prices went down. Good times for the Germans meant bad times for the Nazis. For the time being, no one listened to their hate campaign. The Communist party died down too.

It was during these good times, in 1925, that Otto Frank married a woman named Edith. He and Edith set up housekeeping in Frankfurt, Germany, where Otto had a job as a banker. While living in Frankfurt, they had two daughters. Margot was born in 1926. Three years later, on June 12, 1929, Annelies Marie Frank was born. Her parents often called her Anne or "the Tender One."

The Great Depression Hits

Disaster hit when Anne was just four months old. The stock market on Wall Street in the United States crashed in October of 1929. The result was a worldwide depression, and Germany's economy came tumbling down again. As American dollars and other foreign monies stopped pouring in, Germany's debts increased. When the banks closed, Otto Frank lost his job. Even worse, his parents and many other wealthy Germans lost their fortunes. Thousands of factories stopped production. By 1931, five million Germans were out of work.

The German people became more disgusted with their government than ever before. Now with no jobs, no heat in their homes, and no food on their tables, their lives were miserable. Hungry German families stood in long lines for hours for free bread handouts from the government. Many, evicted from their homes, lived and slept in crude tents on vacant lots.

Fear of Communism Makes Germans Turn to Nazism

The return of bad times made the Communists and Nazis spring back to life. More and more people became convinced that something drastic needed to be done before Germany could get back on its feet again. Many joined ranks with either the radical Communists or the Nazis.

Striving for more and more power, the Communists and Nazis fought each other. They turned the streets of Germany into a battleground of civil war. Both sides rioted. They created so much confusion, the German government was unable to keep order. The two parties grew rapidly.

Many Germans, fearing a Communist takeover, panicked. Most did not want to live under Russian rulers or to have their property seized by the state. Government leaders felt their reins slip away. They began to look to the power group they considered "more German" as the lesser of the two evils—the Nazis. Politicians, people in the monied class, and many of Germany's military leaders began to make deals with the Nazis. Their goal was to get rid of the "Red Menace," their term for the Communists.

What they settled for was not much better. Hitler and the Nazis had offered their cure-all campaign to soothe everyone's fears and worries only as a means to gain power and wealth for themselves.

Jews Become Hitler's Scapegoats

With support now behind him, Hitler unleashed his hatred for Jews. He used Jews as the **scapegoats** for all of Germany's problems. He said Jews were the internal enemy of Germany. He screamed that Jews had caused the inflation, Jews had created the Depression, and Jews had even made the Germans lose the war!

None of Hitler's charges made any sense. For one thing, thousands of German Jews like Anne Frank's grandparents had lost their life savings in the Depression just as many other Germans did.

And what about the 100,000 Jewish soldiers who had defended their homeland in World War I? Of that figure, 80,000 had fought right on the front lines and 12,000 had given their lives in the fight. Thousands more had been decorated for bravery. In fact, Mr. Frank, a lieutenant in the German army, had received medals for heroic efforts in the war.

Besides that, the 525,000 Jewish citizens were such a tiny **minority,** they comprised barely one percent of the entire German population of 66 million. How could a small group like that wield so much influence? After all, the vast majority of leaders in the German government and economy were non-Jewish Germans. In spite of these truths, however, millions, desperate for help, jumped on the Nazi bandwagon. Many paid more attention to Hitler's promises than they did to his hate-mongerings against Jews. Little did they know how far he would go.

"Get rid of Jews to solve Germany's problems!" became the leading Nazi **propaganda** slogan. As Nazi membership increased, so did attacks on Jewish citizens. Jews suffered beatings in the streets. Nazis looted their shops, **vandalized** their synagogues, and even destroyed Jewish cemeteries and burned books by Jewish authors. Many Jews decided to leave Germany, the only home they had ever known.

Hitler Passes Laws Against Jewish Germans

When Hitler came to power in 1933, he took his first legal steps to force Jews out of their own country. He made **persecution** of and **discrimination** against Jews the law. He passed one **anti-Jewish law** after another. First his Nazis ordered the population to **boycott** Jewish businesses. This meant that no German could go to a Jewish place of business for any reason. Other Nazi decrees in 1933 dismissed Jews from government jobs and even Jewish children from public schools. Finally, it was not long before Nazi **storm troopers** boldly murdered Jews in the streets. And the building of the **concentration camps** had begun.

The Franks Flee Germany

Shortly after the law against Jewish children was passed, Mr. Frank and his family fled from Germany with only the clothing on their backs and a few German **marks** in their pockets. The Nazi state seized the rest of their property. By this time, 37,000 other Jews had also left. Unfortunately many others, hoping the Nazi storm would pass, stayed behind.

Anne Frank was now four years old.

Chapter 2:

Nazi Terror Moves to Holland

Holland Is a Haven for the Franks and Other Jews

JEWS HAD lived in the Netherlands for centuries. **Anti-Semitism**, or prejudice against Jews, seemed distant. The Dutch had accepted them as first-class citizens. This relaxed atmosphere offered Jews an illusion of safety from the Nazi persecution that was going on in Germany. Furthermore, everyone believed that if Hitler started another war, Holland would remain neutral just as it had during World War I.

Consequently, many Jewish families, eager to escape the fury of Hitler's hatred, headed toward Holland. By 1938, the Dutch had opened their borders to more than 6,000 Jewish refugees from Germany and Poland. Like the Franks, many settled in the city of Amsterdam, where their numbers climbed to 100,000, or 10 percent of the population. By 1940, approximately 140,000 Jews were living in the country of Holland.

Rabbi Mordecai Haalman had lived in Amsterdam all his life. He became a **Holocaust survivor** who **emigrated** to America after World War II. He describes Jewish life in Holland before the war: "My ancestors had lived in Holland since 1790. Never did we experience anti-Semitism, or anti-Jewish **prejudice**, here. We Jews were very **assimilated**. We lived and thought like all Dutch people. When the German Jewish **refugees** came to Amsterdam with their terrible stories, we didn't really believe them. And we were very, very sure those same things would not happen in Holland."

Mr. Frank had traveled to Holland for many years on business trips, so its friendly atmosphere was not new to him. He and his family arrived in Amsterdam in 1933. For the next seven years, the Franks managed to make new friends and to live a very pleasant life. Mr. Frank became involved with two businesses. He was manager of Pectacon, a wholesale firm that imported and sold spices and part owner of a firm called Opekta. (Anne refers to the first firm as Travis and the second as Kolen in her diary.) A few years before the war, Otto Frank took in another partner named Mr. Van Daan. Also a German-Jewish refugee, Mr. Van Daan had fled from Berlin with his family.

For six years, Anne and Margot Frank attended the Montessori School in Amsterdam. Here Anne had many friends and was usually the center of attention. However, in 1940 the carefree, happy part of Anne's life came to an end. She and her family were never again to enjoy normal lives. In fact, for the next five years, the normal lives of all Dutch people were to be interrupted.

The Nazis Invade the Netherlands

By this time, Hitler's **World War II** had begun. Spreading their stranglehold, his armies had invaded and captured Poland, Norway, and Denmark. But Hitler had vowed to the Dutch many times that he would not invade their land. Holland, which had been neutral during World War I, wished to remain neutral now.

It was one of Hitler's empty promises. When German troops had invaded Poland a few months earlier, Britain and France had come to the Poles' rescue. They had declared open war on Germany. Together with other nations fighting Germany, they were called the **Allies**. Now the German dictator wanted to use Dutch airfields to send missiles to destroy England.

The Hollanders were not fooled. On several occasions, Hitler gave a secret order to invade their country and then changed his mind for any number of reasons, including bad weather. But the Dutch were ready each and every time. Their informers had been on the alert.

Finally, on the night of May 9, 1940, Dutch intelligence received another secret message of possible invasion. It was not another false alarm. Case Yellow, the German military operation to invade Holland, was all set to go. Fifty German divisions had gathered at Holland's borders and planned to attack at dawn. More German troops planned to invade the neighboring countries of Belgium and Luxembourg as well.

Once again the Dutch readied for invasion. They intended to slow down the German attack until they could get help from the French and English armies. To hold back the Germans, they planned to open their dikes and canals. The water would then rush in and drown the attackers. They also mined their bridges to blow them up to bar the Nazis from passing through.

Unfortunately, their clever plan failed to halt the German attack. Before the dawn and out of the darkness came the German **blitzkrieg**. Hitler's men charged ahead with lightning speed. Dressed in Dutch uniforms and armed with machine guns, German parachutists landed behind Dutch lines. They seized the water controls and the bridges. Screeching German **Stuka** dive-bombers careened overhead and dropped explosives. At the same time, **infantry** troops and tank columns swarmed inland.

By the end of the fourth day of battle, the Germans held all positions except the bridges lead-ing to the large city of Rotterdam. The Nazis warned they would bomb this city if the Dutch did not surrender.

Desperate, the Dutch decided to negotiate a peace treaty with the Germans. But while Nazi leaders talked in terms of peace, German dive-bombers roared in and ripped out the heart of this great city. Over 800 people were killed. Thousands more were left homeless. This senseless bombing of Rotterdam made the Dutch furious, and they vowed they would never forget it.

On May 15, just five days after the invasion, the Dutch surrendered. The countries of Belgium and Luxembourg also fell to the Germans. Luxembourg battled, for only one day, while the Belgians managed to hold off the German incursion for 18 days. Thus, as Hitler's armies seized more and more land, millions of Europeans—Jews included—fell into the Nazi grip.

Today Willemina Ratnavale, the mother of two children, lives in Pittsburgh, Pennsylvania. Like Anne Frank (except that she is not Jewish), she was a 13-year-old Dutch girl living in Holland at the time of the German invasion. The boardinghouse where she lived was just one mile from the city of Rotterdam. Mrs. Ratnavale vividly remembers, "The Nazis attacked like thieves in the night. It happened so suddenly and quickly. Three days of night followed the bombing, for the air was so thick with dust and smoke, we couldn't see the light of day. Many, many years later I still had nightmares of the dreadful screaming dive-bombers."

The Dutch Do Not Welcome the Invaders

The Dutch queen, Wilhelmina, with her cabinet, fled to England. She vowed to carry on the Dutch struggle against the Nazis from there. Throughout the war, she spoke to her Dutch people and gave them courage by way of the **BBC**. This radio station, broadcasting from London, England, was called Radio Orange by the Dutch. Though the Nazis had ordered the Dutch to turn in all radios, the people hid them and tuned in anyway.

Many Netherlanders, including Jews who wanted to fight the Nazis right in their homeland, joined the Dutch Resistance. Holland's flat country, large cities, and open highways made **guerilla** warfare almost impossible, however. The Dutch **underground** joined forces with British agents, and together they fought the Nazis, not with guns, but by sabotage. They interrupted and delayed and interfered with German actions. They gathered German intelligence data, helped Allied prisoners to escape, staged labor strikes, and blew up railroads and bridges.

There was also a general will to resist the Nazis among the Dutch. Mrs. Ratnavale recalls, "When Nazi soldiers asked directions, we always told them to go the wrong way. And Dutch people who were Nazi sympathizers were ignored or spit upon by their neighbors."

Even Dutch students gathered the nerve to fight back. For example, June 29, 1940, was the Dutch prince Bernard's birthday. The Nazis would not allow the Dutch to display their national or orange-colored flags in celebration. One week before the prince's birthday, angry Dutch youngsters sent word to many schools and universities in Holland. Their letters suggested that all students wear a white carnation on their lapels, for it was the prince's favorite flower.

The students knew that the Nazis would tear the carnations from their lapels, so they placed pieces of razor blades in these flowers. As a result, Nazi fingers bled over the streets of Holland on the prince's birthday. It was a happy day for Dutch students.

Nazism Spreads Its Stranglehold on Dutch Jews

When the Nazis had invaded Poland in earlier months, Polish Jews had become the objects of pointed attacks. They were immediately harassed,

beaten, and ordered out of their homes and into **labor camps** and **ghettos**. Many were shot on sight. This did not happen in Holland. The invaders went more slowly in their anti-Jewish campaign. Anti-Jewish laws did not come right away. Hitler's soldiers knew that anti-Semitism was not a popular feeling in the West. They realized that mistreating Dutch-Jewish citizens too soon would only further antagonize the Netherlanders. So they played a waiting game.

According to Rabbi Haalman, "We Jews began to relax and say, 'See, we are not really Jews in the sense that the Germans look upon Jews. We are Dutch!'"

But this was false hope. Three weeks after the invasion, Adolf Hitler appointed an Austrian Nazi chief named Arthur Syess-Inquart as head of the new Reich government in Holland. This turnover of power **revitalized** the old Dutch Nazi party. This Nazi movement, part of the activities of the Dutch National Socialists in Holland, had come to be known as the **NSB**. The Dutch Nazis had formed a political party back in 1931. By 1935, eight percent of Dutch voters, mainly for economic reasons, had favored the NSB political platform. Thereafter, though, popular support for the party dwindled. One reason why many voters turned away was the NSB's **outspokenness** against Jews.

By 1940, the NSB still had a following of over 25,000 members. With the invasion of Hitler's troops and Syess-Inquart now holding the reins of government, the NSB had reason to be optimistic. Once again Dutch National Socialism began to flourish in Holland. Eying opportunity for power and wealth, NSB'ers planned to become **collaborators** with the Germans in persecuting Jews and working against all other loyal Dutch people who stood in their way.

Thirty thousand Dutch men also enlisted in the German military forces to fight in Russian territories. Another 30,000, swept along in the war movement, would join German police and military ranks within the next year. Many of these enthusiastic joiners did so for three reasons: (1) they feared the Communist movement in Eastern Europe; (2) they believed the seemingly **invincible** Germans were in Holland to stay; and (3) they underestimated the real dangers of Nazism to Jews as well as to themselves.

In July 1940, just two months after the invasion, the new Nazi rulers, along with the NSB, had Holland firmly in its grip. The invaders announced that, yes, they had signed a peace treaty with the Dutch, but Jews were their enemies forever. Out came the same anti-Jewish laws that had been enforced in other occupied territories. The Nazi all-out war on Dutch Jews had begun.

First, the Nazis required every Dutch citizen to participate in a census. Each person was to designate the number of Jewish parents and grandparents in the family. This set a trap for Hollanders with Jewish blood. A person's religion did not even count. The Nazis labeled anyone with two or more Jewish ancestors as a Jew, even if that individual's family had attended Christian churches for generations.

Some Christians and nonpracticing Jews tried to hide the truth about their Jewish ancestors. This is one instance where neighbor turned against neighbor because of anti-Jewish feelings. It was not uncommon for Nazi sympathizers to contact the Gestapo about unrevealed Jewish backgrounds of people living in their communities.

A short time later, Nazi officials demanded that those labeled as Jews "register for their protection." Jewish passports and other personal identification papers had to be stamped with the large letter *J.* Fear prompted approximately 150 Jews, mostly refugees, to commit suicide.

Five months after the invasion, new decrees called for Mr. Frank and other Jewish merchants to register their businesses. The Nazis carefully wrote and stored all this information in large books. They would later use it to take over Jewish businesses and to deport Jews to camps in the East.

A short time later, a Nazi law passed, freezing all Jewish bank accounts. This law forbade Jewish families from taking money from their own savings.

It also barred them from family valuables stored in their personal safe-deposit boxes.

The torment went steadily on. In her diary Anne speaks of not being permitted to ride in a car, on a bus, or even on her bicycle. If she and other Jews wished to go from one place to another, they had to walk. *(See photo 2.)* Places of entertainment such as movies, swimming pools, and tennis courts were off limits to her and her Jewish friends. Mrs. Frank and all other Jewish housewives had their shopping restricted. They could shop only between the hours of three and five o'clock and just in Jewish-owned shops. Even the use of telephones, both private and public, was forbidden to Jews. So was sitting on park benches. If the need arose, Jews had to find a doorstep or safe street curb as a resting place. And on hot, stuffy summer evenings, Anne and her family could not relax and cool off outside in their yard. All Jews had to be indoors by 8:00 P.M.

By October 1941, no Jew was permitted to be a business owner. Fortunately, Mr. Frank was able to transfer his business to Mr. Koophuis and Mr. Kraler, two good Dutch friends who had worked for him. Later these men would risk their own lives by helping the Franks to hide.

A short time later Nazi law forced Jewish children to drop out of Dutch schools. Anne and Margot had to transfer to a school for Jews only, the Jewish Lyceum, which was a 40-minute walk from their home.

By April 1942, no Jew could walk unnoticed in the street. A new Nazi order made Jews wear the yellow six-pointed Jewish Star of David on their clothing. About four inches across, this black-bordered star had the word "JOOD" (meaning "Jew") printed in black in the center. *(See photo 3.)* To avoid arrest, Jews had to wear the star at all times, placed on the left shoulder of their coats and on all other outer clothing.

As if this weren't bad enough, securing the required stars was an added burden. Like all Jewish mothers who had to sew the stars on the family's clothing, Mrs. Frank needed two things before the

Nazis would hand the stars over: money and **ration coupons**. These were the same ration coupons necessary for food and clothing purchases.

Everything had grown scarce. Food stores, once overflowing with Dutch cheeses, breads, vegetables, and other staples, now were bare. Why? The Nazis did not care whether the people in the Netherlands starved or not. They gathered Dutch food, clothing, and other supplies and shipped them out to ease war shortages in German cities. Even the Dutch Nazis, in exchange for special favors, ignored the welfare of their own compatriots.

By the winter of 1944, hundreds of Hollanders were dying daily. The Nazis had driven them to the point of starvation. In all, at least 20,000—non-Jews and Jews alike—died from hunger and disease. Mrs. Ratnavale recalls this period: "We had to eat sugar beets, which we normally fed to the cattle and even tulip bulbs and crocus bulbs! There was nothing else. Our mothers baked, fried, mashed, and boiled these things to make them taste a little different. After eating crocus bulbs, we usually couldn't speak well for a day. These bulbs had something in them that made our throats raw and sore."

The Nazi Party Shows No Mercy for Jews and Defenders of Jews

The Dutch queen, Wilhelmina, offered comfort by way of the BBC or British Broadcasting Corporation. She promised her Dutch Jewish citizens she would return all their property now stolen by the Nazis.

The Nazis got tougher. In February 1941 they staged their first **pogrom**, or anti-Jewish riot, in Amsterdam where the Franks lived. Jews and their Dutch friends fought back with clubs and other small weapons. Furious, the Nazis took to the streets in armored tanks and ran hundreds of people down.

And they wouldn't tolerate one of their own being hurt. When one Nazi policeman was shot during another incident, the revenge was terrible: 400 Jews were dragged off the streets and shipped

to concentration camps. Enraged Dutch dockworkers staged a strike to protest. Thousands of other workers joined in the demonstration. The Nazis answered with bullets and **martial law**. Anyone who didn't obey their orders was shot on sight.

Sympathetic Dutch citizens still didn't back down. Rabbi Mordecai Haalman recalls, "When the Germans got word of another strike in sympathy for Dutch Jews in 1942, Syess-Inquart, the Nazi Commissioner of Holland, threatened a terrible punishment. Unless people went back to work, the Germans would bomb and completely destroy 10 Dutch cities, to remind the Dutch of Rotterdam." They went back to work.

For many reasons, this strike would be the last outward show of support for Jewish victims. The Dutch Resistance, which **sabotaged** the Nazis, was not well organized until later on in the war. Furthermore, the Nazi iron fist tightened on all Hollanders. The Nazis sent many thousands of Christian Dutchmen, especially younger men, in cattle cars to supply forced labor in German war factories. Most did not want to go. To avoid deportation, at least 250,000 went into hiding. Then the Germans began to grab young men off the streets. This explained why mainly women, children, and older men were seen in public during the occupation of Holland.

Not enough Dutch power could surface. At first, some Catholic and Protestant clergy did urge congregations to help Jewish neighbors. Some Christians even placed a yellow star on their own clothing in support of Jewish friends. And later on when the deportations of Jews began, nearly a dozen churches sent a letter of protest to the Nazi government. The letter was ignored.

An estimated 24,000 Jews did find hiding places with Dutch friends during the war. Unfortunately, that number reflected barely six percent of Holland's Jewish community who desperately needed help. Reasons for this are many.

Hiding from Nazi hunters was a complicated matter, involving sacrifice and high risk on all sides. From the Jewish perspective, seldom could their families stay together in hiding. This meant splitting up and finding several hiding places, one for each family member. Sometimes a family could hide only its children. All this meant that once the family bid farewell to one another, further communication had to stop. Even worse, they had to face the painful truth of possibly never seeing each other again, for Nazi search teams were on the prowl everywhere.

The new rulers also strictly rationed food and other necessities. Only the black market offered goods beyond rationed supplies, and their prices were sky high. This made hiding possible for only those with enough cash reserves to pay for their keep over an indefinite period of time. Furthermore, because most of the 100,000 Jews living in Amsterdam were poor, hiding was not even an **option** for them.

To make matters worse, Nazis used fear and punishment as ways of making sure people would stay away from Jews. First, they issued ironclad laws to strip all citizenship rights from Jews and to deport them from the country. Then they added measures for violating the laws. Helping Jews in any way broke Nazi laws. The treatment for helpers became the same as for Jews: beatings, torture, life in prison, forced labor, and death.

Thousands of brave Dutch helpers paid a heavy price. By the end of their reign of terror, Nazi guards would arrest and imprison 20,000 Christian helpers in concentration camps.

All this hateful effort had a terrible effect. The story of Holland's Jews would come to a tragic and bitter end: 105,000 were to lose their lives in the Nazi Holocaust. That figure translated into this grim statistic: 75 percent of Holland's Jews, one of the highest percentages of any of the **occupied countries** in Europe, were victims.

Among the Dutch Jews who lived, only 16,000 would make it by hiding. Except for one person, Anne Frank and her friends and family would not be counted among them.

Dutch Jews Are Deported

In July 1942, the Nazis began their **deportations** of Holland's Jews. Railway passage for the trains carrying Jews away had top priority. The Nazis even delayed military transports to clear the tracks for the deportation trains.

Each week thousands of Jews received call-up notices to report for "resettlement for labor in the East." They were told to bring along food and work clothes. Then, block by block, Nazi search squads surrounded an area and systematically went from house to house to round up Jewish families. With their machine guns and billy clubs they ushered their captives through the streets. Any Jews seen along the way were arrested on the spot and taken away.

Mrs. Ratnavale remembers clearly, "As Jews walked through the streets to the trains, they held out their young children and begged strangers, 'Please take my child. Please take care of him.' Often Dutch people did take in Jewish children. Many of them survived the war with kind Dutch families."

Like animals on their way to slaughter, the Jewish victims were pushed and packed into railroad cattle cars. Where were they headed? One of two camps in Poland, Auschwitz or Sobibor, was to be their final destination. The nonstop journey across Europe to these camps took several days. In the meantime, the cattle cars had no chairs to sit on, no lights, no heat, no bathrooms.

Often many of the passengers inside died before the trains arrived at the camps. It was just as well, for these camps were not to be places of work but places of death. Gas chambers stood waiting.

Some people in the cattle cars even died standing up. There was no room for their bodies to fall. The cars were too crowded with people.

On Sunday morning, July 5, 1942, the SS ordered Margot Frank, aged 16, to report for deportation to a labor camp in the East. Four days later, the Franks went into hiding.

Chapter 3:

The Franks Go into Hiding

Mr. Frank Prepares the Hiding Place

ONCE THE Nazis occupied Holland, few Jews were able to emigrate to other lands. Dutch borders were heavily guarded: Even if Jews could safely make it to the border, their **passports**, stamped with a large *J,* clearly identified them. Dutch Jews were trapped.

Realizing this and feeling the increasing pressure of Nazi persecution, Mr. Frank wasted no time deciding how to protect his family. Soon after the Nazi invasion, he began to prepare a hiding place. For two years, he set it up. Five very good friends, all Dutch Christians, helped him. Once this hiding place was ready, he planned that he and his wife and daughters would simply "disappear."

Slowly but steadily, Mr. Frank and his helpers carried in small amounts of supplies. Stores of canned foods, dried vegetables, and other necessities grew. Eventually, filled boxes rose to the ceilings in the rooms of the hideaway.

The Franks planned to just walk away from their home and leave everything behind. So they gave clothing and furniture to good Dutch neighbors for safekeeping. If the Franks managed to escape Nazi capture, these neighbors would return their possessions after the war. Otherwise, the Nazis would seize all their holdings, because they were Jews.

The **Aryanization of all Jewish property** was official Nazi policy. The practice of seizing Jewish wealth and possessions had begun in Nazi Germany. Now it spread to every occupied country. Jewish homes, businesses, bank accounts, cars, jewelry, artwork, and every other thing of value became the property of the German state. Nazi thievery was done on a small scale, too. After rounding up Jews for deportation, many Hitlerites simply walked into Jewish homes and pocketed whatever they pleased. They often roughed up their captives in order to unearth more valuables.

Holocaust survivor Freida S. recalls, "At midnight the **Gestapo** pounded on our door. They had arrived to arrest my husband. Their first question? 'Where are your money and jewelry?' Then they proceeded to search our apartment. In their haste, they smashed the windows in my china closet, upset furniture, tore apart the beds, and slashed with their bayonets our wall paintings, which they left behind. It was all senseless destruction."

Fortunately, the transferral of Mr. Frank's business to his Dutch friends had gone smoothly. And the hiding place was nearing readiness. Mr. Frank set the date of their disappearance for July 16, 1942. Time was of the essence, for deportation of Holland's Jews was going full speed ahead.

However, Margot's call-up notice was still a shock to the whole family. They moved up the date to hide by eight days. They dared wait no longer.

Though Mr. Frank had informed Anne and Margot they would hide from the Nazis, he did not reveal how, when, or where they would do it. In fact, they did not learn these answers from their father until they were well on the way to their hiding place.

The Franks Walk to Their Hiding Place

With no time to waste, their last evening home was frantic. Mr. Goudsmit, a man who rented their upstairs room, decided to linger and chat with the Frank family until very late into the night. Not wanting to make this man suspicious, the Franks politely talked. Finally he went to bed. Two good Dutch friends, Miep and Henk Van Santen, then came and helped to carry last-minute needed supplies to the Secret Annexe.

Before dawn the next morning, Thursday, July 9, 1942, Mrs. Frank awakened her two daughters. The girls and their parents quickly piled on heaps of clothing. They did this because no Jew could safely walk the streets with a suitcase. Anne describes their dressing "as if we were going to the North Pole." She had on two vests, three pairs of pants, a skirt, a jacket, a summer coat, two pairs of stockings, shoes, a woolly cap, a scarf, and still more! It was a hot, steamy, rainy summer day.

Soon Miep arrived and took Margot quickly away with her. They rode off on bicycles.

Shortly afterward, Otto, Edith, and Anne Frank walked slowly through the pouring rain toward the Secret Annexe. Margot and Miep had arrived safely before them. Four days later, Mr. Frank's business partner, Mr. Van Daan, his wife, and son Peter joined them. Peter brought along his cat Mouschi. Four months later on November 17, 1942, Albert Dussel, a Jewish dentist, came to hide in the Secret Annexe. Only Mr. Van Daan had met Mr. Dussel before. In fact, the two frightened families had never really been close friends. They now hid together because they were Jews and because they wanted to live.

They Try to Cover Their Tracks

The Franks provided clues to confuse Nazi searchers, their neighbors, and their renter Mr. Goudsmit. They deliberately left their home in a state of disarray. Breakfast dishes remained on the table, all the beds were unmade, and clothing and shoes lay scattered about. A notepad with an address in Switzerland lay on Mr. Frank's desk.

Their plan worked. Later the Franks found out that their neighbors and friends believed they had escaped to Switzerland. Even Mr. Goudsmit was fooled. He later told Lies Goosens, Anne's best girl-friend, that he believed Anne and her parents had made it safely across the Swiss border. Somehow, he said, Mr. Frank must have persuaded a Nazi **SS** (elite guard) to help them.

The Building Housing the Secret Annexe Is Unusual

The **Secret Annexe,** the Frank's hiding place, once had been a laboratory and storage room at the back of the building where Mr. Frank had run his business for the past nine years. This four-story building* dated back to 1635. It was located along the Prinsengracht Canal, one of Amsterdam's many canals. The building had a strange layout. For centuries, the Dutch had used their canals for trade. For this reason, property along the canals had been very desirable and expensive.

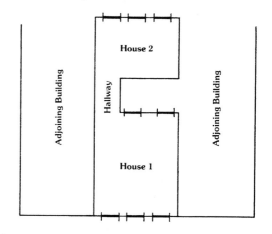

---

* The four stories were the ground floor, first floor, second floor, and third floor. In European countries, the street-level floor is called the ground floor. The next level is called the first floor, the next the second, and so on. We usually call the street-level floor the first floor, and count up from there.

To cut building costs, Dutch builders made structures facing the canals very, very narrow. The length didn't matter, so to provide necessary space, the houses were usually very long and several stories high. They were also side by side, with no space between buildings. The problem with this type of house plan was that windows could be placed only in the narrow front and back. As a result, all the rooms in the long center of the house were dark.

To solve this problem, some Dutch builders constructed two houses in this narrow space with both houses joined by a hallway. (The Dutch word for the rear house was *achterhuis,* or "afterhouse.") An open courtyard lay between the two houses. In this manner, windows could be placed in the middle rooms for needed light. The structure that housed the Secret Annexe was built like this.

There were problems with living in houses like these. They had a very confusing pattern. Because they were so long and narrow and high, the buildings had many hallways, many doorways, and very steep, almost vertical stairways. But for hiding, a house like this was perfect. And few people knew about the construction of Mr. Frank's building. Even better, the Germans had never seen such a plan in their country.

The House Plan of the Secret Annexe Building

The Secret Annexe was located on the second and third floors of the rear house. The ground floor, not pictured, was used by traders for loading and unloading cargo. *(See photo 4.)* You might ask why someone could not see the rear house from the storehouse windows on the upper floor of the front house. Remember that Mr. Frank was a spice dealer. To preserve freshness, spices had to be stored in darkness. For this reason, dark patterned paper was stuck on those storeroom windows. No one could see out. Besides, people standing there by those windows thought they were at the back wall of the building.

Then, for added safety, Mr. Frank had made another provision: he disguised the entrance to the Secret Annexe. A carpenter and good friend, Mr. Vossen, worked in Mr. Frank's warehouse. He built a swinging bookcase over the doorway. A hook on the back kept it in place so that no one could enter unless it was unfastened from the inside. *(See photos 5 and 6.)*

During daylight hours, the people who helped the hidden group worked in the offices on the first floor of this building. However, other workers here knew nothing about Jews hiding upstairs. Therefore, it was extremely important that the **fugitives** above make no noise during working hours.

Two bedrooms and the bathroom were directly above the offices. Because of this, the Secret Annexe people had to be very quiet. They could use the bathroom only in the early morning hours before the workers arrived or late in the evening after the workers left.

Often the Franks and Dussel spent the quiet hours of the day in the Van Daans' upstairs sleeping room. This was higher up and farther away from the ears of unsuspecting workers below. The Van Daans' bedroom, formerly a laboratory, was larger than any of the other closet-sized rooms of the Annexe. Therefore, it also served as the living room, dining room, and kitchen for the whole group. It contained not only folding beds but also two stoves and a sink. The group used one gas stove for cooking and the other one for burning garbage and giving heat in winter. Peter Van Daan's room, also upstairs, had a steep stairway leading to the attic. Here in the attic was the only window that could be opened without fear of discovery. Food and other supplies were stored in this area.

Anne's Diary Covers 25 Months in Hiding

The Franks, the Van Daans, and Dussel were to remain in the Secret Annexe from July 9, 1942, to August 4, 1944, a period of 25 months or 757 days.

15

They were worse off than ordinary convicts who at least have the daily privilege of breathing fresh air in a prison yard. These hidden people never dared set foot in the streets. The walls and sealed windows of this building held them in solitary confinement for the entire time. Because they were eight people crowded into too small a space for too long a time, they got on each other's nerves. It was not an easy time.

However, hiding now was the only way for a Jew to live in Holland or any other occupied country. For a Jew, no alternative existed. Now, stripped of a future, the poor people in hiding were left with only one certainty: the horror of being hunted down. They lived in constant fear of being discovered.

The suffering of all Jewish families at this time was **incomprehensible**. Reports from the outside world of death camps and slave-labor factories in the East would reach the Annexe people by way of radio and their helpers. These stories, plus the dangers around them, would numb their minds with fear. How could they keep their spirits from the breaking point?

Young Anne Frank found her own way to conquer Nazi terror. The Nazis could bully Jews by forcing them into hiding like hunted animals, but Anne refused to take on Nazi definitions of who she was and what she could do. Hitler's guards had no power to imprison her mind. Anne freed her human spirit by openly expressing herself on paper. She kept a diary of their 25 months in hiding, and used it as a control mechanism for responding to everything and everybody around her.

Her writing projects the high drama of the hiding place. Some occasional moments are light-hearted. Others are downright frightening. The reader of her diary smiles when, angered over Mr. Dussel's fussiness, she plants a stiff brush in his bed to get even. At other times, one can sense the terror of the Annexe people. Fear makes them run to the bathroom and causes their hands and knees to tremble.

Anne's diary ends on August 1, 1944, three days before the Gestapo raided their secret apartment and took the group away.

Their Helpers Are Their Lifeline

If Jews wished to hide to escape Nazi capture, their first requirement was a helper in the outside world. How else could they hope to secure food and other supplies necessary for survival? What about keeping their hiding place a secret? The Nazi defiers were not ordinary people. They had to have extraordinary courage, for the penalty for being caught was their own lives. Fortunately, the Franks had the privilege of having good and brave Christian friends who were willing to risk their own safety to act as protectors.

All five of the Dutch men and women who hid and protected their Jewish friends in the Secret Annexe had worked for Mr. Frank before the Nazi occupation. Once the Germans arrived, all five had joined the Dutch Resistance to free Holland from Nazi control. Helping the Franks and the others was just one way they resisted the Nazis.

Included among the group were Elli Vossen and Miep Van Santen, two typists for Mr. Frank's firm. *(See photo 7.)* Henk Van Santen, Miep's husband, also helped. All were in their twenties. Two others, Mr. Kraler and Mr. Koophuis, were Mr. Frank's business associates.

These kind and good people aided the group in hiding in many ways. Every day, they made deliveries of food, books, or medicines. And they provided companionship by visiting, sharing meals, and offering news of Nazi and underground activities. Their visits and deliveries, always highly welcomed, had to be made at times when the workers were not in the building. This was usually before 8:30 A.M., during lunchtime, and after 5:30 P.M. when business shut down for the day. Moreover, Miep and her husband once stayed overnight in the Annexe, just as a special visit of friendship. Sleeping in Anne's bed in the silence of the night, broken by sounds inside and outside the building, they learned how truly frightful it was to be a Jew in hiding. Miep hardly slept a wink.

Providing the eight Annexe people with food was no simple matter. There were food shortages, and the Nazi government required ration coupons for food purchases. But the helpers took the risks of getting food illegally through the **black market**. Naturally, their Jewish friends paid a higher price than the going rate, for such illegal goods were always very expensive.

Two other men also came to the rescue of not only the Franks, but also many other Jews hiding in Amsterdam. They simply ignored government requirements and provided Miep, Henk, and Koophuis with enough vegetables and bread for eight extra persons. Neither of these men knew the Franks or the Van Daans. Nor did they ask any questions. Helping fellow Dutch people escape Nazi terror gave them personal satisfaction. As a matter of fact, the baker refused to collect a cent.

The great risks the helpers took had bad effects on their health. Some could not even safely mention their help to their families. The tension and suspense often built up to such a point they could hardly talk. Mr. Koophuis developed a bleeding ulcer. But in spite of the strain, these good and brave people did not give up. Never complaining, they continued to do all they could for their Jewish friends.

And, as if helping the Franks and their friends were not enough, Miep and Henk were hiding one more person right in their own small apartment. He was a university student, wanted by the Nazis for refusing to sign a required student oath not to act against the German occupation. Miep and Henk kept this to themselves, shielding the matter even from the Franks because they knew it would worry them.

They Try to Occupy Their Time

"Time killers" is what Anne Frank called most of the things they did in the Secret Annexe. That was a good name, for they were really playing a waiting game. They desperately hoped to remain in hiding until the United States and its allies freed Holland from Nazi control, when they could live normal lives again. They needed things to do to pass their time.

During the day, while workers were in the building below, the secret group chose quiet activities which required little talking and movement. It was the time to read the many books Miep supplied weekly. The women did needlework while Mr. Frank supervised the young people with school lessons in algebra, language, and history. Anne passed her time by trying to learn shorthand, and she and Margot did the bookkeeping for their father's business. All of the occupants frequently napped the time away.

However, once the workers left the building for the night, the Secret Annexe came alive. This was the highlight of the long days, when everyone could relax and breathe somewhat normally. Visits from their friends below brightened the atmosphere with lively discussions of business, politics, and the war's progress.

In the evenings, the group often gathered around the radio in the office downstairs. Tuned in to the BBC from London, they heard speeches by Queen Wilhelmina and Prime Minister Winston Churchill. Later, when the Germans demanded that all radios be turned in, Mr. Koophuis salvaged one of his small ones. He gave it to the group in the Secret Annexe. Everyone in the Secret Annexe shared in the daily housekeeping activities of cooking, canning food, and cleaning.

They Contend with Many Problems Inside the Annexe

Hiding in the Secret Annexe had its problems. For one thing, the hidden people had to be extremely quiet as long as workers were in the building. A shoe falling on the floor, a sneeze, a cough might give them away. Therefore, they whispered and moved about in stockinged feet.

Since running water made noises in the building's pipes, the sink and toilet could be used only before and after the workers left. Once when the sewer backed up, water could not be run in the Annexe for three days. Another inconvenience was the absence of hot water and a bathtub in the Annexe. Water had to be heated on the stove. And to take baths, a washtub had to be carried to the hot-water faucets on the floors below.

The Secret Annexe windows at the far end of the building were something else to deal with. Since they could never be safely opened in the daytime, the heat inside the rooms became ever so intense during the summer months. Never could the thin curtains be pulled back, so the only view of the outdoors was through old curtains and dirty window glass. Nor could a light ever be turned on without covering these windows with blackout paper.

Getting rid of garbage was no simple matter either. Using the building trash cans was too risky. So it all had to be burned, even in the summer with all the windows closed!

Rats and fleas caused further misery. Peter's cat Mouschi and the warehouse cat Boche waged war on the building's rat pack. However, the cats were a mixed blessing. At one time their fleas infested the Annexe and all the people in it. But the group still enjoyed having the cats around.

Illness was also a real threat because a doctor could not be safely called to the hiding place. Fortunately, the dentist Mr. Dussel was able to handle some of the dental and medical problems. But for other illnesses, the hidden people took home remedies or simple medicines that their helpers provided. When Anne had trouble with her eyes, Mr. Frank considered sending her to an eye doctor with Miep. But he decided against it. They couldn't take the chance.

Finally, the cramped quarters created a highly stressful situation. The room Anne shared with Mr. Dussel, for example, was hardly more than a closet. A tall man with arms outstretched could touch opposite walls with his fingertips. Never could the people ever really be alone. Week after week and month after month they hovered together looking at the

same walls and the same faces. Tension mounted daily and created many arguments among them.

In spite of all these hardships, however, they were thankful to have this little secret place to hide. For example, after watching Jews in the streets from the curtained window, Anne writes, "It seems like the slave hunts of olden times. . . . I often see rows of good, innocent people with crying children, walking on and on, in charge of a couple of these chaps, bullied and knocked about until they almost drop. No one is spared—old people, babies, expectant mothers, the sick—each and all join in the march of death. How fortunate we are here, so well cared for and undisturbed. . . . I feel wicked sleeping in a warm bed, while my dearest friends have been knocked down or have fallen in a gutter somewhere out in the cold night."

They Face Problems from the Outside

To protect themselves, the hidden occupants could regulate what they did inside the Secret Annexe. Their control over people and conditions in the outside world was another matter, however.

On several occasions outsiders threatened their security. In February 1943 the owner of the Secret Annexe building, which the group's Dutch friends rented, sold it. Much to the shock of Kraler and Koophuis, the new owner arrived one day to inspect his new building. Fortunately, he believed their story of the lost key to the landing door that led to the swinging bookcase. Luckily, he never returned to look around again.

Also, on several occasions thieves broke into the warehouse at night. Each time a burglary occurred, the refugees were off guard, either listening to the BBC in the offices downstairs or laughing and talking loudly. In fact, one thief ran away when he saw Mr. Van Daan walking through the building. These robbers caused the group grave concern. If caught, would the thieves bargain with the police by offering information about Jews in hiding? Would they possibly go for the Gestapo rewards being offered to informers who revealed the hiding places of Jews?

Another person also threatened their safety. One worker in the warehouse occasionally asked Kraler and Koophuis many suspicious questions about the layout of the back section of the building. Both the helpers and the hiders worried about what he might do.

Furthermore, the war was all around them. The Annexe occupants worried that outside conditions might force them to leave the security of their hiding place. As the war progressed, Holland came under fire. **Air raids,** gunfire, and bombings occurred frequently, especially at night. Fires and explosions that erupted nearby made the building tremble. The frightened occupants had no idea if their roof would be next. Just in case, they all had packed a bag for a quick getaway. But for Jews, entering the outside world was suicide. Where would they go? What would they do? Wouldn't they be recognized?

Nothing excited them more than the coming Allied invasion. However, they began to view even this with mixed feelings, for the Germans had come up with some **dire** threats. The Nazis had vowed that if the English invaded, they would flood parts of Holland, including Amsterdam. They also insisted they would drive the entire Dutch population to Germany on a forced march if they had to retreat.

Nor could the Jews in hiding escape the misery felt by everyone else around them. The worsening effects of the war and the terror of the military occupation reached them, too. As all Dutch people suffered from shortages of food, electricity, paper, soap, clothing, and nearly everything else, so did the refugees. Anne speaks many times of having to eat boiled rotten lettuce at each meal for weeks at a time. And the Nazis' special war on Jews made the group increasingly nervous. As the war had dragged on, and the Germans found themselves on the losing side, Nazi roundups had not lessened. Instead, they became more intense and Nazi treatment of Jews became more violent. In fact, by 1941 Hitler had come up with his "**final solution to the Jewish question,**" that is, how to get rid of all Jews in German lands. **Genocide,** the extermination of all Europe's Jews, was his answer.

No Jew was to remain alive. The **Einsatzgruppen,** special shooting squads with orders to wipe out Jewish communities, had followed the German armies into Russian territories. At the same time, Hitler had commanded other SS Jew hunters to "comb the rest of Europe from east to west" to round up every last Jewish man, woman, and child. All were to be deported to **gas chambers** in the **death camps** of Poland.

On March 27, 1943, Anne writes, "Rauter, one of the German big shots, has made a speech. All Jews must be out of the German-occupied countries before July 1. Between April 1 and May 1 the province of Utrecht must be cleaned out (as if the Jews are cockroaches). Between May 1 and June 1, the provinces of North and South Holland."

Anne speaks of hearing about Jewish children coming home from school and finding their parents gone. She writes of Jewish mothers returning from the store to find their homes locked up and their husbands and children missing. Miep also reported that the Van Daans' furniture had all been hauled away, and that many of the Franks' and Van Daans' friends had been deported.

The search for Jews in hiding was stepped up, too. Rewards were offered for information leading to their arrest. Snooping and prying on every street corner were the Gestapo, the plainclothes secret police. *(See photo 8.)* To round up the unarmed Jewish families, they used the German police, the NSB, and the army. All these Nazi activities made the Franks, the Van Daans, and Dussel very fearful and very anxious.

To add to their problems, their helpers got sick or had to be away from time to time. The Nazis called up Mr. Kraler for labor. Koophuis had an ulcer operation. Miep and Elli had illnesses that kept them away. Their absences put the Secret Annexe people more on edge, for these good Dutch friends offered them their only lifeline and security.

Chapter 4:

Who Are the People in the Secret Annexe?

WE KNOW the people hiding in the Secret Annexe were Jews. That fact alone was the reason they hid. But what were they really like as human beings?

Anne Frank

Anne Frank was a very special girl. A typical teenager in many ways, she was also unique in others. She, herself, felt she had two sides. One side she describes as the "chaser-after-boys, flirt, know-it-all" side, while the other is the "finer, purer, better Anne who cares very much what people think."

In school, Anne was a bright, lively, talkative student. With interests focusing more on parties and nice clothes than on making straight *A's*, Anne was always surrounded by a wide circle of friends, both boys and girls. She and her best friend Lies Goosens were inseparable. They giggled and talked so much their teachers always were sure to seat them on opposite sides of the classroom. Once, in fact, her math teacher, annoyed with Anne's constant chatter, insisted she write a paper entitled "A Chatterbox" for punishment. Anne also complained about a few of her teachers; she said some of them were the "greatest freaks on earth."

Anne also loved an audience. She had a real skill in mimicking others' voices. And she could twist her body in such contortions that her shoulder would crack in and out of its socket. To see others become alarmed at this would make her giggle hysterically. She also enjoyed entertaining others with clever impersonations of teachers, famous personalities, and her family cat.

Anne excelled in studies that interested her. On the other hand, she had to repeat sixth-grade mathematics, not because she failed to understand the concepts, but because she lacked interest in the subject.

Nevertheless, because of her genuine sense of humor and her real love of learning, her teachers loved her. Anne was the kind of noisy student who could make the teacher as well as her classmates laugh with her. Later, when the Nazis forced her to leave the Montessori School, she and her teachers cried together.

Sometimes adults found her hard to live with. She once described herself as "a playful little goat who's broken loose." That's exactly what she was—never still, always laughing loudly, talking a mile a minute, and forever playing jokes on people. Her smart answers and "don't care" attitude caused Mr. Dussel and Mr. and Mrs. Van Daan to say many times she "was not well brought up." Anne's mother sometimes found Anne hard to handle, even though she tried to be a friend to her daughter.

Anne reacted to adults in this way because she expected them to be good examples to follow. She was a very good judge of character. All too often those same adults who criticized her behaved badly themselves. And Anne refused to listen to them on those grounds.

Anne adored her father, however, and looked up to him as a perfect model. They were very close. During air raids and bombings, she ran to his side for comfort. Together they read books and plays. When she cut his hair, he said it was a perfect job—even though she had snipped his ear with the scissors. To Anne, Pim—the name she called her father—was without faults. And only from him did she accept advice and scoldings.

The way Anne behaved with adults was immature. However, the war and her position in it as a Jew made her see the childish error in her ways. In fact, by the end of the hiding period, Anne had somewhat distanced herself from her "little girl closeness" with her father, looking to him more as a father figure than as a friend.

Nor was Anne blind to her own faults. She was on a constant path of self-improvement. Throughout her diary, she always analyzes her inner feelings, knowing when she has behaved outrageously and admitting her failings. She criticized her looks, too. Once she called her diary "the unblossomings of an ugly duckling." Anne was dissatisfied with her teeth, which were not perfectly aligned, and was conscious of her "big" ears, which she carefully hid behind curls. She was **vain** about only one thing: her thick, black glossy hair.

Not a selfish girl, Anne cared very much about other people. That she was safe in hiding while other Jews suffered Nazi torture made Anne feel guilty and sad. How bitterly she cried when she heard that her best friend Lies had been deported! In her diary she anguished over the idea that Lies was suffering while she herself was safe in the Annexe.

She also continually worried about their helpers. Always concerned about the risks and trouble they took to help her and the others, she considered them heroes, just like the soldiers in battle against the Germans. And even when the Secret Annexe was already overly crowded, she was kind and welcomed Dussel to share her room.

After a year and a half in the Annexe, Anne fell in love with 17-year-old Peter Van Daan. In the beginning, she regarded him as a bore, but since she was very lonely and needed someone to talk to, she turned to him. During the last seven months in hiding, her visits with him gave her something to look forward to.

However, after getting to know him better, she decided she loved Peter more as a good friend than as a boyfriend. This showed Anne had developed a high level of maturity to know herself and to be able to fit friends into places in her life where they were more suited. Being as lonely and isolated as she was, the decision to avoid "falling in love with love" took strength of character.

But then, Anne Frank was no ordinary girl. Not even the unnatural state of hiding, stressful enough to wither the most hardy adult, could warp this young woman's inner drive to be the person she wanted to be. In March of 1944, she wrote "I want to change in accordance with my own desires . . . even Daddy would never become my **confidant**. . . . I didn't want to trust anyone but myself anymore. . . . I had to face the difficult task of changing myself."

Anne sensed she had little time to waste in her reach for adulthood. By March of 1944, her body had shot up five inches. However, her emotional development was even more striking. She once told her father, "All these troubles have made me older." Today, writing critics who study the pattern of Anne Frank's moral and spiritual development over the two-year course of the diary marvel at the depth of maturity this girl achieved in this brief time and under such horrifying conditions.

Anne was unique in many other ways. Her goals and interests are another example. For one thing, being "just a housewife" was not enough for her. She wanted a career of her own. In April of 1944, she said, "I can't imagine . . . lead[ing] the same life as Mummy and Mrs. Van Daan . . . who do their work and are then forgotten." An ambition like this was uncommon for most girls of the 1940's, who saw themselves as mainly future homemakers, raising children at home while husbands earned the family living in the outside world.

For her age, Anne also was an exceptionally fine writer. She often remarked about expressing herself better on paper than any other way. The writing experience, she said, made her feel "wonderful." Also **analytical**, Anne paid very close attention to what people said, what they were like, and how they behaved. Because of her keen **perception** and sharp writing skills, she gives the reader a very clear picture of life and the people in the Secret Annexe.

Most of all, Anne wanted to be a **journalist.** Three months before her capture, she said, "I want to go on living after my death. And therefore, I am grateful to God for giving me this gift . . . [of writing] . . . of expressing all that is in me."

She also loved reading books, especially history, the history of art, and Greek and Roman **mythology**. The royal families of Europe also fascinated her. She studied their **genealogy,** spending long hours working out their family trees. Princess Elizabeth of England, who was her own age, was one of her favorites. Once she realized that the Nazi invasion of Holland was a real threat, she worried more about the welfare of the Dutch royalty than about her own safety.

Collecting movie stars' pictures and reading about the stars' private lives and latest films were other pastimes for Anne. To admire her favorite stars near at hand, she cut out their pictures from movie magazines and pasted them on the wall above her bed in her Secret Annexe bedroom. Though she never left this hiding place for two years, she always amazed Miep and Elli with how much she knew about Hollywood.

Anne also had visions of being onstage herself. Becoming a ballerina in Paris was one of her future goals. In Amsterdam she had studied ballet for about a year before the Nazi invasion. To keep in practice, she did ballet steps every day in the Secret Annexe. However, after a while her feet had grown so her old ballet shoes didn't fit. **Undeterred**, she tried to convert her gym shoes into ballet slippers. But that didn't work!

Anne Frank was very much her own person. She used writing as an avenue of self-expression to liberate her human spirit from the confines of the hiding place and Nazi regulations. The diary became an instrument for controlling her own life.

For example, in April of 1944, she wrote, "I can shake off everything if I write; my sorrows disappear, my courage is reborn." She therefore seized her mind's freedom to think, talk, and act as an individual, not a cornered prisoner. *She* herself shaped her own image, not on Nazi terms that a Jewish girl had to hide like a criminal or else be deported, but in her own words as *Anne Frank*, a young Jewish woman with the dignity, courage, and optimism to defy the Nazi system.

Anne's writing exercise is far from fantasy. Nor was she naive about the capacity for both good and evil in all people. She wrote about the "destructive urge in people, the urge to rage, murder, and kill." And she was fully aware of her fate as a condemned Jew. However, never once did she **bemoan** her Jewish heritage. In April of 1944, she remarks,

> We Jews mustn't show our feelings, must be brave . . . [and] do what is within our power and trust in God. . . . If we bear all this suffering and if there are still Jews left, when it is over, then Jews, instead of being doomed, will be held up as an example. Who knows, it might be our religion from which . . . all peoples learn good, and for that reason . . . we have to suffer . . . we will always remain Jews, but we want to, too.

She often saw, through the curtained windows of the Annexe, crowds of Jewish people being pushed through the streets with Nazi billy clubs. She repeatedly writes of Jewish suffering, forced labor, and deportation to the death camps. Such thoughts often drove her to depression. But Anne fought it. Though she sometimes shed tears at night in her bed, in the light of day, Anne Frank exhibited a "laugh in your face" mode to offset Nazi pressure. Humor was her weapon. And she relied heavily on God for spiritual strength.

Anne had a rare spirit. Her faith in God even extended to the very world that shut her off from everything and threatened her very life. She writes often of the things she misses:

> I long for a home of our own . . . school. . . .
> When will we be granted the privilege of smelling fresh air? . . .

I feel afraid sometimes of having to be so serious, I'll grow a long face and my mouth will
droop down at the corners. . . .

I can't help feeling a great longing to have lots
of fun for once and to laugh until my stomach
aches. . . .

But she didn't become bitter or hostile, not even
at the end of two long years of hiding. Then she
simply writes, "The world is going through a
phase. . . . It's really a wonder that I haven't dropped
all my ideals, because they seem so absurd and
impossible to carry out. Yet I keep them, because in
spite of everything I still believe people are really
good at heart. . . . It will all turn out right."

Yes, Anne Frank was a very special person. And
some day she would prove this to the whole world.

Edith Frank

An intelligent and refined woman, Edith Frank,
Anne's mother, came from a wealthy family background. It was not easy for her to adjust to the lifestyle of the Annexe, for it was quite different from
what she was used to. Unlike her daughter Anne,
Edith was a reserved, quiet, calm, and serious individual. Since she and Anne were opposites, they did
not understand each other. Their discussions often
led to tears, and Anne usually ran to her father for
comfort.

This barrier between her and Anne hurt Mrs.
Frank, who tried hard to treat both her daughters as
friends. She sometimes cried because she could not
get closer to Anne, but Anne remained unresponsive,
for she believed a mother should be looked up to as
a model, not as a friend. The tension between Mrs.
Frank and her younger daughter eased, however,
as Anne matured and became less headstrong. Edith,
like Anne, always leaned on Mr. Frank for strength
and kind words.

Margot Frank

On the other hand, Margot Frank was very close
to her mother. Just as Anne and her father did many

things together and shared confidences, so did
Margot and Edith. For example, before the families
had gone into hiding, Margot and her mother regularly attended the synagogue together. Anne and her
dad preferred to attend only on holidays.

Gentle, cool, and calm, Margot's personality
was similar to her mother's. Since she was more
obedient, she got along better with the other adults
in the Annexe. And she often tried to make peace
between her mother and Anne. Margot Frank was
an excellent student and planned to be a nurse or
schoolteacher. She also talked about going someday
to live in **Palestine** (now the state of **Israel**), the
homeland of the Jews.

There was little bickering between the two
Frank sisters. They got along well. Nor was there
jealousy or resentment on Margot's part when she
saw that Anne had developed a romantic relationship
with Peter. Margot, too, was a young girl cut off
from people her own age and surrounded continu-
ously by adults she had little in common with.
Nevertheless, she was pleased that at least her sister
had someone with whom to relate.

Margot Frank wrote a diary of the hiding period
in the Secret Annexe too. Her book, however, disappeared after the Nazi raid of the Annexe and has
never been recovered.

Otto Frank

All the Secret Annexe residents looked to Mr.
Frank for leadership; he was their tower of strength.
Without his reassurances and quiet courage, it is
doubtful that the others could have withstood the
everyday tensions and unnatural atmosphere of the
Annexe. He kept everyone reasonably calm, settled
their arguments, and kept up their spirits. And he
never, never showed his own fear and worry. In addition to that, he had the presence of mind to continue
to run his business through Kraler and Koophuis
even under the pressures of his terrifying situation.

That he was totally unselfish was obvious when
he offered to share this crowded Secret Annexe with
another Jewish family and a dentist. His **compas-**

sion even went a step further than that. He did not reserve the best sleeping room for his wife and himself, but instead offered the largest and most private upstairs bedroom to the Van Daans. And his record for caring about others went back to his first years in Amsterdam. This was why five Dutch Christians were now risking their own lives for him and his family. In fact, rather than quitting, these same kind Dutch people had once even taken a cut in their paychecks from Mr. Frank when his business had gone into a slump in earlier years.

Furthermore, this good man was an excellent father and husband. He was able to be very close to Anne and yet not anger Margot or his wife. Equally loving them all, he supported his wife and tended to his two daughters, patiently guiding their education and helping them with their lessons. Finally, he had the **foresight** and courage to prepare the hiding place long in advance in order to protect his family.

The Van Daans

Compared with the Franks, the Van Daans had a different family relationship. Instead of discussing problems quietly and calmly as the Franks did, the Van Daans argued and shouted. They were also far more **indulgent** with their son Peter. Unlike the Franks, who had insisted that Anne leave her pet behind, the Van Daans had permitted Peter to bring his cat along to the Secret Annexe. They also treated their 16-year-old like a child. As a result, he usually went off by himself to his room to escape. Despite these attitudes, however, the Van Daans really were a loving family.

Mrs. Van Daan

A nervous, excitable woman, Mrs. Van Daan rarely kept her feelings to herself. She thought Anne was a naughty girl, and she often said so. During air raids and other tense situations, she became hysterical, making everyone else be more on edge. And she cried and screamed and argued with her husband over little things. She was vain and self-centered too. Once, when they needed more money for food in the

Annexe, her husband asked Mr. Koophuis to sell her fur coat. Then Mrs. Van Daan wanted to save some of the money to buy new clothes after the war was over. She also loved to **reminisce** and brag about all her old boyfriends. Occasionally she even flirted with Mr. Dussel and Mr. Frank.

On the other hand, when she wasn't emotional, she added a spark to life in the Annexe. Friendly and easy to talk to, she cheered up the others in this bleak atmosphere and made them laugh. And she was energetic and helpful. Anne called her "Queen of the Kitchen," because she usually volunteered to do all the cooking.

Mr. Van Daan

Like Mr. Frank, Mr. Van Daan was a spice dealer. Through business dealings, he had met Mr. Frank soon after the Franks had arrived in Amsterdam. Because Mr. Van Daan was so capable and knowledgeable, Mr. Frank had later taken him in as a business partner.

In the Secret Annexe, Mr. Van Daan occupied his time by doing small repairs and helping Mr. Frank to manage the business. But he complained about many things, especially the lack of food and cigarettes. A chain-smoker, he yearned for tobacco almost as much as food. So long as cigarettes were at his side, it seemed he could tolerate almost anything. But he was quite a grouchy person without them.

Mr. Van Daan was also highly **opinionated**. If others didn't agree with his views about politics or the war, he became angry. This same stubborn attitude caused many of his arguments with his wife. However, even though he bickered with her and was overly strict sometimes with Peter, he was still a loving husband and good father.

Peter Van Daan

A typical teenage boy, Peter Van Daan was shy with girls and bored with grownups. He felt very uncomfortable when his parents argued. And how much he blushed when his mother babied him in front of the others. As a result, when he wasn't doing his share of the chores (which he did willingly), he spent most of the first year and a half in hiding alone, locked up with his cat in his room. There Peter daydreamed his hours away and often thought he was sick when he really wasn't.

Nor did he have much confidence in himself. He felt he wasn't too smart, though this was really not so. He was an intelligent boy, a good student with a perceptive mind, but he didn't work at it the way the Frank girls did. It was Mr. Frank to whom Peter usually turned for help with his schoolwork in the Annexe, for he greatly admired and respected the man.

During the last seven months in hiding, Peter and Anne developed a close relationship, but it was Anne who first went to him. Peter's interest in Anne grew steadily. Together they talked about usual teenage concerns: problems with parents, dreams of the future, likes and dislikes. They also developed a romantic relationship.

Anne and Peter Are Not the Perfect Couple

However, Anne and Peter were different by nature. While Anne found pleasure in hard work and studying, Peter preferred to loaf and take it easy. Also, Nazi persecution destroyed neither Anne's faith in people nor her attachment to her Jewish heritage. She was proud to be Jewish and viewed the world with optimism. Peter, on the other hand, had become bitter and hostile. He even had thoughts of becoming a **Christian** after the war. Anne's and Peter's goals varied, too. She had definite plans to travel and study in the future, but Peter was not sure of anything. These differences in their personalities made Anne conclude that Peter was weak. She needed a stronger person to love.

Nevertheless, Peter loved and depended on Anne more and more. In spite of their different personali-

ties, the friendly times they shared helped make a difficult time a bit happier for them both.

Mr. Dussel

Like the Franks and Van Daans, Albert Dussel, the dentist, had taken refuge in Holland to escape Hitler's war on Jews in Germany. But he came much later. He fled Berlin in 1938 soon after **Kristallnacht**, an organized nationwide riot. The Nazis had led this violence against the entire Jewish community of Germany and Nazi-controlled Austria. Dussel had brought along his fiancée, who was non-Jewish.

To escape the Nazi roundup of Jews in Holland, Mr. Dussel had to go into hiding very quickly. He didn't even have time to alert his fiancée, who was then out of the country. When his fiancée returned to Amsterdam, she had no idea where Mr. Dussel was. Nor did she ever find out that he was hiding in this very city, for the secret group could not risk letting her in on their secret hiding place.

As time went on, Dussel, normally a quiet, friendly man, missed his fiancée more and more. Her absence and his arthritic aches and pains made him increasingly bad-tempered. Friction arose between him and the teenagers. Mr. Dussel was rather old-fashioned and had a narrow **perspective** about how young people should be brought up. He thought children should be seen and not heard. Naturally, it was Anne who grated on his nerves the most, for she was in constant motion and talked incessantly. He frequently gave her long sermons about how a young lady should act.

To make matters even worse, he and Anne shared a room together! This arrangement also led to conflict because Mr. Dussel liked to be alone. Consequently, he retreated to the w.c. (water closet), or bathroom, the only place where he could find peace and quiet. He often spent three or more hours there a day. This habit and his loud, strange snoring especially bothered Anne.

Chapter 5:

The Secret Annexe Residents Live and Die in Nazi Prisons

The War Is Coming to an End

BY AUGUST 1944, the Secret Annexe residents were more hopeful of freedom than ever before. Nearing the end, the war had put the Germans on the run. D-Day, June 6, 1944, marked the successful Allied invasion of Europe. The Americans, British, and Canadians had crossed the English Channel to land in Normandy, France. There they had hammered Hitler's soldiers. Also pushing the Germans into retreat from the east and south were more Allied troops.

For the group in hiding, the past 25 months seemed a small payment for their now almost-certain release from the prison of the Annexe walls.

But their freedom never came.

The Secret Annexe Is Raided; Everyone Is Caught by Surprise

It was midmorning on August 4, 1944, when the Nazis entered the building at 263 Prinsengracht. One was a German Gestapo sergeant and the other four were Dutchmen, members of the NSB. Like all good hunters, they hardly made a sound. In fact, only Elli heard their car stop outside. But she did not concern herself when she heard them enter the building, for customers often came and went.

Suddenly, Miep and Elli looked up into the barrel of a pistol. The Jew hunters ordered the two, "Don't move! Not one sound! Not one word!" The

men headed toward the back office. When Miep heard her husband returning to the office after lunch, she ignored the Nazi order to sit still; grabbed the illegal ration booklets, office money, and other items; ran to the doorway; and shoved them into her husband's hands, saying, "Things are not good here." Getting the message, he hastily carried off the **incriminating** evidence.

Meanwhile, in the back office, the German sergeant barked an order to a startled Mr. Kraler, demanding to see the office storerooms. The Nazi search team knew everything. Heading straight for the bookcase, the five drew their pistols and ordered Kraler to open the door. The German officer grew furious when Kraler insisted it was just a bookcase, and the sergeant yanked at it himself.

The bookcase door swung open. The hooks were either not fastened securely or not fastened at all. The Secret Annexe was hidden no more.

The Nazi jammed his revolver into Kraler's back and forced him to walk into the Annexe. As they entered the Franks' room, Kraler's eyes met Edith Frank's. "The Gestapo is here," he announced quietly. Mrs. Frank was silent.

Upstairs, Mr. Frank was coaching Peter with his schoolwork. Moments before they had been discussing the exciting news of the Allied invasion. Mr. Frank had remarked, "For two years, we have lived in fear; now we can live in hope."

As the Gestapo climbed the stair treads, Mr. Frank was pointing out a spelling error to Peter.

"Why Peter," he was saying, "you know that *double* is spelled with only one *b* in English." At that moment, both looked up to see pistols pointed at them. Soon all the hunted people stood with their hands raised in surrender.

The Annexe Occupants and Two Helpers Are Arrested

Ordering the Jewish inhabitants to pack their bags, the Nazis began to **ransack** the Annexe for valuables. After emptying the cashbox and uncovering some jewelry, the Gestapo policeman needed a container to carry his collection. Nearby was Mr. Frank's briefcase filled with Anne's many papers and a book with a red plaid cover. The Nazi reached for the briefcase, shook all the contents on the floor, and replaced them with money and jewelry. The five men continued on their search for more valuables.

Approximately two hours later, 10 people climbed into the back of the police van parked outside. Mr. Kraler and Mr. Koophuis were among them. They, too, were arrested, because they refused to answer questions.

In the meantime, not one of the group had uttered a sound, not even Mrs. Van Daan. Fear and bitter disappointment had numbed them to a point of disbelief.

Fate of the Helpers; Miep and Elli Go Free

Luckily, neither Miep nor Elli was arrested. Elli gave the Nazis no chance to seize her, for as they raided the Secret Annexe above, she was able to run away without being caught or questioned. Elli Vossen remained in Holland until her death in 1982 at the age of 63.

Miep also had the chance to escape, but she couldn't bring herself to do it. In recalling the capture of her friends, she remarked later in an interview, "And I heard them going, first down the corridor, and then down the steps. I could hear the heavy boots and the light footsteps of Anne. Through the years she had taught herself to walk so softly that you could hear her only if you knew what to listen for. I had seen her only the day before, and I was never to see her again, for the office door closed as they all passed by."

After the van carried the fugitives and their two friends to police headquarters, the Gestapo agent returned to question Miep. She **feigned** ignorance, claiming she knew nothing. After intensive examination, he decided to let her go.

Today Miep lives in Amsterdam. She continues to have many sad as well as happy memories of Anne Frank and the others. In fact, she has written a book about these memories. Published in 1987, the book, *Anne Frank Remembered: The Woman Who Helped the Frank Family to Hide*, has now attracted worldwide attention.

Koophuis and Kraler Go to Prison

At Gestapo headquarters, Nazi interrogators cross-examined their 10 captives. Neither Koophuis nor Kraler answered to anything. Koophuis was sent to prison, where he became very ill. After several weeks, a Dutch welfare organization came to his aid and arranged for his release. Today he continues to live in Holland.

Mr. Kraler was sentenced to a concentration camp in Holland, where he was put to forced labor. After seven months of grueling work, he managed to escape. A bombing raid occurred while he and other prisoners were being marched under guard along a roadside. In the midst of the confusion, he and another prisoner managed to hide in the underbrush. For the next few days, the two fugitives stayed undercover. Then Mr. Kraler managed to make his way safely to some relatives in Holland, where he remained until after the war ended.

Mr. Kraler Later Receives a Reward for His Help

Mr. Kraler moved to Toronto, Canada, in 1955. Twenty-two years later, in 1977, the Canadian Council of Christians and Jews honored Mr. Kraler. He was presented with the prestigious Nickolas and Hedy Munk Brotherhood Award for courageous and selfless actions.

And in 1978 more recognition for Mr. Kraler was forthcoming. It was nearly 34 years after the Gestapo had raided the Secret Annexe. The Jewish Institute of Religion of Hebrew Union College in Cincinnati, Ohio, contacted Kraler, then aged 75. The Institute was to give him a reward for his courage and his efforts on behalf of Anne Frank and the other Jews he had sheltered during the Holocaust. Then on June 5, 1978, Mr. Kraler received a $10,000 Ideals Award for "encouraging the values and ideals which derive from religious teachings."

Anne Frank and her family and friends would certainly have cheered all this!

At the time of the Ideals Award, Mr. Kraler dismissed his heroic efforts by saying, "I did nothing special . . . just the human thing."

Mr. Kraler died in Toronto in 1981 at the age of 81.

The Fate of the Annexe People; Police Headquarters Is Their First Stop

Interested in the whereabouts of other Jews in hiding, the Gestapo questioned the Franks, Dussel, and the Van Daans. Did they know of other Jews hiding out? Where were they? Finally, Mr. Frank convinced the interrogators that the group knew nothing. Guards led the prisoners to separate cells, where they were held for several days.

Westerbork Is Next

Without notice, police suddenly ushered the prisoners from their jail cells to the railroad station. There they boarded a regular passenger train. The train headed toward Westerbork, a Nazi prison for Jews in Holland. It was unlikely that they would remain here long, for Westerbork was a **transit camp**, a temporary collection center for Jews on their way to the death camps of Poland.

The Secret Annexe group had heard rumors of those six notorious death houses. The names Treblinka, Auschwitz, Maidanek, Sobibor, Chelmno, and Belzec had sent shivers down their spines. But now they remained almost cheerful, for the news of the Allied invasion was still fresh in their minds. Perhaps they would be lucky.

Westerbork was drudgery. Barracks crammed with thousands of people made the Secret Annexe seem a palace. The workday began at 5:00 A.M. and ended at sunset. For hours on end, adults swung sledgehammers to crush old batteries, while the teenagers assembled cables. All the time, Nazi guards with police dogs pushed them to work faster and harder. Unyielding wooden shoes that didn't fit hurt their feet. And what little food there was—mostly stale bread, a coffee substitute, and watery soup—cramped their empty stomachs.

In spite of these hardships, Anne Frank enjoyed being free of the Annexe walls. She loved being outdoors in the open air and talking to people. Even though men and women prisoners were housed in separate barracks, she and Peter managed to be together often.

They Board the Last Train to Auschwitz

On September 3, 1944, the last shipment of Dutch Jews was deported from Holland. It was the eighty-sixth such trainload to head to either Auschwitz or Sobibor, the two death camps **designated** for Jewish victims from the Netherlands. The unfortunates aboard were the tail end of the more than 105,000 Dutch Jews who had met or would soon meet their deaths at the hands of the Nazis. Two weeks later, what the Franks had hoped for did happen. On September 17, 1944, 20,000 American and British airborne troops fell to the soil of the Netherlands. The invasion was only a partial success. But for the Franks, the Van Daans, and Dussel, the Allies had arrived too late anyway. All eight were on that very last transport to Poland. Their luck had not held out.

Cattle cars carried them to Auschwitz. The three-day nonstop ride was dark, long, suffocating, and unbearable. Few of the 80 people jammed in each car like animals could comfort those around them who expressed embarrassment at having to use the barrel in the corner for bathroom purposes. No one had a choice. One small window high up off the floor let in the only fresh air. It did little to ease the prisoners' bewilderment at not knowing where they were headed. And the lice that infested the cars added much to their misery.

The Men and Women Are Separated at Auschwitz

On the third night, the train screeched to a halt. The cattle car doors swung violently open. Aimed at the loading platform were bright searchlights that blinded the prisoners.

Sam Gottesman, a Holocaust survivor now living in America, clearly remembers this scene of arrival at Auschwitz:

> When the cattle car door slammed open, it was an unbelievable sight. There was so much confusion everywhere. People were screaming, frightened children were crying, prisoners with shaven heads and striped uniforms were running around, and SS guards with large police dogs were pushing the people in different directions. I thought I was in a nightmare.

Camp guards separated the men and women, shoving them to opposite sides of the platform.

There was no time for farewells. This was to be the last time Mr. Frank saw his wife and daughters.

All Arrivals Are Selected for Death or Forced Labor

Next came **selection**. At Auschwitz, which was a combination death-labor camp, 10 percent of the most able-bodied Jewish arrivals were selected for hard labor. The rest were immediately led to the gas chambers.

A young SS officer named Dr. Mengele always did the selecting at Auschwitz. Dressed in his black uniform with shiny silver trim and wearing immaculate white gloves, he met each trainload of Jewish victims. All men, women, and children passed before his scrutinizing appraisal. After a quick look at each prisoner, he jerked his thumb—sometimes his baton—to the right or to the left.

To the left went mothers of children under 14, their children, elderly people, and those who were ill or had physical defects. Those too sick to walk were told to climb into waiting Red Cross trucks, which would deliver them "to a nursing camp." Who wasn't too ill to walk after the long, hard journey in the cattle trains? Many exhausted people eagerly headed toward the trucks at the left.

Mengele directed to the right both men and women who appeared strong enough to work. From the long, protected environment of the Secret Annexe and their short stay at Westerbork, the Franks, the Van Daans, and Dussel were in fairly good shape. All were directed to the right.

Anne, Margot, Mrs. Frank, and Mrs. Van Daan joined a small group of women selected for labor, while Peter, Mr. Frank, Mr. Van Daan, and Mr. Dussel went along with the group of Jewish men destined to work in nearby Nazi mines, factories, and stone quarries.

Those who had gone to the left and the weary souls who had boarded the trucks were never seen again. Told they were to bathe and be **deloused**, they entered large buildings marked with imposing "BATH" signs. Inside, in what appeared to be bona fide shower rooms, were gas jets designed to look like showerheads. For the people here, the Jewish struggle to survive under Nazi terror was over.

The Secret Annexe Occupants Become Slaves

For those who had gone to the right, the struggle was to become a losing battle for life. Living and suffering at Auschwitz were the same. The average life expectancy of camp inmates was nine months! What lay ahead would take its toll sooner than that on all but one of the Secret Annexe occupants. Selection would occur during the next few months many times. The Nazis weeded out the sick and worn-out laborers in order to provide room for the fresh, healthier replacements who arrived daily at the camps.

Now Nazi tools, the Jewish slaves were no longer regarded as human beings with rights, choices, or feelings. They labored for Nazi industry, pushed on by merciless SS soldiers known as the Death's Head Regiment. These guards wore a skull and crossbones **insignia** on their clothing and drove the slave laborers to the limits of endurance.

Other guards were called **Kapos**. They were not SS but camp prisoners themselves—usually hardened criminals, murderers, and **sadists**. These Kapos became the new masters inside the camps during nonwork hours. In exchange for special privileges, Kapos had agreed to supervise camp life. These men and women prison guards were often as cruel and vicious as the SS. However, the life expectancy of Kapos was short, too. The SS regularly exterminated them because the Nazis wanted no living witnesses to tell about their ugly deeds.

The Prisoners Are Prepared for Camp Life

In the meantime, the new arrivals were groomed for camp life. Along with the rest, the Franks, the Van Daans, and Dussel had their heads shaved. How upsetting this must have been to Anne Frank as she watched her prized black tresses fall to the floor! Then they traded their clothes for ill-fitting, dirty pajamas which they had to wear over naked bodies, both summer and winter.

What did the Nazis do with the human hair and Jewish clothing and underwear? They built huge **magazines** at Auschwitz to organize and store these materials until they could be transferred to Germany for use. There, hair was woven into rugs and slippers or used as packing material around pipes in German submarines. All Jewish clothes were shipped to German towns and cities to make up for clothing shortages brought on by the war.

Next, the Jewish prisoners were disinfected and branded like cattle. Body lice and scabies were common problems among prisoners for two reasons. Inmates could not bathe often, and the close contact in the cattle cars and camp barracks spread the lice and scab disease to everyone. To treat both conditions, strong, stinging disinfectant was rubbed into the prisoners' skins. And Kapos followed this by tatooing numbers on the prisoners' arms. The procedure was done with an instrument tipped with a needle and filled with blue dye. Afterward, the tatooed arms swelled and hurt.

Exhausted after all this, prisoners were finally led to their sleeping quarters. Men and women were segregated in separate barracks. Their beds, however, hardly offered a resting place. Wooden or concrete bunks stacked two or three high, the so-called beds had no mattresses and few blankets. Furthermore, the barracks were so overcrowded, five people had to share each bed. For certain, there was not much sleep, only wakefulness and discomfort.

They Labor from Dawn to Dusk

The Franks and other prisoners at Auschwitz began each new day before sunrise. They shared a bathroom with 300 other people and sat down to a meager breakfast, usually a coffeelike drink and dry bread often made of sawdust. Then came roll call, which was held not only before the workday began but also after labor duty was finished. It meant standing at attention, sometimes for two or three hours, outside the barracks in all types of weather: rain, snow, heat.

Dawn to dusk was the regular work shift. There was no lunch, no water to drink in the blistering sun. Anne, Margot, Mrs. Frank, and Mrs. Van Daan spent their workdays digging sods of grass. Mr. Frank, Mr. Dussel, Mr. Van Daan, and Peter performed hard labor with the other men. It was all backbreaking work.

Anne "Shines" Even at Auschwitz

Thirst, hunger, exhaustion, and illness were everyday companions. But Anne, being the kind of person she was, charmed even the heartless Kapos. Once she connived a cup of coffee for a fellow prisoner who was nearly dead from thirst. And another time during the winter she showed up wearing long, white men's underwear. What laughs and howls she drew from the other prisoners!

Others around her also admired and respected her sense of fairness. At Auschwitz, prisoners were told to stay in groups of five, no matter what they did. Even though she was so young, Anne was chosen leader of her group. She was the only one, too, who could distribute bread to the people in her barracks so that they didn't complain about uneven portions. Consequently, handing out the bread became her regular duty.

There was much suffering and pain at Auschwitz. Around the clock the gas chambers did their work. The night sky above was a halo of red from the chimneys of the **crematories** shooting their

flames into the air. And the stench of burning human flesh never went away. Many inmates became numb to it. Not Anne. One day she cried hard at the sight of a group of **Gypsy** children standing naked in the cold and waiting to be led into the gas chambers.

Anne, Margot, and Mrs. Van Daan Leave; Mrs. Frank Dies

Anne, Margot, and Mrs. Van Daan stayed two months at Auschwitz. In October, they were selected to be shipped to Bergen-Belsen, a notorious concentration camp in Germany, often referred to as "the sick camp."

Already very ill from disease and starvation, and now separated from everyone she loved, Mrs. Frank lost her will to live. She died on January 6, 1945, only six months after the Secret Annexe raid.

All the Secret Annexe Men Die Except for Mr. Frank

Meanwhile, in the men's section of the camp, Mr. Frank had lain ill in the **infirmary,** unaware of his wife's or his daughters' fate. Loyal and concerned, Peter had come to visit him every day.

Then on January 16, just 10 days after his wife's death, Mr. Frank was besieged by Russian soldiers who had come to **liberate** prisoners. Auschwitz was no more! Mr. Frank was free! He would not discover for many months that he alone was to be the sole survivor of the Secret Annexe group.

He already knew that Mr. Van Daan had died in the gas chambers, for he had seen him marching toward the building. He would later learn of Mr. Dussel's **demise.** The dentist had died at Neuengamme, a concentration camp in Germany where he had been shipped. And poor Peter was gone, too.

As the Russians had come upon Auschwitz, SS camp chiefs had prepared to abandon the camp. They did not want to be captured, for the Allies had issued several warnings of certain punishments for their war crimes against Jews and other Nazi enemies. Hastily the guards burned as many camp records as time allowed. They even ordered prisoners to smash the three remaining gas-chamber crematory buildings in operation. (Three months before, rioting Jewish prisoners had destroyed the fourth one.) Then the chiefs proceeded to remove remaining prisoners. The physically able were forced to march with the SS to another camp deep in Germany; 3,000 Auschwitz prisoners were in this category. Peter was among them. The rest—the weak and the ill—were to be shot by the Nazi rear guard. The SS took great pains to remove any living witnesses to their crimes.

The **death march** from Auschwitz was to last three weeks. It was in the dead of winter. There was no food or water. Those who lagged behind were killed instantly.

Peter Van Daan ended up in a camp in Austria called Mauthausen. He died there on May 5, 1945, just three days before the Allies arrived to free remaining prisoners.

Bergen-Belsen Is the Final Resting Place for Anne, Margot, and Mrs. Van Daan

In the meantime, Anne, Margot, and Mrs. Van Daan had arrived at the Bergen-Belsen labor camp, a very dreadful place situated in Germany between the cities of Berlin and Hamburg. Located on a heath, or open ground where many pine trees grow, Bergen-Belsen was not a death camp, but it was worse in some respects than even Auschwitz.

Auschwitz, at least, was an orderly hell. Bergen-Belsen, on the other hand, had no order, no roll call, no schedule to follow. In some sections of the camp, there was no food, no water, no latrines, not even enough barracks. In the midst of the barbed wire, prisoners lay among the pines in tents or on the open ground, both summer and winter. No gas chambers here weeded out the sick; they simply lay around and waited to die. Then the prisoners, weak and

dying themselves, were forced to drag the bodies to open mass graves.

To make matters worse, Bergen-Belsen at this time had a raging **epidemic** of **typhus** and **typhoid fever**. The British troops, who would soon liberate this camp, would burn the disease-infested site to the ground in order to stop the spread of the **contagions**.

One living eyewitness to the Frank sisters' last days at Bergen-Belsen is a former nurse named Janny Brandes-Brilleslijper. This woman, imprisoned for being part of the Dutch resistance, remembers once seeing Anne standing in the winter cold, clothed only in a rough blanket. She had given up on the misery of wearing her lice-infested prison pajamas and thrown them away.

It was not long before Anne and her sister and Mrs. Van Daan fell ill. In March of 1945, typhus and starvation claimed the lives of all three. Of the two Frank sisters, Margot lay in a coma and died first. Anne Frank passed away a few days later. She was not quite 16.

Anne Experiences a Bright Spot Before Her Death

Before Anne died at Bergen-Belsen, she had one bright yet bittersweet moment. She met her very best friend Lies Goosens there. Through talking with other prisoners, the two girls found out they were within several hundred yards of one another, staying in adjacent compounds. Lies was the very friend that Anne had worried and pined about so many times in her diary. Anne had always shared everything with Lies—even the measles. The girls had been inseparable companions in Amsterdam since the age of four.

Now they arranged to meet at the barbed wire that separated their living areas. Even though the Nazi penalty for talking at the fence was death, the two friends risked it three times. Though they could not face each other because objects blocked their view, nothing interfered with their excited exchange. Lies even tried to throw Anne some food over the fence that separated them, but the food failed to reach Anne's hands. What a mixture of feelings their meetings must have been!

Lies remembers Anne describing her first days after the Nazi raid of the Annexe as bewildering and scary: the Gestapo had locked them in jail cells for four days before the trip to Westerbork. Anne also cried to Lies about neither of her parents being alive. (She knew nothing of her father's whereabouts and assumed he had died too.)

Fortunately, the two girls did not share death. Lies made it. Today she lives with her husband and children in Israel.

Another bit of **irony** in the Anne Frank story is that just three weeks after the young girl died, British troops arrived to free Bergen-Belsen prisoners. *(See photo 9.)* Isn't it sad that she and her sister couldn't have held on just a bit longer?

Chapter 6:

Mr. Frank and Anne's Diary Testify Against Nazi War Criminals

Mr. Frank Is the Only Holocaust Survivor of the Group

THE HARSH atmosphere of prison life and inhumane Nazi treatment had taken only seven months to kill all the Secret Annexe Jews but one. Mr. Frank was the sole survivor of the Holocaust. That he lived was nearly a miracle.

Before the liberating Russian soldiers had arrived in Auschwitz, Peter and 3,000 other prisoners had been driven off to march to Germany in the ice and snow. Other Nazi rear guards had also followed through with their final orders before abandoning the camp. They stayed to shoot all remaining prisoners too ill or weak to go on the march.

Otto Frank had stayed behind. He had been so sick, he lacked the strength to stand up. But as luck would have it, the rear guards in his section of Auschwitz did not have time to finish their work. Oncoming Russian troops forced the frightened Nazis to run. So Mr. Frank's life had been spared in the nick of time.

Otto Frank Has No Joy in Liberation

However, for Mr. Frank, there was to be little joy in liberation. Once he had regained enough strength to return to Amsterdam, he discovered the painful truth. On his way home, he met a woman survivor of Auschwitz who had shared the same barracks with Edith Frank. She told him of his wife's death.

For several weeks, Mr. Frank roamed the streets of Amsterdam seeking other survivors of the vast number sent to Nazi prisons. Everywhere, he asked about his daughters. Two girls who had outlasted Bergen-Belsen gave him the news he didn't want to hear. Now, with no family, Otto Frank became very, very depressed.

Only one bit of news cheered him. Anne's dear friend Lies Goosens and her younger sister had survived and were now in a distant Dutch hospital. Perhaps being near to them brought him closer to his beloved Anne. Otto Frank repeatedly made the long journey to visit and care for the two girls.

To fill his empty life, he also tried doing many other things. He moved in with his old and loyal friends, Miep and Henk Van Santen, and lived with them for the next seven years. He gave them his spice firm and helped them to manage it. He searched for new homes for orphaned children who had lost their parents and families in the Holocaust.

But no matter how busy he tried to be, it was no use. Amsterdam had too many painful memories. Everywhere he looked, he envisioned his wife and daughters. In 1952 he moved to Switzerland to live with relatives.

Mr. Frank Marries Again

In 1953 Mr. Frank married again. His new wife Fritzi was also a Holocaust survivor who had lost members of her family to the Nazis. Both her son and former husband had perished.

The new Mrs. Frank had once been an old neighbor of the Franks in Amsterdam. In fact, she had once met Anne Frank, who had often played with Fritzi's own daughter. Fritzi's and Mr. Frank's lives had crossed paths again in 1945 on a train bound homeward from Auschwitz, where Fritzi had also been a prisoner.

The Courts Never Convict the Actual Informer in Otto's Lifetime

On August 19, 1980, Otto Frank died at the age of 91 in a hospital in Switzerland. Thirty-seven years had passed from the time he had lost his family to the Nazis. However, for Otto Frank, time had never healed the wounds. From his home in Basel, Switzerland, he had continually worked to keep the memory and ideals of his daughter Anne alive. Memories of his wife Edith and his two daughters often called him back to visit Amsterdam and the Secret Annexe. But he never had the heart to stay more than a few days.

Nor did he ever gain the personal satisfaction of knowing that the informer on his family had been punished. He had always had his strong suspicions about the Nazi sympathizer. Dutch and West German authorities had also arrested and tried several people in connection with the Franks' case. Even Otto himself had testified. But not enough evidence was ever offered to prove the identity of the actual betrayer.

Only two facts had surfaced about their betrayer. A person did make a telephone call to alert the Gestapo of the family's hiding place. And someone had picked up the Nazi reward being offered to informers about Jews in hiding.

A Warehouse Worker Is the Major Suspect

To the very end, Mr. Frank strongly suspected a particular man who had worked in the warehouse below the Secret Annexe. His suspicions were also shared by his wife, the Van Daans, and Dussel for several reasons.

First, during the period of hiding, this man had directed questions to Kraler and Koophuis which indicated he believed people were hidden upstairs. He may have known about the back apartment beforehand and now looked upon the bookcase door with questioning eyes. Or he may have heard the refugees above. Certainly, during a two-year period, the secret occupants upstairs must have forgotten themselves and made noises at the wrong times.

The Annexe people also concluded that this worker could have been the burglar once frightened away by Mr. Van Daan's walking through the building. This thief had entered the building without breaking a window or a door lock. Obviously, he had had a key. Might not an employee of the warehouse have had access to one? And the hidden group believed the thief had had enough time to get a good look at Mr. Van Daan, who was unaware of the robber's presence. It was only four months after this incident that the arrest came.

Another clue was what had happened at the time of the raid after Koophuis and Kraler had been taken away with the rest. The Gestapo sergeant decided to place the building and its keys in charge of this particular man.

In any case, the guilt of this warehouse worker has never been established. Though Dutch authorities did arrest and question him after the war, he had to be released due to a lack of evidence.

The Gestapo Sergeant Who Arrested the Franks Is Brought to Trial

In 1963, a search and careful investigation by **Simon Wiesenthal**, a world-famous **Nazi hunter**, ended in success. The identity of the Gestapo sergeant in charge of raiding the Secret Annexe in August 1944 was revealed. The ex-Nazi was Karl Silberbauer, a 58-year-old policeman then living in Vienna, Austria.

In the fall of 1964, Silberbauer was **indicted** and brought to trial in Vienna. His trial drew worldwide attention. However, he cast little light on the identity of the actual informer, saying only that a woman had made the call that led to the capture of the Annexe residents.

Silberbauer was forced to resign his post with the Vienna police over negative publicity from the trial. Still, he claimed he was guilty of no Nazi **atrocities**. He maintained he had arrested the Franks on orders from his superiors.

Otto Frank was asked to make a statement about Silberbauer's behavior toward him, his family, and his friends during the raid. Frank commented that the Gestapo agent had acted in a businesslike manner. Based on Otto Frank's statement and a lack of evidence to the contrary, Silberbauer was found not guilty of Nazi **war crimes**.

Nazi Chiefs Who Deported Dutch Jews Are Tried

Two years after Silberbauer's trial, his superior officers were arrested. Their arrest was the result of an intensive six-year investigation by West German and Dutch authorities. Three former Nazis were indicted for **complicity** in the mass murder of more than 105,000 Dutch Jews, including Anne Frank. Arrested were 62-year-old ex-Lieutenant General Wilhelm Harster and 58-year-old Major Wilhelm Zoepf. Both had been in charge of the Nazi Depart-

ment of Jewish Affairs in Occupied Holland. Also arrested was their former secretary, 63-year-old Gertrude Slottke, operator of their Department J (for Jews).

Harster had sent out security police units to arrest Jews. (Silberbauer had headed Harster's five-person team to arrest the Franks.) Zoepf had overseen Jewish deportation. And Slottke had prepared the lists of Jewish victims.

The three former Nazis stood trial in Munich, Germany, in 1967. Otto Frank not only appeared as the major **plaintiff** but also questioned them on different points concerning his own family's arrest. Besides that, Anne Frank's diary was now considered a war **document**. As such, it was used as **concrete evidence** against the Nazi chiefs and their secretary. Imagine how Anne would have felt about this!

None of the defendants could offer Mr. Frank the name of the person who turned in his family. However, Zoepf said the caller had received the usual Gestapo reward paid to informers: the equivalent of $1.40 per Jew. Multiplied by eight, the money the betrayer exchanged for the lives of Anne Frank and seven others was less than $12.

Mr. Frank, who told the courtroom of the group's hiding, had hired Robert Kemper as his lawyer. This important attorney was one of the former American prosecutors at the **Nuremberg Trials**. These trials had been held in Germany in 1945 to convict Nazi war criminals.

All the defendants expressed regret over what they had done. In fact, Anne's photograph was on the cover of her diary when it was introduced at the trial as evidence. Zoepf took one look at her snapshot and muttered that the sight of such photographs of Jewish children bothered him.

However, the final sentences imposed on these Nazis hardly seemed just **retribution** for their key role in the murder of Anne Frank and 105,000 other innocents. Harster received a 15-year jail sentence. Zoepf got nine years and Slottke, five years.

Chapter 7:

Anne Frank Lives On in the World

Anne's Diary Becomes An Authentic Leadership Tool

ANNE LOVED people. Talking, laughing, and joking with friends were the things she enjoyed the most. In those tiny, dark Annexe rooms, she had no one. Yes, she and Margot got along well, but they were not intimate friends. Nor did Peter's friendship come very soon. Their closeness developed only after a long and lonely year-and-a-half period.

This expressive girl longed for someone to talk to, to complain to, to share secrets with. With no one else around, she turned to her **diary** and made it her imaginary friend. She called it "Kitty."

Using Kitty as her best friend, Anne confesses very private feelings she reveals to no one else. She was so protective of her secrets she begged Elli over and over again to buy her a diary with a lock. Unfortunately, Elli was unable to find one. Once when Miep came to where she was writing, Anne quickly shut the book. (Miep says she felt as if she had interrupted a very "intimate moment of a private friendship.") Even though everyone knew about her diary, Anne refused to write in anyone's presence. Only in two private places would she do it: her bedroom or her parents' room.

Kitty became Anne's "friend" in a world removed from Nazis and the war. She created this "close friend" and "new world" so her voice could be heard in a way she wanted to be heard. First, she created a record of Nazi brutality as it affected her in the hiding place. From listening to the BBC news and reports about the Nazis from their helpers who

were associated with the Dutch Resistance, Anne recorded everything she heard about the evils of Nazism. Because Anne's book is based on her private view rather than her formal research as a scholar, it is destined to rank, not as an official history book, but as one of the world's most widely read personal documents of Nazi atrocities during World War II.

In addition, the diary "listener" enables her to prove her strength of character and express firm beliefs about appropriate human behavior. She shows up the Nazi cruelty that hems her in by voicing how decent human beings *should* behave toward other people. Anne demonstrates her own ideals by becoming an **authentic** example.

Anne uses the diary in three ways to accomplish this purpose. As a tool for continuous self-improvement and development, she expresses herself openly and freely, analyzing herself and the situation around her. Hers is an unparalleled story of the personal development of a young girl under extreme conditions. Anne's creative spirit propels her forward in personal growth. This early teen displays rapid development into womanhood, despite the trauma of her circumstances. She achieves emotional growth and maturity, no matter how hard her enemies try to put an end to her existence. How can the reader tell this? Anne's patterns of thinking and writing reveal higher and higher levels of mature reasoning and human responses.

Secondly, her diary serves as an artistic vehicle that constructs a new reality away from the Nazi madness. Anne, a skilled writer with a genius far beyond her years, constructs her own world and frees herself from the walls that hold her prisoner. Through the freedom of her mind, she can express and confess private thoughts; reveal her situation as a Jew without condemning herself or the real world; and speak about life to readers through "Kitty," much as a friend talks to a friend. In other words, Anne creates a personal relationship with each and every reader. This **artistry** is an important reason why Anne Frank is able to capture not just the minds but also the hearts of readers everywhere.

Lastly, Anne uses her diary as a connection point between brutal Nazi behaviors "of the past" and the ever-present time of the future reader. By using this technique, Anne Frank emerges as a timeless **role model** for authentic human behavior and her diary stands as an authentic leadership tool for people of all ages.

Anne invites each reader to follow her example. Her call for goodness in people to work things out, "in spite of everything" going on around her, stands true as long as differences among people exist. Her advice shows wisdom and makes the reader want to follow through on her hope. This **accord** between her **legitimate** reasoning and the reader's good sense continues to form a **followership** for Anne's **vision** of a better world. In effect, Anne emerges as an authentic leader with a call for new action, an action that moves away from racism toward community formation. In this sense, the diary serves as a timeless **anchor** for a ***comm-unity-in-action*** movement, swinging away from the disorder of the 1940's to a new order that has yet to settle in place.

Did Anne realize her work would have this effect? Anne certainly had no idea she would become a renowned world figure. But neither did the painters Rembrandt or Rockwell. It appears that Anne Frank, like other highly successful artists, knew precisely her writing purpose. From the harsh reality she faced, she had a message to offer the sympathetic listener, just as a violinist must interpret a melody from sheet music for the music lover or the painter portrays an image on canvas for the art devo-

tee. A skillful writer, Anne knew the key lay in a writer's "voice," a voice that had to: (1) connect with reader understanding; and then (2) serve as an activator for moving both herself and the reader away from the re-formation of the chaotic reality she knew firsthand.

This is why Anne shifts focus from herself and her own pain to an "outsider." Her goal is to appeal to higher levels of human reasoning about human behavior for herself as well as the reader. Her unparalleled circumstances made her sense that few readers would be able to identify with her personal terror. Nor could she reason with the Nazis who tormented her. But to Kitty, a "friend in the sane world beyond," there was hope for a connection to sensible human thinking. This is the only way Anne can escape severe reality and yet get a message across, for the sake of the Jewish people and herself as victims of fierce prejudice.

The outside person of "Kitty," therefore, becomes every diary reader. In addition, the "other" world becomes each reader's setting, right now and into the distant future. The reader, as confidant, even surpasses Pim, her dear father. And Anne surfaces as such an inspiring teacher, her audience is encouraged to mature right along with her. Listener attitude grows as Anne looks past the cruelty to the purer side of human nature, the only side, the reader realizes, where any hope for human survival can ever lie.

The overall effect of reader response to Anne Frank, as Holocaust victim, role model, writer, and friend, is significant. An excess of 25 million readers in 55 nations is adequate testimony to this fact.

Anne, the Writer, Is Prolific

On the pages of the diary, Anne poured out the feelings that overflowed from her mind. She was so **prolific** she soon filled up the diary and ran over onto two more notebooks and 300 other loose pages of diary notes! Actually, all these pages held "two versions" of Anne's diary: the longer one, which

Anne wrote first, and a second, which she edited and revised. She kept all the diary pages safely locked in her father's briefcase.

Anne titled her diary *Het Achterhuis*, Dutch for *Our Afterhouse*, which has been translated as *The Secret Annexe*. Five months before her capture on March 29, 1944, Anne heard the Dutch announcer on the BBC from London remark that a collection of diaries and letters should be made after the war. Hearing this made Anne work more diligently on revising and editing the first version of her diary. She even fantasized about writing a romance novel based on her hiding experience. She wrote "Just imagine how interesting it would be if I were to publish a romance of the *Secret Annexe*. The title alone would be enough to make people think it was a detective story."

A short time later, Anne made a list of make-believe names she would use for the real people in the Annexe. In fact, when the diary was finally published, Mr. Frank used this list to change the real names of Van Pelz to Van Daan, Kugler to Kraler, Bep Voskuijl to Elli Voosen, Mr. Viskuijl to Mr. Voosen, Miep and Henk Geis to Miep and Henk Van Santan, and Fritz Pfeffer to Albert Dussel.

Anne wrote several short stories while in hiding, too. "The Flower Girl," "The Bear Who Discovered the World," and "The Clever Dwarf" are some of the titles of her tales. After the war ended and her diary was published, a collection of her stories was also published in Holland under the title *Do You Remember?* (This same collection was published in the United States in 1983 under the title *Anne Frank's Tales from the Secret Annexe* by Washington Square Press.)

Miep Discovers the Diary

Several days after the Nazi raid on the Secret Annexe, Miep and Elli returned to the apartment. There, scattered on the floor where the Gestapo sergeant had dumped them from Mr. Frank's briefcase, were Anne's diary, notebooks, and papers.

As soon as Miep recognized Anne's writing, she scooped the papers up and took them home for safekeeping, with the idea of giving them back to Anne once the war was over.

Of course, Anne did not return. Instead, Miep gave Anne's writings to Mr. Frank when he came back after the war. Otto Frank found the reading of Anne's thoughts a painfully overwhelming emotional experience. Her words moved him so deeply he could get through only a few pages of them a day.

Because he found his daughter's words so profound, he decided to copy some of the diary for his mother to read. Using Anne's second, edited version, parts of the first version, and a number of Annexe events, recorded in *Anne Frank's Tales from the Secret Annexe*, he left out passages he felt were too personal. He also cut out Anne's criticisms of her mother and some others of the Secret Annexe group because he didn't want people's feelings to be hurt. Later he also shared his copy with a few close friends. One friend loaned it to a Dutch professor to read.

Anne's Diary Is Published

The Dutch professor was also moved by Anne's words, so much so that he wrote an article about the diary for the newspapers of April 3, 1946. This news article stunned Mr. Frank. It also provoked much public interest in what Anne Frank had to say about the war and her role in it. Many friends began to coax Mr. Frank to publish Anne's diary. In the spring of 1946, a Dutch publisher approached Anne's father.

Mr. Frank was undecided about publication. Should he make public his daughter's very private thoughts? The urging of his friends and the memory that Anne herself had hoped to publish her book made him finally give in.

A year later, the book came out in the Netherlands. Word of it began to spread. A publisher in the United States put it on bookshelves in 1952. Then several New York dramatists decided to adapt Anne's diary into a stage play. The play became a very successful Broadway production. It was after this that Anne's diary began to attract worldwide attention. Her story touched people's hearts everywhere.

From the four corners of the earth, letters written in every language imaginable—from Bengali to Japanese—began to pour in to Mr. Frank's Switzerland address. Many said they had read the diary over and over again. Others proclaimed Anne's book as the most important they had ever examined.

Mr. Frank tried to answer all the letters himself. Finally, the flood of mail became so great, he retired from his business to dedicate full time to his daughter's book. All the money earned from it he donated to charities.

By 1996, Anne's diary had been translated into 55 different languages. Over 25 million copies have now been sold. Considering those sold to lending libraries alone, the number of readers must go way beyond 25 million. Just think how shocked Anne would be if she knew this!

1989—Anne's Full Diary Is Published in English

Otto Frank kept his daughter's original diary in a safe-deposit box in a Swiss bank until he died. After his death it became a part of the Netherlands State Institute of War Documentation. In February of 1981, the Institute made an announcement. For the first time, Anne's full diary would be published in Dutch. This volume came out in Holland in 1986. Three years later, the English translation, *The Diary of Anne Frank: The Critical Edition*, was published. This new book includes both versions of Anne's original diary plus the one edited by Otto Frank and published in America in 1952. *The Critical Edition* also features background on Anne's situation and the results of an exhaustive study of Anne's diary, based on years of scientific research and analysis.

Why have scholars examined Anne Frank's diary so closely? The study emerged because a number of extremists had claimed Anne's book was a hoax! For example, they said only Otto Frank or some other adult could have written it, asserted the ink and paper used in the diary were manufactured after the 1940's, and questioned whether Anne's handwriting changes over the two-year writing period were genuine. Not one of these charges is based on facts.

Fortunately, no one can any longer state false claims like this about the diary. The findings of the 250-page study, done by the State Forensic Science Laboratory of the Netherlands State Institute for War Documentation, has proven, beyond question, that Anne Frank's diary is authentic in every way.

The Diary Becomes a Broadway Play

In 1953 American **playwrights** Albert Hackett and Frances Goodrich sought out Otto Frank. They received his permission to adapt Anne's diary into a theatrical production. Much work lay ahead. To convey from a stage the dilemma of the people in hiding, their suffering, their personalities, and the atmosphere in and around the Secret Annexe was no simple matter. Portraying the layout of the Annexe itself was difficult, too.

The writers dug in. They pored over books on Nazi Germany and the occupation of Holland. To learn more about the Annexe and the two-year hiding period, the two dramatists traveled across the ocean to talk with Mr. Frank and to visit the warehouse building. For days they questioned Otto Frank, visited the Secret Annexe with him, and lingered there to try to capture the feeling. They even borrowed old World War II news broadcasts from the BBC in London to listen to reports once heard by the Annexe occupants.

Recalling the past was an ordeal for Mr. Frank. But because furthering Anne's memory and ideals was so important to him, he agreed to give the writers the details they needed. However, the interviews took their toll. Otto Frank experienced such emotional trauma from the interviews that he later had to be kept at complete rest for many days.

Once equipped with the necessary background, the two dramatists set to work. They read and reread Anne's diary entries. Dialogue and actions for the characters had to be created so their stage personalities would emerge as Anne viewed them. Stage settings reminiscent of the Annexe arrangement were important. And the mood and atmosphere of fear and horror could not be overlooked.

Like most playwrights seeking certain effects, Hackett and Goodrich used **dramatic license** to change the original story in some respects. With eight Annexe people continually in view of the audience, the portrayal of five helpers crowded the stage. The writers limited the helpers to two instead, Kraler and Miep. They cut the number of cats down to one, Peter's Mouschi. And to call attention to the tension, terror, and suspense felt by the people in hiding, they even added a few incidents that never occurred. For instance, there is a burglary during **Hanukkah** when Peter falls off a chair and frightens the burglar away.

Not satisfied until the effects were just right and intent on receiving Otto Frank's approval, the dramatists wrote and rewrote the script eight times. (However, Otto Frank never would see the play; he couldn't bring himself to do it.)

All their efforts were worth it. Under the direction of Garson Kanin, their play, *The Diary of Anne Frank,* opened on Broadway at the Cort Theater on October 5, 1955. What a success it was! For 86 weeks, full-house audiences bravoed for repeated curtain calls after Susan Strasberg as Anne Frank and Joseph Schildkraut as Otto Frank had taken their final bows.

Then the awards started to pour in. The Antoinette Perry Medallion called the play the season's most outstanding drama. The Drama Critics' Circle Award named it the production of the year. It even won the coveted **Pulitzer Prize**.

The success of the Broadway play caused a chain reaction. Soon theatrical Anne Franks, portrayed by young dark-haired girls in every land, were uttering Anne's words in their native tongues. Like American audiences, theater crowds everywhere fell in love with that unforgettable Jewish teenager from Holland. Their reaction to her situation and her ultimate death was emotional and powerful.

Tokyo audiences sobbed. Londoners, drained and emotional, felt they had witnessed an historical event firsthand. So did weeping Parisian theatergoers. But in Amsterdam, the crowds received the play in strained silence, for it was a painful reminder of why one in ten of their neighbors was gone. Even Queen Juliana and Prince Bernhard attended the first performance, given on a stage just a few hundred yards away from the Secret Annexe building.

German audiences, too, were taken aback with grief. In October 1956, in seven major German cities, the play **premiered** simultaneously. The reaction was the same everywhere. No applause. Only stunned silence for several minutes after the final curtain, and then, tears.

Shortly afterward, West Berliners were moved to name their new youth center The Anne Frank Home. One student in Hamburg made a suggestion: to make a **pilgrimage** to Bergen-Belsen to lay flowers on the mass grave where Anne Frank and her sister lay buried. That's exactly what 1,000 German teenagers did. On March 18, 1957, they pedaled their bicycles from Hamburg to Belsen, a distance of 80 miles, through a driving rain to pay homage to Anne Frank. One man who was a former member of **Hitler Youth** gave a talk at the gravesite. He told the crowd he had become a citizen of Israel to work for that Jewish homeland as a means of repentance for the death of Anne Frank and other Jews killed in the Holocaust. The following year, the German youths made this same pilgrimage again.

These two incidents were just a beginning. In the next two seasons alone, Anne's play was performed more than 3,400 times throughout

Germany! As more and more Germans saw the play and read the diary, they would continue to commemorate Anne Frank in many, many ways. So would thousands of others throughout the world.

Anne Goes to Hollywood

A few years later, film director George Stevens decided to take on the task of creating a movie from Anne's book. He worked under contract with 20th Century-Fox in Hollywood, California. As with the playwrights who had adapted the diary to the stage, Mr. Stevens began to prepare himself thoroughly before film production.

He read voraciously. He flew to Amsterdam to study the layout of the Secret Annexe. For further advice, he brought in Mr. Frank to visit the set in Hollywood. Moreover, he devised special effects so that his film would be realistic. Though he used essentially the same script as the stage version of the diary, Mr. Stevens added a few changes for dramatic effect. For example, to increase suspense, he had Peter's cat make noises behind the bookcase door while Nazi soldiers searched the warehouse after a burglary.

Stevens wanted just the right people to portray the Annexe occupants. He chose famous actress Shelley Winters to play the role of Mrs. Van Daan, but only if she agreed to gain 40 extra pounds for the role. Quickly shedding this extra poundage during production was also part of the bargain. If the movie audiences could witness the shrinking of Ms. Winters's frame, then they could better appreciate the severe food shortages the group suffered while in hiding. Ms. Winters complied.

Who would play the role of Anne Frank was Stevens's biggest concern. For a time, he considered young actress Audrey Hepburn for both her beauty and her Dutch background. But he changed his mind. It was a beautiful but unknown girl he wanted for Anne's part. After all, wasn't that really what Anne had been when she had written the diary?

Finally, after an international search, Stevens found her: a lovely 20-year-old model named Millie Perkins, a girl out of the public eye and with no acting experience whatever. She had the same rich, shiny black hair of which Anne was so proud. Her dark, thick-lashed eyes seemed just right, too, to reflect Anne's many moods on the movie screen.

What finally emerged from Stevens's efforts was a first-rate black-and-white film. Running for two hours and 50 minutes, it opened at the Palace Theater in New York City on March 18, 1959. A real success, Stevens's film attracted large movie audiences all over the United States. Then it traveled through Europe. Its European premiere was in Amsterdam, where once again Dutch royalty graced the theater to watch Anne Frank. This time it was Queen Juliana and Princess Beatrix who headed the audience.

Awards were forthcoming, too. For her excellent portrayal of Mrs. Van Daan in the film, actress Shelley Winters was honored with the highest reward Hollywood can offer a star: the Oscar. The movie also gained international recognition when it won the grand prize from the International Catholic Film Bureau in Cologne, Germany. The Bureau called it "the best film of 1959 which contributed the most to spiritual progress and human values."

Thousands Pay Tribute to Anne Frank

Anne Frank often said she wanted to live after her death through her writing. That she has. American President John Kennedy once said, "Anne Frank has left a gift [her diary] to the world that will survive her enemies. . . . Of the multitude who throughout history have spoken for human dignity in times of great suffering and loss, no voice is more compelling than that of Anne Frank."

Millions throughout the world share President Kennedy's sentiments, and many have honored Anne with **testimonials**. The list is endless, the creators both famous and average, young and old.

Admirers of Anne have always extolled the haunting expression of her eyes, often comparing it with that of Mona Lisa. Artists, from the renowned Marc Chagall down to schoolchildren, have tried to capture that look on their canvases. And wax has been shaped into her 16-year-old figure. Standing next to the noted Dutch figures of Queen Wilhelmina, Rembrandt, and van Gogh in Madame Tussaud's Wax Museum in Amsterdam is the lifelike replica of Anne Frank.

A great number of things bear Anne's name: at least five dozen schools (including the former Montessori School Anne attended in Amsterdam) and other public buildings throughout the world, a Dutch tulip, a Belgian rose. A postage stamp with her name and picture was issued by the West German government in 1979.

Even a small town in Germany is named after her. In February, 1960, Otto Frank was asked to attend the inauguration of the building of the Anne Frank Village, near the Ruhr city of Wuppertal. This village was to be a refuge for displaced persons. Mr. Frank brought along a handful of earth from Belsen, the gravesite of his daughter Anne, to lay the first foundation stone.

There was more. In January of 1957, in an Israeli Theater in Tel Aviv, a cast director of *The Diary of Anne Frank* emerged on the stage after the final curtain. He read to the audience a special cable being sent to Otto Frank. A wooded area would be planted in the Jerusalem hills to honor Anne. Today more than 10,000 green trees growing in the Judean Hills offer a sharp contrast to the golden arid land around them. It is the Anne Frank Forest, a living testimony to the young girl's eternal spirit.

Other nations have **revered** Anne, too. To remind them of their heroine, the Dutch unveiled in 1977 a three-foot bronze statue of Anne in Amsterdam, just around the corner from the Secret Annexe building. It is inscribed "Anne Frank, 1929–1945." A bronze plaque with another inscription is posted on a house located at Ganghoferstrasse 40 in Frankfurt,

Germany. This is the place where Anne grew up. The plaque says:

> In this house lived Anne Frank
>
> Who was born June 12, 1929, in Frankfurt am Main.
>
> She died as a victim of National Socialistic persecution in the concentration camp at Bergen-Belsen.
>
> Her life and death—our responsibility.
>
> *The Youth of Frankfurt.*

June 12, 1979, was made a special day of tribute among many people in major cities throughout the world. Why? This was Anne Frank's birthday, the day she would have been 50 years old had she lived. To honor the occasion, Otto Frank and Queen Juliana of the Netherlands made a special pilgrimage to the Secret Annexe. Americans also joined in to commemorate the day.

The Judaic Heritage Society of America issued a special medal as both a remembrance of Anne's fiftieth birthday and a tribute to her human spirit. The beautiful medal is inscribed with Anne's face surrounded by many symbolic images. On the reverse side are her words: "In spite of everything, I still believe that people are really good at heart."

At the Central Synagogue in New York City, a special **memorial** service was held on June 12. People from all walks of life and of many races and religions attended. Among the main speakers was Ernest Nives, the president of the American Friends of the Anne Frank Center in New York City, a group dedicated to keeping the memory of Anne Frank alive. The audience listened to selected passages from Anne's diary. Governors from many of the states also sent word. Thereafter, June 12 was to be named Anne Frank Day in Pennsylvania, Arkansas, Tennessee, Virginia, Delaware, Florida, Georgia, Massachusetts, Mississippi, New Jersey, New Mexico, and New York.

By 1996, 17 years later, every state in the nation had followed suit. June 12, 1996, became the first national Anne Frank Day. And special memorial services in many major cities commemorated the occasion.

Anne Frank **memorabilia** is extensive and ever-growing. As more and more people come to know her through her writing, more and more paintings, busts, statues, wood carvings, books, poems, songs, and numerous other things created in her honor continue to surface.

Worldwide Anne Frank Centers

As of 1997, four worldwide Anne Frank Centers serve educators who use Anne Frank's diary as a classroom tool and communities who wish to combat intolerance and discrimination. The American site, called The Anne Frank Center USA, is located in New York City. The other three centers are located in Germany, Australia, and Chile.

Professionals at the Anne Frank Centers, together with those from the Anne Frank House and other experts, have created traveling exhibitions of Anne's experience, featuring pictures and other documentation. The American exhibit, named "The Anne Frank Story," started a tour of major cities throughout the United States and Canada in 1984 and still continues to this day. Similar exhibits have also been circulating abroad.

The 50th Anniversary of Anne's Death Is Commemorated

March of 1995 marked the 50th anniversary of Anne's death in Bergen-Belsen. People from all parts of the world commemorated the event in many ways. For example, the Anne Frank House in Amsterdam approached British film director Jon Blair to see if the real essence of Anne Frank could be captured through memories of people who knew her at various stages of her life.

Blair accepted the challenge, and his film ended up winning the Academy Award for the Best Docu-

mentary Feature of 1995. The film, *Anne Frank Remembered,* is an eyewitness portrait of Anne, created by the voices of family, friends, and concentration camp survivors and never-before-shown photographs, including the only moving pictures of Anne in existence. The documentary portrays Anne's life and Otto Frank's role in spreading his daughter's spirit of hope throughout the world.

A newer translation of Anne's diary also came out. On March 9, 1995, more than 2,500 people, including nearly 1,000 children, gathered in the Fifth Avenue New York City Presbyterian Church to read passages from Anne's book during a special memorial service. Miep Geis even came to America to speak at this ceremony and to be interviewed on national television about her years with Anne and the others in hiding.

And on March 10, 1995, in Times Square in New York City, a huge screen displayed Anne Frank's image every 15 minutes. Just think how overwhelmed Anne would feel about all this!

Anne Frank Web Site

People can even learn about Anne Frank and the Holocaust on the Internet. The Anne Frank Center USA World Wide Web site came on-line in the autumn of 1995. From this resource, people can learn about: (1) Anne Frank's life and times; (2) current events related to her presence in the world; (3) new educational materials on Anne Frank and the Holocaust; (4) resources for combating anti-Semitism and other forms of racism in the community.

To gain access to the Web, contact: http://www.bdd.com

The Anne Frank Center USA may also be contacted at: afexhibit@aol.com

The United States Holocaust Memorial Museum Home Page address is: http://www.ushmm.org

The Anne Frank House

Not only has the person of Anne Frank been commemorated, so has her hiding place. In fact, the entire building housing the Secret Annexe has become a museum and an international tourist attraction.

On May 3, 1957, the twelfth anniversary of Holland's liberation from Nazi occupation, the Anne Frank Foundation came into being. This group of Dutch people pledged to buy the Secret Annexe building and restore and preserve it for future generations. They would use it to further Anne Frank's ideals of hope and confidence in the good of humanity. Not one of the founders was Jewish.

By 1960, the Foundation had met its goals. Officially opened in May of that year, the Anne Frank House has been an international tourist attraction ever since. Millions representing 65 nations have been drawn here. And the yearly average figure of over a quarter of a million visitors is steadily growing. (In 1979 the greatest percentage of tourists came from Germany.)

In 1960, Otto Frank worked with the Anne Frank Foundation to make the Anne Frank House an international educational center. Here, young people and their teachers would congregate to study and discuss the causes of prejudice and discrimination as well as the dangers of **fascism**. The building next door at 265 Prinsengracht was acquired for this purpose. Lecture halls and classrooms were set up, in addition to offices for the foundation staff.

Thus far, many teenagers and civic groups have held discussions there. An educational exchange program between Dutch and German students has been initiated. In addition, what once were the warehouse rooms, offices, and storage rooms of the Anne Frank House are now used as display rooms for educational materials and exhibits pertaining to prejudice and discrimination. For example, in 1978 an exhibition entitled "2,000 Years of Anti-Semitism" was on display. Visitors to the Anne Frank House generally walk through the display rooms on their way out of the building.

In 1996, architects started a new project to restore the Anne Frank House to its Holocaust period atmosphere. The new plans also include a library, a bookstore, new displays, and a lecture room.

The Secret Annexe Today

What is there that tourists flock to the Secret Annexe to see? Not much. It's what they feel that counts.

The rooms are empty and dark. They look exactly as they did in 1942, except that the furniture has been removed—to make room for the large crowds. Only a few permanent fixtures remain, such as the gas stove used for cooking and the incredibly small toilet bowl. Most visitors shake their heads when they look at those.

To give onlookers an idea of how the rooms had been furnished, the foundation has provided two glass display cases holding miniature models of the rooms with furniture.

Seldom do the people talk in the long lines. When the author of this book visited the Secret Annexe in the summer of 1980, the silence was broken only once. A moment of nervous giggling broke out when a floorboard creaked under the weight of a man's shoe.

For the most part, people stand and stare. They linger at Anne's bedroom wall where the old and faded pictures of Hollywood stars still hang. Lines on the wall where Mr. Frank had measured how tall the children were are still visible too. They are a pitiful reminder of how small the children were when inhuman Nazi treatment froze their growth in the concentration camps.

Another relic makes the reality of World War II hit home. It is the wall map where Mr. Frank and the others, hopeful of invasion, had charted the positions of the Allies. "Why couldn't the Allies have arrived just a few weeks sooner?" has to be a question on the mind of everyone who is familiar with Anne's story.

Nearly every visitor also takes the time to climb the really steep, narrow ladder to the attic room where Anne and Peter spent many hours by the window. And no one in the crowd complains about being held up. All willingly wait until each and every one carefully ascends the stairway, takes a long look, then eases back down.

It takes time for the people in lines to walk through these tiny rooms, to stare at the faded walls, to look out the back windows, now uncurtained, from which Anne must have gazed many times. Tourists there seem to have the patience to wait their turn though. Even the people standing shoulder to shoulder on the steep, dark, narrow stairwells leading from the street entrance to the Secret Annexe remain patient. Never turning back, they wait. And they come—by the millions—to look and to feel.

Anne Frank Lives On As an Indestructible Spirit of Peace

Anne Frank Is a Symbol and a Reminder

Who was Anne Frank? She was, most of all, a typical teenager with feelings and dreams just like you. Why did she die? She was sick from neglect and she was deliberately starved to death, not because she had hurt anyone, but only because she was Jewish. She was a totally innocent girl, an innocent victim of hatred based on prejudice.

What has Anne Frank become? Circumstances of her life and death, now known throughout the world, have made her a symbol of the most honorable human qualities, as well as a reminder of the dark side of human nature.

First, she is a symbol of innocence. Her suffering and innocence stand for the suffering and innocence of all six million Jews murdered in the Holocaust: the 1.5 million children under the age of 14 and the 4.5 million adults who were their mothers, fathers, families, and friends.

Anne Frank also symbolizes belief in the ultimate goodness and capacity of people to make "everything . . . turn out right." She proves this by her very example. Nothing, not even the Nazis and their cruelty, destroyed her faith in people. Never once does Anne mention "hating" her enemies. Because this teenager had the insight to look beyond

Nazi hatred to the other side of human nature, her trust that most people wish to do the right thing has encouraged readers everywhere to strive for that purpose.

Furthermore, Anne Frank's example offers courage to never give up a life goal, no matter how forceful the resistance. Her role in today's world is exactly what she had hoped. She once said, "If God lets me live I shall work in the world and for mankind." Isn't she doing that very thing? Doesn't she continue to live through her book and in people's minds and hearts? And with her in our thoughts, isn't it easier to be kinder and more tolerant toward others who differ from ourselves? Anne Frank did reach her ideal, in spite of her death.

Anne's death also serves as a reminder that modern culture still has not weeded out primitive human behaviors, those tendencies to crush others in the way of achieving desired goals. First, she reminds us that horrible crimes against humanity did take place in situations of uncontrolled power and during modern times among highly civilized and cultured people. The Holocaust, remember, was a 20th-century event. Survivors of the Holocaust still live, haunted by memories of the 1930's and 1940's. Aging Nazis, actually war criminals guilty of carrying out Hitler's orders to exterminate the Jewish people, are still around today too.

Secondly, Anne's interrupted and tortured life nags us about the racial, cultural, and class prejudices very much alive today. In recalling her death in a prison camp, unfit for hardened criminals let alone harmless teenage girls, we can imagine Anne saying, "Please remember me as one of the six million victims killed in the Holocaust, *only because we were Jewish.* Every time you feel you are better than someone else because you are this religion or live in that neighborhood, you trigger the same storm of hatred again."

Anne's Story Points to Ancient Truths

Anne's story also attracts worldwide attention because it points to ancient truths about good versus evil and peace versus conflict that people still need to learn. Why does Anne's situation capture the essence of these truths?

Anne assumes two roles in the Holocaust, and two opposite messages emerge. First, as a tragic victim in the brutal environment of a Nazi prison, her life is cut short. Anne suffers an agonizing death just months after her capture. The message here is clear: *The Holocaust evolved because evil forces linked and grew, causing suffering and destruction beyond human imagination, even to defenseless children, and occurred among highly sophisticated and educated people right in today's world.*

The anti-Jewish prejudice in Nazism, fueled by hate-filled political leaders, linked common, ordinary people to the cause of getting rid of Jews. The evil force destroyed people like Anne Frank, who had hurt no one, and consumed millions of other harmless people who stood in the way of the real Nazi goals: gaining land, power, and wealth. Eventually the Nazis themselves ended up in the mess they had created. This end, an important part of humanity's lesson about the consequences of evil, fits the picture of ultimate destruction that evil forces always project.

On the other hand, Anne's other position, as writer and fugitive, propels her so far ahead of the evil forces that she becomes a messenger of hope and a leader for goodness. Anne demonstrates, both in life and after death, that people can overrule evil surrounding them. Anne displays this greater power through her human will and spirit. The main source of her strength is a strong belief in God. In April of 1944, she says,

> Who has inflicted this upon us? Who has made us Jews different from all other people? Who has allowed us to suffer so terribly up to now? It is God that has made us as we are, but it will be God who will raise us up again.

In Anne's case, exactly that did happen.

Anne Achieves Victory in Defeat

Anne displays spiritual strength and willpower to break through the cloud surrounding her. She defies Nazi wickedness in many ways. Her first move is to keep a record of their vile deeds during her hiding experience. Her response is so moving, it will later evoke a powerful chord in the reader. As her book is published and widely read, Anne's voice continues to grow far above the **din** of the crowds that once consumed her. In effect, Anne manages to **actualize** her presence in the minds and hearts of millions of readers in almost every nation on earth.

Touching the eyes and ears and understanding of every decent person who cares about the good of others, Anne's voice projects a vision in people's minds of a better world. Her voice reaches beyond the dreadful Nazi story in her diary and in this book, *The World of Anne Frank.* As a result, the spirit of Anne Frank emerges in several ways:

- Despite the humiliation and abuse she suffered in hiding, she retained her personal dignity and integrity;
- Her example serves as a living witness to the ultimate destructiveness of anti-Semitism and the Holocaust, which wiped out innocent

people along with so many human talents that might have benefited society;

- Her story remains a timeless and powerful warning to stop the same potential of brute force in all **racist** ideologies;

- She leaves a living record of unparalleled personal development, from child to mature young woman, at a time when outside forces were most likely to destroy mental and moral development;

- She captures the spiritual strength, feelings, and responses of many other Jewish victims of the Holocaust who refused to acknowledge the labels and abuse of their persecutors;

- A victim of unparalleled discrimination herself, Anne looks to the future and clings to a hope in **humanity** for herself and the sake of others, a wish of every ethical person who views the Holocaust;

- Her expectation that "in spite of everything, people [who] are good at heart" will connect and interact "to make things turn out right," has become an immeasurable motivation to do so, as millions continue to relate to her story;

- The wisdom contained in her child-woman voice makes a rich historical statement about human behavior, far surpassing any record of

hateful warmongers with advanced military weapons and **coffers** to fill.

The essence of Anne Frank is a call for peace among all people. Her invitation to form a peaceful **community**, where people of differences coexist, takes shape every time there is a positive **interaction** between her writing and reader understanding of Anne's call. The product of tens of millions of such interactions, given the immense popularity of her book, projects a second clear message: *Anne Frank, Holocaust victim, achieves victory in defeat.*

Through her victory, Anne shows that goodness can overpower evil in the end, no matter how brutal the force. Her call for fellowship breaks through barriers of language and culture as millions in many nations continue to respond in a universal yearning for harmony, found only in community formation. She becomes an ongoing peacemaker, creating a unity in human understanding that removes her from the hopelessness of a prison camp in 1945 to the prominence of a legendary figure rising above her tragedy.

Consequently, there is no end to the life of a young Jewish girl called Anne Frank, as the Nazis had planned. On April 11, 1944, Anne said, "I shall not remain insignificant!" She proves her point, beyond a shadow of a doubt. And that is the enduring gift Anne Frank receives and gives back to the world.

Chapter 8:

Time for Reflection: Anne's Message of Peace Through the Perspective of Holocaust Experience

The Holocaust Is a Documented Crime

The Holocaust is one of the most **documented** crimes in history. Despite Adolf Hitler's order to destroy all evidence of crimes against Jews and others, many incriminating files remained after the war. There were several reasons. Hitler's men lacked the time and the resources to get rid of records at the end of the war. Many people had ignored Nazi laws; they took pictures of Jewish victims, seized and hid files, or wrote diaries as Anne Frank did. In fact, the Allies gathered up so much evidence verifying the Nazi war on Jews they had to use dozens of huge trucks to transport it all. All this proof would show the Nazis had violated not only every principle of human **decency**, but also international laws of war.

This mass of physical evidence provides history with an **indisputable** record of the Nazi attempt to commit a genocide of European Jews.

Following the war, at the Nuremberg Trials held in Germany, the Allies used the overwhelming evidence to convict many Nazis of being war **criminals.** Accused of **crimes** against humanity, a number of Nazi criminals claimed to be "not guilty," arguing they had "only followed orders of superior officers." The judges at the Nuremberg Trials disagreed. They gave a number of the Nazis the death penalty.

Unfortunately, some had escaped after the war because they knew their actions would someday surface in a court of law; a large number of these runaways have never been brought to trial. (To this day, there are well-known Nazi hunters, such as Simon Wiesenthal, who have rooted out many old Nazis and still continue to search the world for others.)

The Holocaust Stands As History's Model of Racism-in-Action

Many historians consider the Holocaust as the most **evil** crime ever committed in the history of human experience. Why is this? First, the Nazis' motive to commit mass murder on an entire people was unique. Not one Jewish life was to be spared. Though outrageous, this plan took on its grotesque mission and charged ahead against innocent people.

A second distinctive feature is the remarkable use of Nazi propaganda. Some deceptions were swallowed whole by followers, and others deceived the victims about their true fate. The deceitful **nature** of the Nazi **scheme** provided a host of human responses that forwarded the momentum of destruction. The Nazis devised **cunning** and deceptive strategies, never before tried. The plan to turn people against Jews as an inferior race and then to destroy the Jews touched every level of society. It began as fake propaganda, called "new scientific racial theories," and moved on to use the chaos of World War II as a cover for mass murders taking place in Poland and Russian territories after 1939.

The third and fourth distinctive features of the Holocaust were the growth of the power in racism and the great effect on the victims and the perpetrators. Huge numbers of people were consumed by the actions of racism. On one hand were the millions of Jewish people who suffered and died at Nazi hands. And on the other were those millions who climbed on the Nazi bandwagon of racist policies and acted out evil in a number of ways.

In summary, these four features make the Holocaust outrank in scope the evil committed in other crimes in history:

1. Genocide, an unmatched criminal motive, seeking total death of a group

2. The deceptive nature of the racist scheme, giving it momentum

3. The growth displayed in the power of racism, causing widespread destruction

4. The magnitude of the horrible effects, resulting in chaos and confusion

The Holocaust stands as history's model for **racism-in-action**. Because it happened, we must face a most difficult truth about the power of evil in human nature. The Holocaust serves as a **summons** to each of us. It challenges us with its success. It boasts, "Look at this monumental crime. It proves a racial-hatred plan can **network** and mushroom into a massive movement that can change the faces on the earth. All you need is just one obscure person with the nerve to fire up hidden biases into open prejudice. The documented evidence is abundant. So is proof that Adolf Hitler engaged millions in his plan to obliterate Jews and ravage Europe. Now, what do *you* plan to do about it?"

We can do exactly what Anne Frank did: use the example of the Holocaust to promote the value of positive relationships and fruitful interactivity among all people. Like her, we can promote a positive, forceful action to stop anti-Semitism and every other kind of prejudice. From such an effort, some good may come from all the suffering of the Holocaust.

Neither Words Nor Numbers Can Define the Holocaust

History has documented the hard cold facts about the Holocaust. Hitler wanted to create a "new world order" by destroying Jews and having his "master race" rule over all. Though this idea sounds crazy, millions followed it.

Yes, attempted murder of the entire Jewish people really *did* happen! Human beings, in modern society and under a legal framework called Nazism, *did* carry out this bizarre crime. They killed six million defenseless Jewish men, women, and children in Europe, and Jews throughout the rest of the world were targeted next. They almost got away with it!

The facts are undeniable. However, a true examination of the crime must also include minute details about the circumstances, backgrounds, and **experiences** of all the parties.

The following questions need to be addressed: Was the Holocaust a **premeditated** act? If so, who had inside information? And what was the real motive? Who knew from the beginning that every Jew would be slain? What did uninformed others believe about the circumstances? What prompted them to take some part of the action? What did the victims see, hear, and understand about the events taking place? How did they respond? And how did each human experience affect a person's mind, body, and spirit? What about the effect on friends, family, and others in this person's environment? on the larger world?

Such questions, when applied to a crime of the magnitude of the Holocaust, defy our understanding because the human experiences were as diverse as the people and all their relationships put together. And the action was mostly lopsided, with force coming from one side and landing on millions of defenseless people. Because almost no human **inter-actions** occurred between the two sides, **brute force** stood supreme. As a result, the degree of suffering and **irrational** behavior became so extreme and varied, the true effect escapes **definition**. Words of description or numbers of victims fail to capture it. What's more, the ramifications still affect many Jewish families today.

Words defining the Holocaust actually become a limitation, no matter how gifted the writer. For a definition to be clear, one must understand the **meaning.** To derive meaning, we must be able to (1) observe the **phenomenon** in some way; (2) see how it is related to both its parts and the sum of its parts; (3) draw analogies or explain how the thing corresponds to other similar things; and, if possible, (4) determine the degree of its effect on other relevant phenomena.

Applying such logic to derive meaning from the Holocaust makes only two messages ring true. First, in relation to human life, this tragedy emerges as the exact opposite to the **creative** processes that give life new shape and meaning. Its essence was all chaotic, **destructive** forces, which robbed life of any **growth**. So people can be certain about a second truth inherent in this event: just as the solution to the Jewish question denied every Jewish man, woman, and child a future, any potential effect of a similar action on the future of human culture can only be called **catastrophic**.

Confusion and Chaos Reign in the Holocaust

No matter where we look, chaos and confusion can be found in nearly every area of the Holocaust. Even a single sample of Holocaust experience reveals this truth. In fact, examining samples is the only way a student can grapple with the Holocaust or almost any subject. All researchers, including students of the Holocaust, need to study as many samples as possible. Unfortunately, however, avail-able Holocaust samples present only a limited perspective on what people experienced.

The biggest limitation is that the vast majority of victims are no longer alive. Fortunately though, the **oral history** of Holocaust survivors is available. Even though many survivors have now died, a large number have had their personal testimonies taped and filmed. Some still willingly lecture to groups about their experiences. However, some survivors have refused to share experiences because the memories are too painful. Many live, haunted by memories of many forms of inhuman treatment.

Another highly complex issue, the **psychological** explanation for the actions of the perpetrators, also raises more questions than answers. Blatantly criminal actions against innocent people were carried out, not just by hardened Nazi executioners, but by average, ordinary people without former criminal records. For example, law-abiding citizens, including doctors, publishers, lawyers, teachers, engineers, policemen, and many others adjusted their routines and mindsets in order to accommodate the Nazi regime. The identities and true number of these individuals is not known. And those who have testified about their actions most often shift the blame and rarely admit personal guilt. Their responses suggest they were caught up in a natural disaster, having no free will to control the course of events.

It is true that harsh Nazi repercussions did intimidate people into following their orders. Rule by fear does work. But where did human conscience, guilt, and personal **responsibility** lie in all this? It is true that small-scale attempts on behalf of churches, government leaders, and other influential groups tried to stay the hands of the Nazis on Jewish families. But could sweeping, coordinated actions of these groups have made a real difference? The same question holds true for responsible individual choices. Could responsible choices, on behalf of caring people on a large scale, have delayed or restricted the gruesome Nazi business of persecuting Jews?

Furthermore, how many people willingly acted out of selfish motives, perhaps from petty grudges toward Jews in the workplace or a desire to get ahead politically or professionally under Nazi rulers? Were some focused simply on their own safety and unconcerned about the welfare of anyone else, whether Jew or non-Jew? If so, why did this mentality exist then, and what **justification** explains why it still exists today?

And finally, to what extent was either ignorance or knowledge of the real Nazi motives toward Jews a factor in every person's behavior on both sides of this crime?

There are no ready or simple answers to any of the above questions.

Analyzing the Holocaust

This brings us to a final question about the Holocaust: how can we make any sense of a subject as complex and confusing as the Holocaust? The answer to this question is the prime objective of this whole book. How can we be sure we do not let anything like the Holocaust happen again?

No matter how large or small the evil encounter, the answer is this: (1) first, identify the forming action as evil; (2) stop to analyze and investigate the confusing circumstances that led to it so they can be avoided; (3) make a conscious choice to refuse to become enmeshed with it; (4) keep in mind a "higher purpose"—perhaps calling on a spiritual source; (5) search for building blocks of goodness in the form of helpers and work together to build a foundation of safety; (6) build an open forum where caring and serving others is the main objective; (7) keep working on this foundation to make walls of racism disappear; and finally (8) rally and celebrate in the wholeness of the true community of fellowship.

Considering the state of the world today, you will note that a good number of people are lagging between stage 3 and stage 4. Evil continues to attract followers in the world who are eager to gain power

and wealth in many disguises. On the other hand, many more billions of good people avoid destructive actions most of their lives. The point is: nowadays evil actions attract the most attention as "newsworthy." Good actions remain largely invisible. So the human tendency can be to give up hope on any sizable goodness.

But remember, goodness surfaced during the Holocaust years, too, in tens of thousands of Europeans who lived under Nazi harshness and yet risked death to help Jewish victims. And rising above the chaos and confusion, the spirit of Anne Frank has managed, in the words of an old Hebrew expression, "to draw hearts closer together" for close to 70 years. Her undying faith in the invisible power of God has moved millions to a stage where helpers are willing to build a foundation and walls of safety against the same kind of prejudice that destroyed her and millions of others.

Goodness in Anne, Her Helpers, and Jewish Survivors Are Linking Mechanisms

Anne Frank has already given us the best way to deal with the senseless tragedy of the Holocaust. The most effective way is to focus, one at a time, on the level of an individual Holocaust experience, such as reading a story or listening to a survivor's testimony. From an observer's perspective, an intimate view of another's problematic experience is far more significant and easier to grasp than large-scale human issues. Also important, too, is to listen for some mechanism of goodness.

The evidence of goodness is already there in the form of the storytellers, the survivors themselves. They now serve as critical living lessons from history and spiritual building blocks to a better society. We also should listen with a **hope** of hearing that some goodness may have surfaced even back then, so that it will continue to serve as a connecting link to today.

As we well know, the **spirit** of Anne Frank has done that very thing. Her positive attitude toward others and the good-spiritedness she projects have inspired readers for decades. Her story also rests on the support of the goodwill of helpers who protected her and the others for nearly two years. This combination of good has and will continue to serve as a timeless linking mechanism from the past. It prompts a caring attitude about victims of prejudice and discrimination. Only this, a caring attitude, can move an observer of wrongful situations to make a rightful choice and say, " Yes, I will help that victim of intolerance!"

All sympathetic readers, whether they know Anne's plight beforehand or not, usually respond to the diary in a similar way: (1) they appreciate the good deeds of the four helpers more and more as Anne's story unfolds; (2) they delight in the evolving of Anne's unique personality and writing talent; (3) they identify with the humanness of the other hiders; (4) they empathize in the attempts to normalize life in a totally abnormal environment; (5) they shudder as the fugitives fear for their lives yet cling to survival; (6) they are left hanging as the diary ends abruptly; (7) they become filled with the dreadful awareness the aftermath has on Anne and the others; (8) they worry and breathe a sigh of relief about the fate of the helpers; (9) and then they experience **grief**, accompanied by a powerful **motivation** to take positive action against anti-Semitism, too, as they recall Anne's hope in humanity's goodness to make things "turn out right."

Only Anne's Call Makes Sense of the Chaos: "Goodness-in-Action"

The combined product of these reader responses is a **meaningful relationship** between what has been learned and what should be done about it. In other words, Anne Frank's faith in people manages to create a positive human force, the only kind from which any meaningful action can develop. In its

effect, some order and sensible thinking arise out of the confusion and disorder that destroyed her.

This movement of human desire toward community formation is human **progress**, a **progression** from chaos to **order** and from total destruction of life toward a **formation** of **constructive** human relationships. It is the **fruit** of Anne's effort to form meaning from her hopeless and meaningless existence in hiding, which assumes worldwide proportions because it is based not on a naive belief in humanity's goodness but in a promotion of people's **inherent** goodness to change things for the better in the future. A bond of understanding has taken hold in "the goodness of the hearts" of millions of readers everywhere: "Never again should the likes of this happen."

This **unity** of understanding acts as both an individual **promise** and a group **com-promise** that: (1) neither Anne Frank nor any other Jewish person should suffer this way anymore; (2) the rights and welfare of the Jewish people, as well as every other minority group in society, must be protected; (3) good people everywhere need to link spiritually to push evil prejudice into **oblivion**; and (4) the movement of goodness must form and grow through a continuous **inter-connectedness** and **inter-activity** of many groups working to assure these very things.

In conclusion, a *meaningful purpose* emerges from the hope Anne Frank had in mind. This becomes her message: *let goodness in people form a comm-unity-in-action movement to achieve a unity through diversity, where human relationships generate wholesome and constructive experiences, built on the* **common ground** *of mutual respect and celebration of cultural differences and human and spiritual fulfillment.*

Society still has a long, long way to go. That is why the memory of the Holocaust and Anne Frank must be kept alive, in order to drive her meaningful message home, again and again and again.

Student Activities

Suggestions for Using the Student Activities

Vocabulary

Each chapter includes a list of vocabulary words. Before your students read each chapter, you might introduce them to these words and concepts. Or, you can use the vocabulary list as a pretest, or as a posttest to check their understanding. The list for Chapter 8 is longer than that of the earlier chapters, addressing some of the higher-level concepts introduced in that chapter. The vocabulary study for this chapter may be spread out over several teacher or learner activities. For example, teachers can select groups of words for: (1) a pretest or posttest for certain reading sections; (2) introducing concepts before students read various reading sections; (3) forming questions for classroom discussion purposes; (4) independent student work in defining words and writing sentences; (5) use in students' creative writing assignments; (6) essay test questions about chapter concepts; (7) ideas for students to use in projects like posters or artistic representations; (8) a study/review list for students, prior to reading or testing; (9) a list for cooperative learning groups to draw on for investigation; and (10) background reference for you to use as you introduce the ideas and concepts in the chapter.

Reading Comprehension

Each chapter also contains a reading comprehension exercise that can be used as an oral quiz, or as a reproducible written quiz. Or, if you prefer, you may use it as a source of discussion questions after the students have read the chapter. Answers are provided for the reading comprehension quiz.

Discussion Questions

Each chapter contains discussion questions relating to the topics in the reproducible student reading. These questions can be used to lead a class discussion, or you may choose to use some or all of them for a short-answer essay test. Answers are provided for the discussion questions.

Short Essays

Chapters 1–7 also contain critical thinking activities you might offer to students to help them think about what it might be like to be Anne Frank or one of the people who lived and supported the Jews during the time of the Holocaust. You can use these activities as short essay assignments or as long essay questions on a test. These essays would also make good class discussion topics.

Possible Topics for Research Reports

These topics, in Chapters 1–7, offer a wide variety of ideas and resources to extend students' understanding and awareness of the events of the Holocaust. These can be used for term paper research or for weekly research assignments.

Cooperative Learning Activities

At the end of Chapter 8, you will find two cooperative learning activities designed to offer extended research and reflection on the life and experience of Anne Frank and other Holocaust victims. Anne Frank's hope and the study of Holocaust experience calls for people to look for ways to erase racism and anti-Semitism so that people of different cultures can live together in peace. The two cooperative learning activities offer a stepping stone for such a call to action to become more mindful of the forces and confusion that led to the Holocaust. Included in the cooperative learning activities are research, reports, summarizing, reflection, and activities for active participation in the community. Students will also learn the value of supplementing research and oral reports with visual aids and three-dimensionl projects.

Extending Student Interest

After the cooperative learning activities, you will find an extensive bibliography for conducting further research and creating reports on Anne Frank and the Holocaust and many other related topics. This bibliography includes books, audiovisual materials, as well as a complete bibliography of the materials consulted to create *The World of Anne Frank: A Complete Resource Guide.*

The Franks Suffer Persecution in Germany

Vocabulary

1. **Adolf Hitler**
Adolf Hitler was the Nazi dictator of Germany between 1933 and 1945.

2. **anti-Jewish laws**
Nazi discriminatory laws denied Jews many rights and privileges, including citizenship, civil rights, and property ownership.

3. **Aryan**
During the Hitler era, the Nazis incorrectly used the term "Aryan race" to mean "German race." Actually, Hitler and his men were confused in two ways. First, there is no such thing as an "Aryan" or "German" race. Second, "Aryan" really means a family of languages often referred to as Indo-European. Not just Germans but half the world's population speaks a language belonging to this group, including English, French, Polish, Italian, and many others.

4. **boycott**
To boycott is to refuse to do business with a specific group. The Nazis boycotted Jewish businesses and kept all Germans from buying from or selling to Jewish merchants.

5. **concentration camp**
A concentration camp is a place where political enemies and prisoners of war are held. Without trial or explanation, the Nazis imprisoned Jews and everyone else they wanted out of the way. They used their camps to terrorize people and silence opposition.

6. **discriminate**
To discriminate can mean to make a distinction, but it also means to act on the basis of prejudice or unfairness. The Nazis used laws to discriminate against Jews or treat Jews unfairly, because they regarded Jews as non-Germans.

7. **Jew**
A Jew is a person whose religion is Judaism, a member of a group that once lived in Palestine but now lives in many countries throughout the world. German Jews comprised barely one percent of the total German population when Hitler came to power.

8. **Judaism**
Judaism is the religion of the Jewish people, based on the belief in one God. The foundation of Judaism is in precepts of the Old Testament and teachings of rabbis found mainly in a book called the Talmud.

9. **mark**
The mark is a unit of German money.

10. **minority group**
A minority group is comprised of a number of people who differ in some way from the dominant group that has greater control in society. Differences in culture and religious belief made Jews a minority in German society. Nazis also singled Jews out as an "inferior race."

11. **Nazi**
Nazi is an acronym, or abbreviated name, for

the Nazionalsozialische Partei, or National Socialist German Workers' party. This was a fascist group under the leadership of Adolf Hitler.

12. **persecute**
To persecute is to harm often and unjustly. The Nazis persecuted Jews and other groups they called "inferior races," such as Slavs and Gypsies.

13. **propaganda**
Propaganda is a plan for spreading opinions. Nazi propaganda to discredit Jews and to promote the master race theory bombarded the German public through every communication channel possible: schools, the press, radio, books, magazines, paintings, stage plays, films, songs, etc.

14. **scapegoat**
A person or thing made to take the blame for the mistakes of others is called a scapegoat. Nazis used German Jews as the scapegoats for all the economic, social, and political problems following World War I.

15. **storm troopers**
Hitler created a private army who helped him to power by fighting opposing political parties like the Communists and Democrats.

16. **synagogue**
A synagogue is a building used by Jews mainly for the purpose of religious worship and instruction.

17. **Third Reich**
The German government under Nazi control between 1933 and 1945 was called the Third Reich.

18. **vandalize**
To vandalize is to willfully destroy another's property. To harass Jews, Nazis vandalized synagogues and other Jewish property.

19. **World War I**
World War I was fought in Europe, Asia, and Africa between July 28, 1914, and November 11, 1918. On one side were the United States, Russia, France, Great Britain, and their allies. The other side included Germany, Austria-Hungary, and their allies. The Nazis came to power after World War I largely because the existing German government was unable to solve severe postwar problems.

Name _____ Date _____

Reading Comprehension Quiz

DIRECTIONS: This is a true and false exercise. Write a *T* if a statement is true. Write an *F* if it is false. Write your answers in the blanks next to each statement.

_____ 1. Otto Frank was a German army officer.

_____ 2. From the time World War I ended in 1918 up to the time that Hitler took power in 1933, Germans experienced no breathing spell from all their economic problems.

_____ 3. Nazis gained the most power during times of trouble in Germany.

_____ 4. The Communists who battled the Nazis in the streets were Russians.

_____ 5. The Nazis were just like the Communists.

_____ 6. Anne Frank was born in Berlin, Germany.

_____ 7. That Hitler blamed Jews for German problems made no sense.

_____ 8. The Nazis persecuted Jewish adults but left their children alone.

_____ 9. Many Germans who supported the Nazis did not realize how far Hitler would go in his hate campaign against Jews.

_____ 10. Nazis called Jews an inferior race.

_____ 11. Hitler's anti-Jewish laws were a means of forcing Jews out of Germany.

_____ 12. The fear of Communism and severe post-World War I problems brought Nazism to Germany.

_____ 13. Germany was a democracy before the Nazis came to power.

_____ 14. Jews comprised five percent of the total German population when Hitler came to power.

_____ 15. Otto Frank's family were Orthodox Jews who strictly followed all precepts of the Jewish faith.

Discussion Questions

1. Why did the Franks and other German Jews believe they were true Germans?

2. Give three reasons why the morale of the German people was low at the end of World War I.

3. Why did the inflation that occurred after World War I cause Germans to lose more faith in their government?

4. What common goal did the Nazis and the German Communists share?

5. What were Hitler's two goals? Why did he want Jews out of Germany?

6. What was the Communists' way to solve all of Germany's postwar problems?

7. When Anne Frank was born, why had conditions improved in Germany? What economic disaster struck shortly after her birth?

8. Describe life in Germany during the Depression.

9. Why did so many Germans decide to join ranks with the Communists?

10. What fear made many sensible Germans turn to the Nazis for help?

11. Why did Communists and Nazis battle in the streets? How did this chaos shake people's faith in their government even more?

12. For what problems did Hitler blame Jewish Germans?

13. Why were Hitler's charges against Jews false?

14. Discuss how Hitler tried to force Jews to leave their country.

15. What happened to all Jewish property whenever Jewish families emigrated? Do you think this was a factor in holding some families back?

16. In what year did the Franks flee?

Word Derivations

Below are five activities related to the derivation of words from this chapter. Working alone or with a partner or groups, complete one or more of these activities.

1. *Scapegoat.* Tell the derivation of the word. Give its meaning once used by ancient Jewish high priests, and tell how that meaning is related to the current use of the word.

2. The word *Nazi* is an *acronym.* First define *acronym.* Then look up the derivation of the word *Nazi.* Also look up the derivation of these acronyms in your dictionary:

ALCOA	GASP	Nabisco	scuba
Amerasian	Gestapo	NASA	SEATO

Amerind	HUD	NATO	snafu
AMOCO	laser	NOW	UNESCO
BASIC	LEM	PanAm	Wac
CORE	MASH	radar	

3. *Holocaust.* Give the derivation of the word, its literal meaning, and the reason it is used to describe the mass killing of Jews by the Nazis.

4. *Propaganda.* Give the origin of the word. Tell how the original meaning is related to the current use of the word.

5. *Boycott.* In addition to your dictionary, use the encyclopedia for the origin of this word. Tell how the current use of the word came to be.

Short Essays

1. Using at least eight vocabulary words from this chapter, write a short essay explaining how post-World War I conditions led to the rise of Hitler in Germany and to the persecution of Anne Frank and other German Jews.

2. Pretend you, like the Franks, are a German Jew whose ancestry in Germany dates back hundreds of years. Write a short essay describing your feelings about being persecuted and being labeled "non-German." Include such things as your reactions and questions related to you and your family's military service record, the law forbidding you to attend public schools, and the seizing of your property.

Answers to Reading Comprehension Quiz

1. T; 2. F; 3. T; 4. F; 5. F; 6. F; 7. T; 8. F; 9. T; 10. T; 11. T; 12. T; 13. T; 14. F; 15. F

Answers to Discussion Questions

1. Germany was their only home, and their ancestors had lived in Germany for hundreds of years.

2. a. Germany had lost World War I.

   b. Countries the world over blamed Germany for causing World War I and insisted Germans pay war damages to other European nations.

   c. A severe inflation shook the already weak German economy.

3. Prices rose so high that people could not afford to buy food and other necessities, businesses closed, and thousands lost jobs.

4. They both wanted to take over the German government.

5. Hitler wanted to create two things: a master race of Germans and the Third Reich, an all German-speaking nation which would rule the world. He considered Jews "non-Germans" and called them an inferior race.

6. The Communists wanted to make Germany a Russian territory in which all property would become state-controlled.

7. Before Anne was born, America and other nations poured money into the German economy, people went back to work, and prices stabilized. Soon after Anne's birth, the Great Depression began.

8. Millions were unemployed, hungry, and homeless. Many had no choice but to accept food handouts from the government and to live in crude sheds on vacant lots.

9. The Communists promised that all workers would share in the wealth of the state.

10. Many did not want to live under Russian rulers or have their properties seized by the state. The Nazis who promised to create a new, powerful Germany also pledged to get rid of the Communists.

11. They wanted to create chaos in the country so that the German government could not keep order. This lack of order caused people to look elsewhere for stable government leaders.

12. He blamed them not only for every post-World War I problem, but also for causing Germans to lose that war.

13. All Germans—Jews and non-Jews alike— suffered from the war and the problems that followed it in exactly the same way. Jews had more than done their share to defend their homeland in the war. And Jews were a tiny minority of the German population.

14. He passed many harsh anti-Jewish laws, ordered Jewish businesses boycotted, and encouraged mistreatment of Jews.

15. The Nazi government siezed it. Yes, for many resented giving up everything they had.

16. The Franks emigrated in 1933.

Possible Topics for Research Reports

1. Contrary to what Hitler said, Jews were great contributors to the culture and welfare of not only Germany but also the world. Along this line are two possible topics:

   a. **Famous German Jews**
   By 1933, of the 38 Germans who had won the Nobel Peace Prize, 11 were Jewish. Find out who these Jewish winners were and what their accomplishments were.

   b. **World-famous Jews**
   Good sources: *Index to Collective Biographies for Young Readers* by Judith Silverman; *American Jewish Heroes* by Rose G. Lurie; *Great Jewish Women* by Elma Levinger.

2. **Hitler as a politician**
   Read Chapter 6, "The King of Munich and His Court," in the book *Adolf Hitler* by Frank Gervasi.

3. **Hitler's character**
   Good sources: The chapters "A Man Possessed" and "The Anatomy of a Liar" in *Hitler and Nazism* by Louis B. Snyder; *Hitler's Hang-ups* by Mina C. and Arthur H. Klein; *The Mind of Adolf Hitler* by Walter Langer.

4. **The Reichstag fire**
   The Nazis used this incident to destroy two things: the German democracy and the German Communists. Good sources: *Reichstag Fire* by Henry Gilford; *Reichstag Fire: Ashes of Democracy* by John Pritchard.

5. **The Nazi's "Lebensborn" program**

6. **The Jews as a race**
   The Nazis claimed the Jews were a race. Investigate this claim. Good sources: Chapter 6, "Are Jews a Race?" in *Man's Most Dangerous Myth: The Fallacy of Race* by Ashley Montagu; the topics "race" and "Jews" in encyclopedias.

7. **Germany in the 1920's and 1930's**
   This period was characterized by inflation and depression. A good source of photos from this era is *Seig Heil: An Illustrated History of Germany from Bismark to Hitler* by Stefan Lorant.

8. **Dr. Leo Baeck (1873–1956)**
   Dr. Baeck was the leader and spokesman of the German-Jewish community during the Hitler years.

9. *Mein Kampf*
   Research Hitler's book. Did he do the actual writing? What was it about? When and where was it written? Most books on Nazi Germany and Adolf Hitler will serve as good sources.

10. **Anti-Jewish laws**
    Most of these laws were passed in Germany in 1933. Good sources: *The War Against the Jews* and *Holocaust Reader* by Lucy Dawidowicz; *The Holocaust: The Destruction of European Jewry, 1933–1945* by Nora Levin; *Hitler's War Against the Jews* by David A. Altshuler.

11. **The Versailles Treaty**
    The peace treaty that officially ended World War I blamed the Germans for causing the war and called for many punishments against them. How did the Germans feel about the Versailles Treaty? How did Hitler use the treaty to gain power? Encyclopedias and books on world history are good sources.

12. **Hitler's life**
    Good, short biographies are: *Horn of the Moon* by Gene Smith; *Hitler and Nazism* by Louis B. Snyder.

13. **Fascism**
    What is fascism? Why is Nazism a form of fascism? How are Nazism and Communism similar? How are they different?

Nazi Terror Moves to Holland

Vocabulary

1. **Allies**
   The nations that fought against Germany, Japan, and Italy during World War II were called the Allies. The Franks hoped for an Allied invasion of Holland.

2. **anti-Semitism**
   This term is often used to mean hateful feelings for or actions against Jews. It was incorrectly used by Wilhelm Marr, a German writer who coined the term in 1879. He defined anti-Semitism as "prejudice against the 'Jewish or Semitic race.'" Marr didn't realize that *Semitic* refers not to a "race" but to a group of languages that includes not only Hebrew, a Jewish language, but also a number of other languages, such as Arabic and Ethiopic. Nevertheless, Marr's inaccurate definition of anti-Semitism has been used ever since.

3. **assimilate**
   To assimilate is to absorb or become alike. Both German and Dutch Jews had assimilated the non-Jewish culture around them.

4. **BBC**
   BBC stands for British Broadcasting Corporation. During World War II, the BBC broadcast radio messages to occupied Europe.

5. **blitzkrieg**
   Blitzkrieg is a German word meaning "lightning war." It is used to describe a rapid, overwhelming attack.

6. **collaborate**
   During a war, to collaborate means to aid or cooperate with the enemy. Compared with some other Europeans living in occupied Europe, few Dutch collaborated with the Nazis.

7. **deport**
   To deport a person is to exile or remove that person from a country. Nazis deported European Jews from their native lands to concentration camps and ghettos.

8. **emigrate**
   To emigrate is to move from one's own country to live in another. Like the Franks, thousands of Jewish refugees emigrated to Amsterdam, Holland, to escape Nazi terror.

9. **ghetto**
   A ghetto was the part of a city where Jews were forced to live. The Nazis first set up ghettos in cities in central occupied Poland immediately after their invasion of that country in 1939. Later, ghettos were spread over much of occupied Eastern Europe.

10. **guerilla**
    A guerilla is an independent fighter in a war who is not part of the regular army. Many Dutch Jews and non-Jews became guerillas who harassed the Nazis in many ways.

11. **Holocaust survivor**
    A person who lived through the persecution of the Nazis is called a Holocaust survivor. Most of the Holocaust's victims were Jews. Of the

more than nine million Jews in occupied Europe, only one third survived.

12. **infantry**

Soldiers trained to fight on the ground or on foot are infantry.

13. **invincible**

To be invincible is to be incapable of being defeated. Many young Dutchmen who joined the German army did so because they believed the German army to be invincible, and they wanted to be part of a winning cause.

14. **labor camps**

Labor camps were Nazi prisons where inmates were forced to work. Except for most death camps, nearly all Nazi camps used prisoners as a cheap labor force.

15. **martial law**

During a time of war or trouble, soldiers and military authorities might rule a country. This is martial law. The Germans declared martial law in Holland.

16. **NSB**

NSB is a name for the Dutch who joined the Nazi party, the Dutch National Socialist Movement.

17. **occupied countries**

The countries taken over by German forces during World War II were called occupied countries.

18. **option**

The power or right of choosing is an option. Because most of the 100,000 Jews living in Amsterdam were too poor to have large reserves of cash necessary for one's keep over an extended and indefinite time in hiding, this option was closed for the vast majority of Holland's Jews.

19. **outspokenness**

The act of speaking with frankness and boldness is outspokenness. Nazi outspokenness about dislike of Jews was cruel, caring not at all whether Jewish families felt hurt or insulted.

20. **pogrom**

A pogrom is an organized and, often, officially approved attack on a minority group. The first Nazi pogrom against all the Jews of Germany and Austria occurred November 9–10, 1938. It was called *Kristallnacht,* or "Night of Broken Glass."

21. **prejudice**

A prejudice is an opinion or judgment made in advance without good reason. The Nazis had strong prejudices against Jews.

22. **ration**

To ration is to allow only fixed amounts. Germans strictly rationed food and other supplies to the citizens of their lands. They gave out **ration coupons**, which severely limited the number of items people could purchase.

23. **refugee**

A person who flees for safety in times of war or persecution is a refugee. The Franks were refugees from Germany.

24. **revitalized**

To revitalize means to give new life to. The Dutch National Socialists or Dutch Nazi party, which had gained attention in 1931, joined forces with the German National Socialists or German Nazis in 1940 when the German armies seized Holland.

25. **sabotage**

To undermine or interfere in a cause is to sabotage. The Dutch Resistance, which included both Jews and non-Jews, sabotaged Nazi efforts in many ways, such as giving false information, blocking military efforts, making defective war equipment in factories, helping refugees to get food and supplies, and destroying enemy forces.

26. **Stuka**

A Stuka is a German airplane, a bomber.

27. **underground**

An underground is a secret organization that resists foreign domination and works to free its country. The people who helped the Franks were members of the Dutch underground or Resistance.

28. **World War II**

The war fought mainly in Europe, Asia, and Africa from September 1, 1939 to August 14, 1945, is called World War II. It began when Hitler's armies invaded Poland, and Britain and France came to the Poles' rescue. Eventually the war involved most of the world. The major conflict was between Great Britain, the United States, and the Soviet Union on one side, and Germany, Italy, and Japan on the other.

Name _____ Date _____

Reading Comprehension Quiz

DIRECTIONS: Each incomplete statement in Part A tells about Jews under Nazi occupation in Holland. Part B gives reasons that complete the statements. Match the lettered statements in Part B with the numbered statements in Part A to make complete sentences. Write your answer in the blank after each incomplete statement in Part A.

PART A—Incomplete Statements

1. Jews like the Haalmans considered themselves truly Dutch because _____

2. Mr. Frank was aware of friendly attitudes toward Jews in Holland because _____

3. Hitler ignored the Dutch wish to remain neutral in the war because _____

4. The Dutch could not stop the German invasion because _____

5. The German bombing of the city of Rotterdam was totally unnecessary because _____

6. We can safely say that Nazi ideas influenced fewer Dutch people than any other group of Europeans under Nazi rule because _____

7. The Dutch queen and her cabinet fled to England because _____

8. Dutch resistance consisted of people from all walks of life because _____

9. Nazis felt freer to persecute Polish Jews than Dutch Jews because _____

10. The anti-Jewish laws against Dutch Jews were not new because _____

11. Jewish registration was really a step toward deportation of Jews because _____

12. Nazi laws against Jews really segregated the Jews from the rest of their fellow citizens because _____

13. Though the Dutch fiercely defended their Jewish fellow citizens, they could not stem the tide of Nazi persecution because _____

14. The Nazis lied, telling Jewish deportees they were going to work in the East, because _____

15. The Franks went into hiding because _____

16. The Dutch Nazi party was optimistic about the German occupation of Holland because _____

Name _____ Date _____

PART B—Reasons Why

A. this was the Nazi way of identifying Jews to be shipped out of the country.

B. the Dutch were negotiating a peace treaty with the Germans at the time.

C. they could no longer get out of Holland, and Margot had received a call-up notice.

D. their ancestors had lived in Holland for centuries.

E. they were no match for the powerful German armies.

F. if the victims knew they were destined to die in the gas chambers, they would resist.

G. the Nazi invaders usually killed or imprisoned the heads of state in the countries they occupied.

H. he had done business in Holland for years.

I. obviously anti-Jewish feelings among the people were stronger in Poland than they were in Holland.

J. Nazi power, organization, and weapons used in carrying out the anti-Jewish war were too great to stop.

K. the laws were made to isolate and confine Jews to certain areas until they could be deported.

L. there were fewer Nazi collaborators among Dutch people than among any other group of occupied persons.

M. this meant they could gain political power and wealth by joining forces with the German Nazi party.

N. he wanted to use the airfields in Holland to send missiles to destroy nearby England.

O. not only the queen and her cabinet but also workers, other men and women, and even the children opposed the Nazis.

P. they were the same laws enforced against the Jews in Germany and all Nazi-occupied lands.

Discussion Questions

1. Give two reasons why Mr. Frank decided to emigrate to Holland.

2. Explain why the Franks would have been better off to have left Europe altogether.

3. Discuss how the Dutch planned to bar the German invasion. How long did they hold out?

4. Describe the German blitzkrieg attack.

5. Why did most of Europe's Jews fall into the Nazi grip?

6. Why did Holland's terrain make guerilla warfare difficult?

7. Compare the way Nazi invaders treated Jews in Poland with the Nazi treatment of Jews in Holland. Why did the Nazis move more slowly in Holland?

8. What was the Nazis' first step in identifying Jews among the Dutch population?

9. What happened to all Jewish property?

10. Discuss the many anti-Jewish laws Anne Frank mentions in her diary.

11. When did Nazis begin to deport Dutch Jews to camps in the East?

12. When did the Franks decide to go into hiding?

13. Give three reasons why as many as 30,000 Dutchmen decided to join the German military forces after the German invasion of Holland.

14. Why did only six percent of Jewish families in Holland go into hiding?

15. How many of Holland's 140,000 Jews would be consumed in the Holocaust before it ended with the war in 1945?

Short Essay

Pretend you are a close friend of Anne Frank's who used to sit beside her at the Montessori School before the Nazis forced her to leave. You are not Jewish. You really miss Anne. You live across town from her, so you two can no longer get together. You can't telephone; Nazi restrictions have removed her phone and stop her from using another.

Write Anne a letter. Tell her how you feel about her being persecuted by the Nazis.

Answers to Reading Comprehension Quiz

1. **D**; 2. **H**; 3. **N**; 4. **E**; 5. **B**; 6. **L**; 7. **G**; 8. **O**; 9. **I**; 10. **P**; 11. **A**; 12. **K**; 13. **J**; 14. **F**; 15. **C**; 16. **M**.

Answers to Discussion Questions

1. Not many anti-Jewish feelings existed in Holland, and Mr. Frank, who had been a frequent visitor to Holland before the war, enjoyed its friendly atmosphere. Also, Holland opened its borders to Jewish refugees.

2. The Nazis eventually took over Holland and caught up with the Franks.

3. They intended to hold back and stop the invaders by opening their dikes and blowing up their bridges. They held out for five days.

4. It was a heavy, intense attack by land, air, and water forces all at once.

5. The Nazis seized nearly every European country and persecuted Jews living in all their occupied lands.

6. A mostly flat wide-open country with large cities, Holland had few places to hide.

7. After their invasion of Holland, the Nazis waited for two months before attacking Dutch Jews, but in Poland, they persecuted Jews as soon as they entered the country. Anti-Semitism was not popular among Dutch people.

8. They required that all Jews register "for their protection."

9. First, Jews were ordered to register all their property with the Nazi government in Holland. Then, the Nazis took it all away.

10. The laws included having to walk everywhere, being barred from places of entertainment, having restricted shopping, being barred from use of telephones, and having to be indoors by 8:00 P.M.

11. Deportations began in July 1942.

12. The Franks went into hiding in July 1942, four days after Margot Frank was ordered to report for deportation.

13. The three reasons included—(1) they feared Communism would seep into Holland, and the Germans seemed less of a threat than the Communists; (2) they believed Holland would remain in German hands because the German army could not be defeated; (3) they did not realize the evil potential in the Nazi movement that would bring destruction to all of Europe, including Holland.

14. Among the many reasons: helpers were scarce, for Nazis threatened anyone who helped Jews; many non-Jews were hiding young Dutchmen who wanted to avoid deportation to German factories; black-market goods, the only supplies people in hiding could get, were scarce and very expensive; the majority of Dutch Jews did not have enough cash to maintain themselves for an indefinite time period; some families hesitated to send individual family members to separate hiding places; some could afford to hide only their children.

15. 105,000 men, women, and children, reflecting 75 percent of the total number, or one of the highest percentages of Jewish victims in Nazi-occupied lands.

Possible Topics for Research Reports

1. **Star of David**
   Look into the historical and religious significance of the Jewish Star of David. Good sources: *Book of Knowledge* (look up David, the second king of Israel); encyclopedias (look up "David").

2. **The Nuremberg Laws**
   These anti-Jewish laws were passed in Germany in 1935 and enforced in all of occupied Europe. Describe their extent and impact. Good source: *Holocaust Reader* and *The War Against the Jews* by Lucy Dawidowicz; *The Destruction of European Jews* by Raul Hilberg.

3. **Rationing**
   Rationing took place in most countries during World War II. Research the products rationed. Good source: encyclopedias.

4. **German-occupied countries**
   Name the European countries in the order that they were occupied by the Germans in World War II. How many Jews were living in each country at the time of occupation? Give the total number of Jews in occupied lands. Good sources: *The War Against the Jews* by Lucy Dawidowicz, pages 359–403; *American Jewish Yearbook,* Volume 63.

5. **Deportation routes**
   Trace the path of the deportation trains enroute from Holland to Auschwitz in Poland. Give the total distance in miles. Make a map to show your class. Good source: *The Holocaust* by Martin Gilbert.

6. **Dutch resistance**
   Good sources: The chapter entitled "The Low Countries: The Netherlands, Belgium, and Luxembourg" in *European Resistance Movements* by Trevor Nevitt Dupuy.

7. **Nazi invasion of Holland**
   Good sources: *The Rise and Fall of the Third Reich* by William Shirer; *Story of World War Two* by Robert Leckie; *The Story of World War II* by Stewart Graff.

8. **Nazi occupation of Holland**
   Good source: *The Holocaust: The Destruction of European Jewry, 1933–1945* by Nora Levin.

9. **Polish Jews**
   How did the traditional lifestyle of the Jews of Poland differ from the modern lifestyle of Jews in western European countries? Why was anti-Semitism stronger in Poland than in the West? Good sources: *The Destruction of European Jews* by Raul Hilberg; *Harvest of Hate* by Leon Poliakov; Chapter 10 in *The War Against the Jews* by Lucy Dawidowicz; *Image Before My Eyes: A Photographic History of Jewish Life in Poland 1864–1938* by Beth Hatefutsoth.

10. **Ghettos**
    Of the ghettos of Poland and eastern Europe, the Warsaw ghetto was the largest. Describe living conditions in the Warsaw ghetto. How many Jews were crowded into it? Find out the names and locations of other large ghettos holding tens of thousands of people. Tell how long the ghettos lasted. Good source: *Harvest of Hate* by Leon Poliakov.

11. **The Dutch Nazi Party (NSB)** before the German occupation of Holland.
    Who were the followers of this movement? Why did it lose followers after 1935? Why did it gain strength after the German invasion? Good pictorial source: pages 28–29 in *Anne Frank in the World: 1929–1945* Anne Frank Stichting.

The Franks Go into Hiding

Vocabulary

1. **air raid**
   An air raid is an attack by enemy airplanes, usually bombers.

2. **Aryanization of Jewish property**
   The Nazis took over all property owned by Jews in Germany and the occupied lands. This was called Aryanization of Jewish property.

3. **black market**
   Goods sold at illegal prices or in illegal amounts are sold on the black market. Jews in hiding had to secure food and other necessities through the black market.

4. **death camp**
   A death camp is a place expressly designed for the purpose of killing. Of the six major death camps in Poland, only two—Auschwitz and Maidanek—reserved a small percentage of inmates for forced labor. At the other four—Chelmno, Treblinka, Sobibor, and Belzec—all prisoners were killed as soon after arrival as possible.

5. **dire**
   Dire means disastrous, causing great suffering, terrible. The Franks hid to escape the dire consequences of Nazi capture.

6. **Einsatzgruppen**
   The Einsatzgruppen consisted of four SS squads of 3,000 men assigned to shoot Jewish men, women, and children living in western Poland (then under Russian occupation) and other Russian territories. The Einsatzgruppen followed the regular German forces in Hitler's invasion of Russia in June 1941.

7. **"final solution to the Jewish question"**
   The "final solution to the Jewish question" was a Nazi euphemism, or inoffensive term, for the extermination of all Jewish people in Europe.

8. **fugitive**
   A fugitive is someone who flees. The Franks became fugitives from Nazi deportation.

9. **gas chamber**
   A gas chamber was an airtight room designed with gas jets that secreted lethal fumes to kill the occupants within. Nazis built death camps in Poland equipped with gas chambers to kill Jews and others.

10. **genocide**
    Genocide is the planned killing of an entire racial or cultural group of people. The word "genocide" was coined in 1945 by R. Lemkin to describe the Nazi crime of murdering six million Jews.

11. **Gestapo**
    The Gestapo was a division of the SS. A plain-clothes secret police force, the Gestapo was in charge of imprisoning all Nazi enemies, including Jews.

12. **incomprehensible**
    Incomprehensible means impossible to understand. Jewish suffering at the time of round-ups and deportation is incomprehensible for people to grasp today.

13. **passport**

    A passport is a document given to a citizen by his or her own country that grants permission to travel to other countries. Jews' passports in all Nazi-occupied countries were labeled with a large letter *J*.

14. **Secret Annexe**

    Secret Annexe was the name for the Franks' hiding place. The Secret Annexe was located on the second and third floors of a warehouse-office building in Amsterdam, Holland.

15. **SS**

    SS was the acronym for Schutzstaffel. The SS was a private army of elite, highly trained Nazi guards. Hitler placed Jews under the complete control of the SS.

Name _____ Date _____

Reading Comprehension Quiz

DIRECTIONS: Below are the beginnings of 14 sentences. Under each beginning are four possible endings. One of the four possible endings is not true. Write the letter of the untrue ending in the blank next to the beginning of the sentence.

_____ 1. The Franks fell victim to the Nazis because
   A. they had not emigrated far enough from Germany.
   B. they could not emigrate from Holland.
   C. they were Jews.
   D. in Holland they were not citizens but aliens.

_____ 2. In their own way, the Franks resisted the Nazis by
   A. moving out of Germany.
   B. hiding from them.
   C. joining the underground.
   D. transferring their business to Dutch friends.

_____ 3. Aryanization of Jewish property
   A. was a way of seizing Jewish wealth.
   B. meant the Nazi takeover of all Jewish holdings.
   C. was always done in a businesslike fashion.
   D. included everything of value owned by Jews.

_____ 4. Mr. Frank took pains to keep the hiding place a secret by
   A. preparing it little by little so as not to be noticed.
   B. telling none of his friends about it.
   C. not informing his daughters about the location until the last minute.
   D. hiding the entrance with a swinging bookcase door.

_____ 5. Dutch Jews did not feel so threatened by Nazi prejudice because
   A. anti-Jewish laws did not come until two months after the invasion.
   B. not all the invaders were against Jews.
   C. they were not used to being persecuted because of their Jewishness.
   D. they thought the German-Jewish refugees exaggerated Nazi persecution.

_____ 6. The Franks tried to make it appear as though they had disappeared by
   A. walking to their hiding place without any parcels or luggage.
   B. talking late into the night with their roomer.
   C. sneaking one by one into the Secret Annexe.
   D. leaving dishes on the table and their clothing scattered about their house.

_____ 7. The Secret Annexe was
   A. in the attic of a warehouse building.
   B. part of the building where Mr. Frank had his business.
   C. really an old laboratory and storage room.
   D. situated above rooms where business was going on.

(continued)

Name _____ Date _____

_____ 8. The people in the Secret Annexe
    A. went out into the streets only at night.
    B. had to be still and quiet during the day.
    C. were protected and provided for by good Dutch friends.
    D. had to keep the hooks fastened on the bookcase door.

_____ 9. People who protected Jews
    A. put their own lives in danger.
    B. had a hard time securing food.
    C. considered Jews Dutch like themselves.
    D. were few and far between in Holland.

_____ 10. Problems inside the Secret Annexe included
    A. no running water.
    B. little fresh air.
    C. no privacy.
    D. too much heat in the summer and not enough in the winter.

_____ 11. Problems in the outside world that affected the Franks and the other Jews in hiding included
    A. air raids.
    B. having to deal with the military rulers face to face.
    C. food shortages.
    D. being aware that the SS was looking for them.

_____ 12. The security of the Annexe people was threatened by
    A. thieves who robbed the building at night.
    B. being seized off the streets by SS squads rounding up Jews for deportation.
    C. a warehouse worker who asked the helpers suspicious questions.
    D. Gestapo rewards offered to those who informed on Jews hiding out.

_____ 13. Hitler's "final solution to the Jewish question"
    A. was the dictator's way of getting rid of all Jews in the occupied countries of Europe.
    B. included the shooting of Russian-Jewish communities.
    C. meant that European Jews not killed by shooting squads were to be deported to gas chambers in Poland.
    D. excluded young children and their mothers.

_____ 14. Nazi cruelty against Jews
    A. was carried out right in the open.
    B. was reported to the world by radio and newspapers.
    C. was no different than the way Nazis treated others under their rule.
    D. was totally indecent and inhumane.

Discussion Questions

1. In your opinion, why did Mr. Frank wait until the family was on its way to tell his daughters where their hiding place would be?

2. Why do you think Margot quickly left with Miep to go to the Annexe before anyone else was ready to go? Why did Margot take a chance riding a bicycle?

3. Think of going on a vacation. Compare how you might pack to go on vacation with the way the Franks packed for their two-year "trip."

4. In case of bombing or fire, why would leaving the building be very dangerous for the Annexe occupants?

5. Why were black-market goods more expensive than the same goods on the regular market?

6. Why was outside help necessary if a Jew wished to hide from the Nazis?

7. How long did the Franks hide?

8. Why did the Franks give friends some valuables for safekeeping until after the war?

9. Why were the houses along the Dutch canals very, very narrow?

10. To provide necessary space, how did Dutch builders make up for the narrowness of their buildings along the canals?

11. Why couldn't the inner courtyards of some buildings be seen by neighboring buildings?

12. Why was it important that the people in the hiding place make no noise during the day?

13. Discuss some of the problems the Franks faced while hiding.

14. What made the Franks go into hiding earlier than they had planned?

15. Discuss some of the activities the people in the Annexe used to keep themselves busy during the day.

16. Why did Miep and Henk believe the Franks would worry if they knew about the university student hiding in their apartment?

Short Essays

1. Pretend you are one of the people in the Secret Annexe. Make two lists: (1) the advantages of living in the Secret Annexe; (2) the disadvantages. Now write a paper in which you compare the good and bad points of hiding there.

2. Put yourself in the place of a Dutch Jew in occupied Holland. How would you feel about the Nazis? about your fellow citizens? about yourself and your Jewishness? Write a paper about your feelings.

Answers to Reading Comprehension Quiz

1. **D**; 2. **C**; 3. **C**; 4. **B**; 5. **B**; 6. **C**; 7. **A**; 8. **A**; 9. **D**; 10. **A**; 11. **B**; 12. **B**; 13. **D**; 14. **C**

Answers to Discussion Questions

1. Student opinions will vary, but will probably express the safety factor—if the girls didn't know where they were going, they couldn't inadvertently mention the location to anyone.

2. Since the Nazis had called up Margot to report for deportation, she had to "disappear" quickly. Although Jews were forbidden to ride bicycles, Margot used one to get away fast.

3. Answers will vary.

4. They might be recognized and turned in by people who were Nazi sympathizers.

5. The sellers of these illegal goods risked going to jail if caught and demanded higher prices for their supplies.

6. People in hiding needed an outsider to supply them with food and other necessities while keeping their hiding place a secret.

7. They hid for 25 months.

8. The Nazis seized all Jewish possessions.

9. Because property along the canals was sought after by traders, such land was both desirable and expensive. The Dutch builders made the buildings here very narrow to cut costs.

10. They made the buildings very long and several stories high.

11. No windows were placed along the sides of the buildings, only in the front or back; nor was there any space between buildings.

12. Workers on the lower floors of the building might hear them.

13. Answers will vary, but should include at least three problems.

14. Margot was scheduled for immediate deportation to a concentration camp.

15. Answers will vary, but should include at least three activities.

16. If this student were discovered in Miep's apartment, she and Henk could be sent to prison.

Possible Topics for Research Reports

1. **Anne Frank's diary**
Read Anne Frank's diary. Find passages in which she describes her feelings about: the Nazi invaders, going into hiding, herself and her place in the world as a Jew, and the group's activities in hiding. Read and discuss these passages.

2. **The Einsatzgruppen**
Describe what type of men the Einsatzgruppen had been in private life, from whom they took orders, and what their activities in Russia included. Good sources: *The Rise and Fall of the Third Reich* by William Shirer; *Licensed Mass Murders* by Henry V. Dicks.

3. **The Secret Annexe**
The Secret Annexe was located at Prinsengracht 263, Amsterdam. Describe what the Annexe looked like in the 1940's and how it looks today. Give some of its history. A good source of photos is *A Tribute to Anne Frank* by Anna Steenmiejer.

4. **Adolf Eichmann**
Eichmann was Nazi Deportation Chief in charge of the trains to carry Jews to the death camps. Research who he was, how he organized the deportation process, what happened to him after the war, and his capture and trial in Israel in 1961. Good sources: *Justice in Jerusalem* by Gideon Hausner; *Laws and Trials That Created History* by Brandt Aymur.

5. **Heinrich Himmler**
Himmler was Hitler's SS chief in charge of the Holocaust and all death camps. Find out more about him and his wartime activities. Good source: *Infiltration: The SS and German Armament* by Albert Speer.

6. **Reinhard Heydrich**
Heydrich was head of the SD, the intelligence division of the SS. He was third in command after Hitler and Himmler in the organization of the mass murder of the Jews. Find out about his assassination in Czechoslovakia and the resulting Nazi punishment—the destruction of the town of Lidice.

7. **Aryanization of Jewish property**
Find out more about the seizure of the Jewish-owned property by the Nazis. Good sources: *Holocaust Reader* by Lucy Dawidowicz; *The Holocaust: The Destruction of European Jewry, 1933–1945* by Nora Levin.

8. **Going into hiding**
What were some other experiences that Jewish children had in hiding? Good sources: *Quiet Heroes: True Stories of the Rescue of Jews by Christians in Nazi-occupied Holland* by Andre Stein; *Hidden Children, Forgotten Survivors of the Holocaust* by Andre Stein;. *The Hidden Children: The Secret Survivors of the Holocaust* by Jane Marks; *We Are the Witness: Five Diaries of Teenagers Who Died in the Holocaust* by Jacob Boas; *The Hidden Children* by Howard Greenfield.

Activities for Chapter 4

Who Are the People in the Secret Annexe?

Vocabulary

1. **analytical**
   To be analytical is to examine carefully each part of a thing or situation. Anne's analytical mind gives the reader of the diary a vivid picture of people and life situations in the Secret Annexe.

2. **bemoan**
   To bemoan is to grieve, moan, weep. Anne never bemoaned her Jewish heritage, even though this very heritage stood as the *only* reason why she was being persecuted.

3. **Christian**
   A person who believes in and follows the teachings of Christ is a Christian. Miep, Elli, Koophuis, and Kraler were Christians.

4. **compassion**
   To have compassion is to have pity for suffering, with a desire to help. Compassion moved Miep, Elli, Koophuis, and Kraler to shelter and protect their Jewish friends.

5. **confidant**
   A confidant is a close friend or associate to whom secrets are confided or with whom private matters and problems are discussed.

6. **foresight**
   Foresight is the capacity to see ahead or to figure out what is likely to happen in the future. Mr. Frank had the foresight to prepare a hiding place long before the Nazi deportation of Dutch Jews began.

7. **genealogy**
   A genealogy is a list of ancestors and their descendants, a family tree. Anne Frank's hobby was creating genealogies of European royal families.

8. **indulgent**
   Indulgent means lenient, kind, yielding. Allowing Peter to keep his cat in the Annexe showed that the Van Daans were indulgent with their son.

9. **Israel**
   Israel is the part of Palestine that was declared a Jewish state by the General Assembly of the United Nations on May 15, 1948. During the Holocaust, there was no national Jewish homeland for Jewish refugees wanting to escape Nazi tyranny.

10. **journalist**
    A journalist is a person who works in writing, editing, or producing newspapers or magazines. One of Anne Frank's goals was to be a journalist.

11. **mythology**
    A mythology is a collection of a people's legends or stories. Anne Frank loved to read Roman and Greek mythology.

12. **opinionated**
    A person who is opinionated is stubborn or overly sure of his or her own opinions. Mr. Van Daan was opinionated about the war and politics.

13. **Palestine**
    Palestine is the ancient homeland of the Jews and other peoples, located on the eastern coast of the Mediterranean Sea. Margot Frank wanted to emigrate to Palestine.

14. **perception**
    Perception means observation or understanding. Mr. Dussel's perception of how young people behaved was limited because he had no children of his own.

15. **perspective**
    To have a perspective is to have an idea of the relationship between objects or facts, a viewpoint. Anne's perspective of people and life in general reflected a wisdom far beyond her years.

16. **reminisce**
    To reminisce is to talk about or look back on the past. The people of the Secret Annexe frequently passed time by reminiscing.

17. **undeterred**
    Undeterred means not discouraged or hindered. Anne's belief that people were good at heart remained undeterred in spite of Nazi cruelty.

18. **vain**
    To be vain is to be proud of oneself. Anne was vain only about one thing: her beautiful dark hair.

Name _____ Date _____

Reading Comprehension Quiz

DIRECTIONS: Each set of personal qualities below describes one of the people in the Secret Annexe. Choose the letter of the person who matches the description best and write it in the blank before the number.

_____ 1. cranky, fussy, set in his or her ways; a loner; an admonisher
    A. Mr. Dussel
    B. Mr. Van Daan
    C. Mrs. Van Daan

_____ 2. loud, excitable, good-natured, self-centered, materialistic
    A. Mrs. Frank
    B. Mrs. Van Daan
    C. Anne

_____ 3. always right, competent, outspoken, nervous, stubborn
    A. Mr. Dussel
    B. Mrs. Frank
    C. Mr. Van Daan

_____ 4. reserved, quiet, cultured, liberal, calm
    A. Anne
    B. Mrs. Frank
    C. Mrs. Van Daan

_____ 5. studious, gentle, easygoing, bright, peace-loving
    A. Peter
    B. Margot
    C. Anne

_____ 6. life-of-the-party, witty, fun-loving, keen, good-hearted
    A. Peter
    B. Margot
    C. Anne

_____ 7. wise, strong, calm, kind, perceptive
    A. Mr. Dussel
    B. Mr. Frank
    C. Mr. Van Daan

_____ 8. shy, reserved, insecure, bright, obedient
    A. Peter
    B. Anne
    C. Margot

Discussion Questions

1. At times, why did Anne not get along so well with the adults in the Annexe?
2. Discuss the many ways in which Anne showed her unselfishness.
3. In which ways was Anne unique?
4. Point out Anne's actions that are typical of most teenage girls.
5. How was Margot more like her mother?
6. In your opinion, did Peter's parents' treatment of him have anything to do with his lack of self-confidence?
7. Compare the family relationship between the Van Daans and the Franks. Which of the two does your family resemble most?
8. Do you think Margot's relationship with her sister Anne is typical? Explain why or why not.
9. Anne felt that parents should be good models for their children, rather than trying to be friends with them. Do you agree with Anne's opinion? Explain why or why not.
10. Anne and Peter were different types of people, yet they were romantically involved. There is an old saying that "opposites attract." Do you agree that opposites attract, or are you more comfortable with a person who shares your goals and interests?
11. Anne loved her father dearly and thought he was perfect. Isn't it common for us to overlook the faults of those we love, and, at the same time, find fault with those we don't like? Point out instances in your own life when you've done one or the other.
12. Anne became annoyed with people who gave advice but didn't follow it themselves. Do you feel the same way? Can you remember someone who was guilty of something that he or she also preached to you about?
13. In what ways was Mr. Frank everyone's "tower of strength"?
14. Can you explain why Anne was so popular at school? Do you think you would like her as a friend? Tell why.
15. How does Anne use her diary as an instrument to control her life?
16. Was Anne a "naive Miss goody-two-shoes" type who failed to see either evil in anyone or the real danger surrounding her as a Jew?
17. How does Anne gain the strength to cope with the extreme level of anxiety in hiding?

Short Essays

1. Anne Frank said she had "two sides." Most of us do have both a better side and a darker side. Think of yourself, then make two lists of at least five points each in which you write your better points and then your faults. Now write a composition describing your two sides.
2. In this chapter, reread the section entitled "Anne and Peter Are Not the Perfect Couple." Notice how the first paragraph is developed to point out the differences between the two young people. Note the transitional words that are used to state the differences: *however, while, on the other hand, too, but.*

   Using this paragraph as a model, write your own paragraph comparing yourself to someone else you know well. Try to use the same transitional words listed above.
3. Imagine yourself as a parent. Make a list of five things you would do in raising your child. Now make a list of five things you definitely would not do. Write a two-paragraph paper on being a parent, using the items from your lists.
4. Read the pages again about Anne Frank's personality. Write your own paragraph or poem about what Anne was like.

Answers to Reading Comprehension Quiz

1. **A**; 2. **B**; 3. **C**; 4. **B**; 5. **B**; 6. **C**; 7. **B**; 8. **A**.

Answers to Discussion Questions

1. That she was noisy, active, and outspoken annoyed some of the adults, and she refused to accept their criticisms quietly.

2. and 3. Answers will vary.

4. She liked attractive clothes, boys, and parties.

5. She was reserved and serious, just as her mother was.

6. through 12. Answers will vary.

13. Always reassuring others and easing their fears and worries and never allowing his own anxieties to show, Mr. Frank was a group leader and advisor.

14. Answers will vary.

15. The diary allowed Anne the control to: (a) say what she wanted to say; (b) express her own "being" on her terms, not the Nazis', (c) defy Nazi orders by keeping a diary of their deeds; (d) create an *Anne Frank* mindset about Jewish identity, life's meaning, and other people; (e) fashion a "world" where she could openly communicate with an "outside person," removed from the Nazi occupation; (f) release herself from the hiding prison into her own "free reality"; and (g) use humor as a weapon against Nazi scorn of Jews.

16. Absolutely not. Anne squarely faced facts about the presence of evil, destructive urges in all people. She witnessed Nazis battering Jews in the streets, heard reports of Nazi persecution from her helpers who were tied to the underground movement, reported knowledge of every type of Jewish persecution that was going on at the time, and endured living through torture and the dangers of hiding out for two long years herself.

17. She gains the spiritual strength and courage to endure hardships from her deep faith in God.

Possible Topics for Research Reports

1. **The Montessori School**
   The Montessori School that Anne attended in Amsterdam is but one of many schools throughout the world with the same name. Research the Montessori method of education. Tell about founder Maria Montessori (1870–1952). Do you think Anne had developed the self-awareness and self-confidence which this educational method promises to develop in a child? Explain.

2. **Anne Frank**
   A good source for reporting on Anne Frank through the eyes of the people who knew her is *Anne Frank: A Portrait in Courage* by Ernst Schnabel. Another good source is *Anne Frank Beyond the Diary: A Photographic Remembrance* by Ruud van der Rol and Rian Verhoeven, which features over 100 pictures, many never before published.

3. **The Franks, the Van Daans, Dussel, and their Dutch helpers**
   Good sources for reporting on the Franks, the Van Daans, Dussel, and their Dutch helpers are *Anne Frank: A Portrait in Courage* by Ernst Schnabel and *A Tribute to Anne Frank,* edited by Anna Steenmeijer. Another good source is *Anne Frank Remembered* by Miep Geis with Alison Gold. (Miep, the Franks' helper, enlisted Gold as the principal writer for her book.)

4. **Anne Frank's other writings**
   Read and report on one of Anne's stories. Good sources: *The Works of Anne Frank* by Anne Frank has the diary plus the rest of her work; *A Tribute to Anne Frank,* edited by Anna Steenmeijer, has several of Anne's stories, never before published, on pages 64–69.

5. **Anne's analysis of her good and bad features**
   Report on Anne's list of "12 Characteristics of a Beauty" and her appraisal of whether she had any of them or not. You'll find "12 Characteristics of a Beauty" on page 68 of *A Tribute to Anne Frank,* edited by Anna Steenmeijer.

6. Read and report on one of the magazine articles listed below.

   Pick, Lies G. "I Knew Anne Frank." *McCall's.* Vol. 85, July 1958, pp. 30+ (An excellent, comprehensive article.).

   Johnson, Marilyn. "The Unknown Anne Frank." *Life.* Vol. 16, June 1993, pp. 66+.

   Elliot, Lawrence. "Anne Frank's Enduring Gift." *Reader's Digest.* Vol. 146+, May 1995, p. 137.

   Kline, Reva. "An Inspiration of Our Times." *Times Educational Supplement.* May 31, 1996, p. 139+.

   "Memories of Anne Frank: Reflections of a Childhood Friend." *Publishers Weekly.* Vol. 244, July 7, 1997, p. 69.

The Secret Annexe Residents Live and Die in Nazi Prisons

Vocabulary

1. **contagion**
   A contagion is a disease that can be transmitted by direct or indirect contact. From unsanitary conditions in Nazi prisons, typhus and typhoid fever became the most feared contagions among inmates.

2. **crematories**
   Crematories are furnaces for burning bodies to ashes. At all the death camps, crematories were used to dispose of gas-chamber victims.

3. **death march**
   A death march was a long forced march of concentration camp prisoners led by Nazi guards retreating from Allied invasion. Death marches were so named because weak and starving prisoners who could not keep up the pace were shot instantly. The marches—generally dozens of miles long—ended at prison camps farther away from front lines than the original camps.

4. **delouse**
   To delouse means to remove lice. Because Nazi prisoners seldom were granted the privilege of bathing, they often had to delouse their lice-infested bodies and clothing.

5. **demise**
   Demise means death. All but one of the Secret Annexe residents met their demise in Nazi prisons.

6. **designate**
   To designate is to point out, select for. Auschwitz and Sobibor were the two death camps designated for deported Dutch Jews. Other people were sent to the two camps as well.

7. **epidemic**
   An epidemic is the fast spreading of disease to many people. Anne and Margot became caught up in a typhus epidemic at Bergen-Belsen.

8. **feign**
   To feign means to pretend. When questioned by the Gestapo, Miep feigned ignorance about the Jews in hiding.

9. **Gypsy**
   Some scholars calculate the loss of European Gypsies to Nazi execution to be as high as 80 percent.

10. **incriminating**
    Incriminating is presenting proof of a crime or a fault. Illegal ration coupons in Miep's possession, at the time of the Secret Annexe raid, could have stood as incriminating evidence of breaking Nazi laws for helping Jews.

11. **infirmary**
    An infirmary is a hospital in an institution. When Auschwitz was liberated, Mr. Frank lay ill in the infirmary there.

12. **insignia**
    An insignia is a special emblem worn by

soldiers or others to show rank or to give evidence of some accomplishment. The death's head insignia—a skull and crossbones—worn by SS camp guards seemed an appropriate badge for their service.

13. **irony**
An irony is a situation that results in the opposite of what might be expected. It is an irony that Bergen-Belsen was liberated just three weeks after Anne died.

14. **Kapos**
Kapos were prisoners of concentration camps who agreed to supervise other prisoners inside the camps in exchange for special privileges from the Nazis. Kapos were most often sadists or hardened criminals.

15. **liberate**
To liberate is to set free. Allied troops eventually liberated all the Nazi concentration camps.

16. **magazine**
A magazine is a building used for storage. At the concentration camps, Nazis built huge magazines to hold all their prisoners' belongings. Items such as clothing, eyeglasses, shoes, and suitcases were stored until they could be shipped out and used by others in Reich cities.

17. **ransack**
To ransack is to rob, plunder. Nazi teams in charge of rounding up Jews for deportation often ransacked their prisoners' homes and pocketed valuables.

18. **sadist**
A sadist is a person who derives pleasure from inflicting pain on someone else. SS camp guards were frequently sadists.

19. **"selection"**
"Selection" was a term used by Nazis to describe the process of choosing incoming Jewish prisoners for immediate death or forced labor.

20. **transit camp**
Transit camps were Nazi concentration camps, set up mainly in western European countries, that served as temporary collection centers for Jews on their way to the death camps of Poland. While held at transit camps, Jewish prisoners were put to forced labor.

21. **typhoid fever**
Typhoid fever is an often fatal infectious disease spread by contaminated food. Symptoms include high fever and inflamed intestines. Typhus and typhoid fever claimed the lives of thousands of concentration camp prisoners.

22. **typhus**
Typhus is an often fatal infectious disease spread by fleas and lice. It is characterized by a rash, extreme weakness, and brain irritation.

Name _____ Date _____

Reading Comprehension Quiz

DIRECTIONS: Listed below are 20 incomplete statements with three possible endings each. Choose the ending that best completes each statement. Write the letter of the ending in the blank next to the number.

_____ 1. At the time of the Secret Annexe raid, the German armies were
    A. in control of Europe.
    B. losing ground fast.
    C. pushing the Allies into retreat.

_____ 2. The Nazi squad that arrested the Secret Annexe occupants was made up of
    A. all Germans.
    B. all Dutchmen.
    C. one German and four Dutchmen.

_____ 3. When the Nazi squad entered the warehouse building,
    A. no one heard them.
    B. they came in the back entrance.
    C. they shocked everyone by their presence.

_____ 4. The Nazi search team came because
    A. they knew precisely where the secret group was hiding.
    B. they wanted to search the building.
    C. they were searching all buildings on that block.

_____ 5. When the searchers entered the Secret Annexe,
    A. the residents were taken by surprise.
    B. the residents became hysterical.
    C. the residents tried to fight them off.

_____ 6. The Gestapo
    A. arrested all the Franks' helpers.
    B. did not know Miep and Elli helped the group in hiding.
    C. imprisoned Kraler and Koophuis for life.

_____ 7. The Franks' helpers
    A. remained loyal to their Jewish friends to the end.
    B. all still live in Holland today.
    C. never received any thanks for their help.

(continued)

Name _____ Date _____

_____ 8. The camp that was only a temporary stopover for Dutch Jews on their way to death camps in
Poland was
A. Auschwitz.
B. Bergen-Belsen.
C. Westerbork.

_____ 9. Selection at Auschwitz meant
A. being separated by sex.
B. being chosen to die or to work.
C. being quarantined for illness.

_____ 10. The Franks, the Van Daans, and Dussel became laborers at Auschwitz because
A. their physical condition was fairly good.
B. they had important work skills.
C. they had volunteered their services.

_____ 11. Once the Annexe residents arrived at Auschwitz
A. they never left.
B. all but one died there.
C. the men and women never saw one another again.

_____ 12. Selection at Auschwitz
A. occurred only once, upon arrival.
B. spared the lives of some.
C. was done over and over again.

_____ 13. Kapos were camp guards who were
A. members of the SS.
B. prisoners themselves.
C. hired civilians.

_____ 14. Grooming for camp life included
A. being branded with one's name.
B. having one's head shaved.
C. the assignment of a morning or night shift for labor.

_____ 15. In prison, Anne Frank
A. became a different person.
B. resisted the authority of the guards.
C. never lost her ability to make friends.

(continued)

Name _____ Date _____

_____ 16. Bergen-Belsen
    A. was located in Poland not far from Auschwitz.
    B. was a death camp.
    C. was called the "sick camp" because most prisoners were infected with typhus.

_____ 17. The Secret Annexe resident who died in the gas chambers of Auschwitz was
    A. Mr. Dussel.
    B. Mr. Van Daan.
    C. Mrs. Van Daan.

_____ 18. Before the liberation of Auschwitz, Mr. Frank, weak and ill, was earmarked for death by
    A. the SS rear guard.
    B. the gas chambers.
    C. the shooting squads.

_____ 19. Peter probably
    A. died from starvation and exposure.
    B. was shot for refusing to march.
    C. died from illness.

_____ 20. The SS guards of Auschwitz
    A. willingly gave themselves up at the end of the war.
    B. tried to destroy all evidence of the crimes committed in their camps and then ran away.
    C. never dreamed they would be punished for their war crimes.

Discussion Questions

1. Why were the occupants of the Annexe particularly hopeful of their freedom right before their capture?

2. How long had the Secret Annexe residents been in hiding before they were captured?

3. Why weren't any of the helpers or the Secret Annexe people aware that the Gestapo had arrived to arrest them?

4. Why was Mr. Koophuis released from prison?

5. How was Mr. Kraler able to escape from prison? Where did he live for the last 25 years of his life?

6. Which helper hid from the Nazis after the Annexe raid until the end of the war?

7. Which helper received a money reward for aiding the people in the Secret Annexe? How many years after the Annexe raid did the reward come?

8. How did the Nazis make use of prisoners held temporarily at Westerbork?

9. What aspects of prison life at Westerbork did Anne not mind?

10. Why were the Annexe people still hopeful even after their capture?

11. How many weeks after the Franks' deportation did the Allied invasion of Holland come? Was it totally successful?

12. Describe the ride on the cattle trains.

13. Explain selection on the loading platform at Auschwitz.

14. Why do you think the Nazis destroyed not only young children but also their mothers?

15. Give two reasons why the people from the Secret Annexe still remained in fairly good condition by the time they arrived at Auschwitz.

16. Describe a few of the ways the Nazis tricked Jewish victims into entering the gas chambers.

17. In your opinion, does this trickery make the Nazis seem even more evil? Why or why not?

18. How did the SS make room for new and healthier slaves to replace those who became sick and worn-out?

19. In your opinion, was the skull and crossbones insignia worn by the SS an appropriate label?

20. From all you've learned about the Nazi persecution of Jews so far, discuss the many ways in which Jewish victims were exploited or taken advantage of for the Nazis' own profit.

Short Essays

1. Go back and reread parts of the chapter about life in Nazi prisons. List some of the key words used to describe that life. Then add your own words to the list that describe:

   a. how Anne Frank probably felt physically;

   b. what she probably saw at camp;

   c. what she might have heard there;

   d. what her thoughts could have been about living in the barracks;

   e. how she viewed the work, the food, other prisoners, and the Nazis who tormented her.

   Now, using words from the list, write a poem entitled "Anne Frank at Auschwitz" or "Anne Frank at Bergen-Belsen." Make your poem include a variety of words that will appeal to your readers' senses.

2. Reread the chapter section describing Anne meeting her very best friend Lies at Bergen-Belsen. Now write this paper:

   a. Write a short introductory paragraph or two describing how both girls looked and felt as they approached the barbed-wire fence to talk to each other.

   b. Then write a dialogue of what you think they may have said to each other. (Perhaps you will first need to review the proper way to write direct quotations and to indent lines of a conversation.)

   You might want to take this exercise one step further and dramatize the dialogue of the two girls in front of the class.

3. Leah Gottesman and her mother are Holocaust survivors. Like the Franks, they had also lived and suffered in Auschwitz. When friends learned Leah and her mother were together in the camp, they say this was probably a comfort to them. However, Leah says that having her mother beside her made her life in the concentration camp harder to bear. Can you give several reasons why? Do you think the Franks and the Van Daans felt as the Gottesmans did?

4. Contact a local synagogue to ask whether any member is a Holocaust survivor who would be willing to discuss his or her experience during the Nazi occupation. Either interview the survivor and report your findings to your class, or invite the Holocaust survivor to speak to your class.

Answers to Reading Comprehension Quiz

1. **B**; 2. **C**; 3. **C**; 4. **A**; 5. **A**; 6. **B**; 7. **A**; 8. **C**; 9. **B**; 10. **A**; 11. **C**; 12. **C**; 13. **B**; 14. **B**; 15. **C**; 16. **C**; 17. **B**; 18. **A**; 19. **C**; 20. **B**.

Answers to Discussion Questions

1. Nearing an end, the war was all but lost by the Germans. And the Allies were on their way toward Holland.

2. They had hidden for 25 months.

3. The Nazi searchers entered the building without calling attention to themselves.

4. He became very ill.

5. He ran for cover during a bombing raid while on a march. He escaped and went to live with relatives until the war's end. He lived in Toronto, Ontario, Canada.

6. Mr. Kraler hid.

7. Mr. Kraler was rewarded 34 years later.

8. They put them to work.

9. Anne loved being outdoors and talking with people. She also enjoyed seeing Peter.

10. The Allied invasion of Holland was soon coming.

11. It came two weeks later. It wasn't totally successful.

12. Descriptions will vary.

13. Mengele, a Nazi officer, decided which prisoners were to live or die. To the left he sent those destined to die. To the right were those selected for hard labor.

14. Answers will vary.

15. Their long stay in the Secret Annexe and a relatively short period in Westerbork left them in fairly good condition.

16. and 17. Answers will vary.

18. They sent worn-out and sick laborers to their deaths.

19. and 20. Answers will vary.

Possible Topics For Research Reports

1. **D-Day and VE-Day**
Describe the German armies' positions and circumstances leading to their unconditional surrender.

2. **First Allied invasion of Holland**
Describe the first Allied invasion of Holland on September 17, 1944, and why it was not totally successful. When did the Allies succeed in liberating Holland?

3. **Locations of Westerbork, Auschwitz, and Bergen-Belsen**
Locate these camps where the Secret Annexe people lived and died. A good map can be found on page 48 of *The Holocaust* by Martin Gilbert. Make a similar map of your own. Try to calculate the total number of miles that Anne Frank was transported from camp to camp.

4. **The capture of the people in the Secret Annexe**
Describe the event in detail. Good source: *Anne Frank: A Portrait in Courage* by Ernst Schnabel. This book also tells how Miep tried to "bribe" the Gestapo into letting the Franks go free!

5. **Life in Auschwitz**
Find out more about life (and death) in Auschwitz and write about it. Good sources: *In the Hell of Auschwitz* by Judith Newman; *Eichmann's Inferno: Auschwitz* by Miklos Nyiszli (an excellent book); *Night* by Elie Wiesel.

6. **Jewish slave laborers**
Describe the Nazi system of slave labor. Good source: *Never to Forget: The Jews of the Holocaust* by Milton Meltzer.

7. **Gypsies under Nazi occupation**
The Nazis planned to exterminate another group besides Jews whom they considered an "inferior race": the Gypsies of Europe. What percentage of the European Gypsy population did the Nazis murder? Good source: *The Holocaust* by Martin Gilbert.

8. **Reports on individual death camps**
The death camps were Auschwitz, Treblinka, Maidanek, Sobibor, Chelmno, and Belzec. Make a map showing the location of each camp.

9. **Dr. Mengele**
Mengele, the evil doctor who sent millions to their deaths at Auschwitz, escaped capture after the war. He has been the object of an international hunt ever since. Find out what you can about him.

10. **The Sonderkommando**
The Sonderkommando was the name for prisoners (usually Jews or Poles) whom the Nazis forced to work in the gas chambers and crematories. Good source: *Eichmann's Inferno: Auschwitz* by Miklos Nyiszli. This is an autobiography of a Jewish doctor forced to do medical experiments on the inmates at Auschwitz. It gives a firsthand account of the lives of the Sonderkommando.

11. **Medical experiments by the SS doctors**
SS doctors did many medical experiments on concentration camp prisoners. Good sources: *The Rise and Fall of the Third Reich* by William Shirer; *Doctors of Infamy* by Alexander Mitscherlich.

12. **Anne Frank in Westerbork, Auschwitz, and Bergen-Belsen**
Good sources: *Anne Frank: A Portrait in Courage* by Ernst Schnabel; "A Tragedy Revealed: Heroine's Last Days," by Ernst Schnabel, *Life*, Vol. 45, August 18, 1958, pp. 78–80, 82–90; *The Last Seven Months*

of Anne Frank by Willy Lindwer is the testimony of six teenagers who entered the camps with Anne and Margot, survived, and recall memories today.

13. **Lies Goosens**
Lies Goosens tells about her friendship with Anne Frank and also about their meeting at Bergen-Belsen in "I Knew Anne Frank," by Lies Goosens Pick, *McCall's,* Vol. 85, July 1958, pp. 31+. Other good sources: "Anne Frank's Friend," by Moshe Brilliant, *New York Times Magazine,* April 21, 1957, p. 30; "The

Sequel to a Sandbox Snapshot," by Paul Schutzer, *Life,* Vol. 47, October 12, 1959, pp. 111–12.

14. **Auschwitz riot**
On October 6, 1944, a riot by prisoners of Auschwitz totally destroyed one of the four gas chamber-crematory complexes there. Good sources: *They Fought Back: The Story of Jewish Resistance in Nazi Europe* by Uri Suhl; *Eichmann's Inferno: Auschwitz* by Miklos Nyiszli.

Activities for Chapter 6

Mr. Frank and Anne's Diary Testify Against Nazi War Criminals

Vocabulary

1. **atrocity**
   An atrocity is a cruel and brutal act. Nazis committed atrocities against not only Jews but also millions of non-Jewish civilians.

2. **complicity**
   Complicity is partnership in crime. Many SS personnel in charge of rounding up and deporting Jews were guilty of complicity in genocide.

3. **concrete evidence**
   Concrete evidence is solid proof. *The Diary of a Young Girl* by Anne Frank was used as concrete evidence in the trials of Nazi war criminals.

4. **document**
   A document is printed or written material that offers proof of something. Anne Frank's diary is considered a World War II document.

5. **indict**
   To indict is to charge with a crime. Even today, Nazi war criminals are being indicted and brought to trial for their mistreatment of Jews during the Holocaust.

6. **Nazi hunter**
   A Nazi hunter is a person who searches for Nazi war criminals in hiding in order to bring them to justice.

7. **Nuremberg Trials**
   The Nuremberg Trials were post-World War II trials held in Nuremberg, Germany. During these trials Nazi war criminals were tried for war crimes. One of the Nuremberg prosecutors became Mr. Frank's lawyer in a trial of a Nazi war criminal accused of deporting the Franks.

8. **plaintiff**
   A plaintiff is a person who brings on a lawsuit. Using his family's experience in the Secret Annexe and Nazi prisons as evidence, Mr. Frank became one of the plaintiffs in the court trial of Nazi chiefs in charge of deporting Dutch Jews.

9. **retribution**
   Retribution is punishment for evil done. Some Nazi war criminals found guilty of crimes against the Jewish people received the death sentence as retribution.

10. **Simon Wiesenthal**
    Simon Wiesenthal is a world-famous Nazi hunter who has succeeded in rooting out over 1,100 war criminals. Wiesenthal, himself a Holocaust survivor, located the Gestapo sergeant who arrested the Franks.

11. **war crime**
    A war crime is a violation of the rules of warfare set up by international agreement at the Geneva Convention. Nazis who persecuted Jews were guilty of numerous war crimes.

Name _____ Date _____

Reading Comprehension Quiz

DIRECTIONS: Each incomplete statement in Part A tells something about the circumstances following the deaths of the Secret Annexe people. Part B gives reasons that complete the statements. Match the lettered statements in Part B with the numbered statements in Part A to make complete sentences. Write your answer in the blank after each incomplete statement in Part A.

PART A—Incomplete Statements

1. Mr Frank survived because _____

2. The rear guards ordered to shoot Mr. Frank did not do so because _____

3. To learn the fate of his family, Mr. Frank had to ask questions of people in the street because _____

4. After the war, Mr. Frank tried to help other Holocaust survivors because _____

5. After the war, Mr. Frank moved from Amsterdam to Switzerland because _____

6. The new Mrs. Frank and Otto shared a common personal tragedy because _____

7. Mr. Frank believed he knew who their informer was, but that man was never convicted because _____

8. Mr. Frank worked to keep Anne's memory alive because _____

9. The Secret Annexe group had believed a certain night burglar was a warehouse employee because _____

10. The German sergeant who arrested the Franks was released after his trial because _____

11. The Nazi chiefs in charge of deporting most of Holland's Jewish victims to the death camps were given jail sentences because _____

12. Anne's diary was used as court evidence against Nazi war criminals because _____

(continued)

Name _____ Date _____

PART B—Reasons Why

   A. no one could prove him guilty of any actual crime.

   B. that thief had entered the building without breaking in and obviously with a key.

   C. luck, timing, and location were in his favor.

   D. he had no family to care for, so helping others made him feel useful.

   E. it is a documented war record of Jews being persecuted by the Nazis during World War II.

   F. he wanted others to remember her and other innocent Holocaust victims so that their deaths wouldn't be in vain.

   G. Amsterdam held too many painful memories of his family.

   H. the Nazis destroyed most records of their crimes against prisoners in their camps.

   I. they both lost members of their families in the Holocaust.

   J. there was not enough evidence to prove he was the one who either turned them in or collected the reward.

   K. they were guilty of being involved in the crime of mass murder.

   L. oncoming Russian troops made them run away before they had finished their job.

Discussion Questions

1. How long did inhumane Nazi treatment take to kill seven of the eight Secret Annexe occupants?

2. Explain why you think Mr. Frank had to resort to questioning strangers about the whereabouts of his family after the war. Why couldn't he go to some government source to find out?

3. That Mr. Frank gave his business to Miep and her husband is further proof of the bond of friendship between these people. Explain in your own words.

4. In your opinion, does it seem fitting that the new Mrs. Frank knew Anne?

5. Discuss why the Secret Annexe people suspected the warehouse worker as the informer who turned them in.

6. If Mr. Frank had been a hateful person seeking revenge for his family's deaths, how might his statement about Silberbauer at Silberbauer's trial have been different? If you had been Mr. Frank making this statement, would you have been tempted to lie about this ex-Nazi's behavior during the raid? Explain why or why not.

7. Do you think the penalties received by the Nazi chiefs and their secretary in charge of deporting Dutch Jews were fair or unfair? Explain your reasons.

Short Essays

1. Pretend you are a member of the jury in the court trial of Karl Silberbauer. This ex-Naxi who arrested the Franks and the other Annexe occupants claims he is not guilty of any war crimes. He says he had carried out the arrest on orders from his superiors. Do you think he is guilty or not guilty of being involved in the deaths of Anne and the others? Explain your verdict.

2. Write another ending for Anne Frank and the others in hiding. Have your story begin in Auschwitz but end the way you would like it to end.

Answers to Reading Comprehension Quiz

1. **C**; 2. **L**; 3. **H**; 4. **D**; 5. **G**; 6. **I**; 7. **J**; 8. **F**; 9. **B**; 10. **A**; 11. **K**; 12. **E**.

Answers to Discussion Questions

1. Seven months was all it took.

2. The Nazis destroyed records of their crimes, so there was no record of what had happened to the Frank family. The government in charge had been the Nazi government, so there were no government sources to go to.

3. and 4. Answers will vary.

5. The man had asked suspicious questions, and he may have been the burglar who saw Mr. Van Daan. Also, the Gestapo left him in charge of the building after the raid.

6. He could have claimed that Silberbauer had mistreated him and his family during the raid of the Annexe. Answers will vary when students put themselves in Mr. Frank's place.

7. Answers will vary.

Possible Topics for Research Reports

1. **The Nuremberg Trials**
   Read and report on these war-crime trials.
   Good sources: *Justice?* by L. Gribble; *Trials at Nuremberg* by William Shapiro; *Trials That Made Headlines* by A. Fleming; *Laws and Trials That Created History* by Brandt Aymur.

2. **Silberbauer's arrest and trial**
   Read more about this ex-Nazi's arrest and trial. Good source: *The Murderers Among Us* by Simon Wiesenthal. Simon Wiesenthal is a famous Nazi hunter. Wiesenthal's biography, *Nazi Hunter: Simon Wiesenthal,* was written by Iris Noble.

3. **Nazi war criminals still in hiding**
   Find out more about these people and write about some of them. Good sources: *Wherever They May Be* by Beate Klarsfeld, the famous German Nazi hunter; *The Bormann Brotherhood* by William Stevenson; *Wanted! The Search for Nazis in America* by Howard Blum.

4. **Geneva Convention and rules of war**
   Discuss how the SS in charge of the Holocaust violated the rules of war.

5. Read and report on one of the newspaper articles listed below.

   "*The Diary of Anne Frank* Introduced at Trial of Nazis." *New York Times,* January 31, 1967, col. 8, p. 14.

   "Ex-Nazi on Trial in Dutch Killings." *New York Times,* January 24, 1967, col. 1, p. 11.

   "Franks' Betrayer Got Nazi Reward." *New York Times,* February 1, 1957, col. 3, p. 12.

   Godfrey, Peter, "How Anne Frank's Father Has Made Sure That the World Will Not Forget." *The London Times,* April 16, 1977, col. a, p. 12 (an excellent article).

   "Nazi Who Hunted Dutch Jews Held." *New York Times,* January 14, 1966, col. 3, p. 10.

   "A Play on Anne Frank Theme Given Premiere on French TV." *New York Times,* January 18, 1967, col. l, p. 46. This play is based on the real-life case of Karl Silberbauer. Written by an Austrian playwright, it was presented on television in at least eight European countries.

   "Three SS Sentenced in Death of Jews." *New York Times,* February 25, 1967, col. 7, p. 1.

6. **Neo-Nazis, the Ku Klux Klan, and Racism in America**

   Good sources: *The Racist Mind: Portraits of American Neo-Nazis and Klansmen*; *KKK* by Ben Haas; *The Nazi/Skokie Conflict: A Civil Liberties Battle* by David Hamlin; *American Swastika* by Charles Higman.

Activities for Chapter 7

Anne Frank Lives On in the World

Vocabulary

1. **accord**
   Accord is to be in agreement or harmony. An accord exists between Anne Frank's reasoning and the understanding of millions of readers, regarding the value of authentic human behavior in erasing racism from the world.

2. **actualize**
   Actualize is to make real. The Nazis deprived Anne of her life on earth, but through the diary she achieves victory in defeat, for her voice actualizes her presence all over the world.

3. **anchor**
   An anchor is any person or thing that can be relied on for support, stability, or security; a mainstay. Anne Frank's voice can be thought of as an anchor to support a "comm-unity-in-action" movement to promote unity through diversity.

4. **artistry**
   Artistry is showing skill and excellence in execution. Anne's artistry was a combination of her positive human spirit at work, excellent writing skills, and the effective technique of using "Kitty" to form a friendly relationship with every reader.

5. **authentic**
   Authentic is not false but is real; genuine. Just as Anne was an authentic person who advocates a higher mode of life for others than the miserable one she experiences herself, her diary is an authentic piece of Holocaust litera-

ture, and her voice continues to carry the only authentic message which can be drawn from the senseless destruction of the Holocaust.

6. **coffers**
   A coffer is a box or chest, especially one for valuables. The Nazis filled their coffers with everything of value they could take from conquered people in their territories, including artwork, gold, jewelry, money, cars, deeds to property, and all else.

7. **community**
   A community is a social, religious, occupational, or other group, sharing common characteristics and interests and perceiving itself as distinct in some respect from the larger society within which it exists . . . [and in an ecological sense] . . . is an assemblage of interacting populations occupying a given area. Anne's hope is true community, where differences in ethnicity, color, and creed prevail in uniqueness and yet are mutually cherished, welcomed, and celebrated.

8. **comm-unity-in-action**
   This is a coined expression by the writer of this book, meaning a coming together of differences and merging as one in a goodness of spirit that benefits the whole. This spiritual unity springs from positive human interactivity and grows as more and more people of differences connect, interact, and build on the common ground of mutual respect and celebration of cultural differences and human and spiritual fulfillment. (The same idea of "unity

through diversity" is projected in the Latin phrase "E pluribus Unum," printed on American money, and in the word "university." You can make two good analogies here!)

9. **diary**
A diary is a book for writing a day-by-day account of what is done, thought, said, and so forth. Anne Frank kept a diary of the three weeks of events leading up to going into hiding and also of the 25-month stay in the Secret Annexe.

10. **din**
A din is a loud sound with persistent repetition. Anne's voice, as a call for peace and fellowship, has risen far above the din of Hitler's audiences who were often heard thundering the words, "Seig! Heil!" over and over again.

11. **dramatic license**
Dramatic license is artistic liberty which permits playwrights to alter factual events to achieve a desired effect in their plays. Dramatic license was employed in the stage version of Anne Frank's diary both to add situations that never really occurred and to delete others that did happen.

12. **fascism**
Fascism is a reactionary or totalitarian system of government. A fascist government controls the economy, encourages extreme nationalism, and suppresses all opposition.

13. **followership**
This is the willingness to follow a leader; a group of supporters. Anne has inspired a followership of people all over the world because she portrayed herself as person with high ideals.

14. **Hanukkah**
Hanukkah is a Jewish holiday, the Feast of Lights, which lasts for eight days and usually occurs in December.

15. **Hitler Youth**
Hitler Youth was a Nazi organization of the Third Reich for German boys aged six to 18. A similar organization for German girls was called League of German Maidens.

16. **humanity**
Humanity is the human race; the quality of being humane; kindness. The cruel Nazis showed no humanity in the way they treated other people who did not belong to the "Aryan race."

17. **interaction**
This is reciprocal action, effect, or influence. The relationship between Jews and Nazis was hardly one of interaction; in fact, it was more action and reaction. Brutal action spilled forth from the Nazis, and unarmed Jewish victims had little choice but to react in the only way they could—through suffering and dying.

18. **legitimate**
Something that is legitimate is in accordance with established principles, rules, or standards or laws of reasoning. Anne Frank's reasoning about human behavior remained legitimate, even though her circumstances could have made her bitter toward all non-Jews.

19. **memorabilia**
Memorabilia is a set of things worthy of remembrance or record. The list of Anne Frank memorabilia is ever-growing as more and more people come to know her through her book.

20. **memorial**
A memorial is a reminder of some person or event. The building housing the Secret Annexe, known today as the Anne Frank House, is a memorial visited by tourists from all over the world.

21. **pilgrimage**
A pilgrimage is a long journey, especially to a shrine or a sacred place. Thousands of German teenagers have made pilgrimages to Anne Frank's gravesite at Bergen-Belsen.

22. **playwright**
    A playwright is a dramatist, a writer of plays. Two playwrights adapted Anne's diary into a successful Broadway show.

23. **premiere**
    A premiere is a first public performance. The drama *The Diary of Anne Frank* premiered on Broadway at the Cort Theater on October 5, 1955.

24. **prolific**
    Prolific is producing abundantly. Anne was a prolific writer who produced two versions of her diary and several short stories.

25. **Pulitzer Prizes**
    The Pulitzer Prizes are awards given each year in the United States for outstanding achievement in journalism, drama, music, and literature. In 1956 *The Diary of Anne Frank* received the Pulitzer prize for drama.

26. **racist**
    A racist is a person who believes that by nature some races are superior to others. The Nazi belief that the German or "Aryan" race was superior to all others was a racist philosophy, built on falsehood. There is no such thing as a "German master race" or even a "German race," for that matter.

27. **revere**
    Revere means to love and respect highly, to honor deeply. People in nearly every country of the world have revered Anne Frank.

28. **role model**
    A role model is a person whose behavior, example, or successes can be emulated by others, especially by younger people. Anne Frank serves as an exemplary role model for leadership: though barely 16, she shows exceptional maturity and sensitivity, refusing to take on the meanness of people who oppress her. Instead she uses her bad situation as a lesson for promoting fellowship among other people.

29. **testimonial**
    A testimonial is a token of regard or admiration. Thousands of admirers the world over have offered a variety of testimonials to Anne Frank.

30. **vision**
    Vision is the act of anticipating that which may come to be. Anne's vision of a better world where positive human relationships prevail and Jews are held in high regard sharply contrasted to the Nazi vision of a master race who would destroy Jews and rule the world.

Name _____ Date _____

Reading Comprehension Quiz

DIRECTIONS: This is a true and false exercise. Write a *T* if the statement is true. Write an *F* if it is false. Write your answers in the blanks next to each statement.

_____ 1. Anne hid her diary from everyone by locking it in her dad's briefcase.

_____ 2. Anne wanted to publish a book based on her diary after the war.

_____ 3. Otto Frank looked for a publisher to print Anne's diary once he found out how interesting it was to others.

_____ 4. Had the Gestapo sergeant read the diary, he would have known Miep and Elli were guilty of helping the people in the Secret Annexe.

_____ 5. The diary lay scattered on the floor of the attic until the war ended.

_____ 6. The Broadway play based on the diary made the diary even more famous.

_____ 7. Mr. Frank made the diary his main business and full source of income.

_____ 8. When Mr. Frank saw the play, he highly approved of what had taken place on the stage.

_____ 9. Creating a stage play from a diary was not that difficult.

_____ 10. Unlike the stage play, the motion picture about Anne Frank was seen only by audiences in the United States.

_____ 11. Neither the diary nor the play received much attention in Germany.

_____ 12. The motion picture based on Anne's diary came out before the stage play.

_____ 13. Millions flock to the Anne Frank House in Amsterdam because there are many relics of World War II there.

_____ 14. Anne Frank is a living force in the world today.

_____ 15. Anne believed her secrets, confessed to only "Kitty," would someday be revealed to the public whenever her diary was published.

_____ 16. Anne wanted to have her diary published and probably thought she would be the one to decide which parts would be exposed.

_____ 17. Anne reached adulthood even though her life was cut short.

(continued)

Name _____ Date _____

_____ 18. The rapid rate of Anne's personal and emotional growth during the hiding period made her reach maturity in just two years.

_____ 19. Anne had no way of mentally escaping from the prison of her hiding place.

_____ 20. We can call Anne an artist because, like painters or sculptors, writers use their skills to create an overall effect in the mind of the outside person who will look for meaning in their work.

_____ 21. Anne is so unusual in her outlook on life that she could never be a leader for ordinary people.

_____ 22. Anne uses her diary as a tool to connect the past to the present time of the reader, which can be right now or any time in the future.

_____ 23. Everybody who has ever read Anne's diary has developed a great sympathy for the suffering of the people in the Secret Annexe.

_____ 24. Anne Frank's spirit and the popularity of her book proves that goodness not only overcomes evil but also outlasts it.

_____ 25. Anne Frank is a leader in the world of today because through her book her voice continues to promote peace and authentic human behavior.

Discussion Questions

1. Why did Anne think of her diary as a friend?

2. What was included in the hundreds of pages Anne called her diary?

3. Explain how the publication of the diary came about.

4. Why was it pure accident that the diary survived the war?

5. After the diary was published, why did Mr. Frank retire from his regular job?

6. How many people had read Anne's diary by 1995? In how many languages has the book been printed? Where has it been sold?

7. The "full version" of Anne's diary printed in 1982 includes which sections left out previously?

8. Discuss some of the problems the playwrights faced in adapting Anne's diary into a stage play.

9. Name the most outstanding award received by the playwrights.

10. Discuss how the play affected different audiences throughout the world.

11. Where did German students decide to bicycle? Why?

12. Why did the movie producer want an unknown girl rather than a star to portray Anne on the screen?

13. Discuss the many ways people have memorialized Anne Frank. Which memorials do you approve of most?

14. German youth of today claim that Anne's death is their responsibility. Do you agree?

15. How do you think Anne felt about sharing her diary "secrets," the very private thoughts about herself and others, with other people? Would you feel the same way?

16. How does Anne's diary serve as a leadership tool?

17. Why was a thorough study recently done on Anne's diary? What does this say about the presence of anti-Semitism in today's world?

Short Essays

1. Find out the meaning of *poetic justice*, a term used to describe how circumstances sometimes turn out in narratives. Now write a paper explaining how the Anne Frank story reveals "poetic justice" in a real-life situation.

2. With your teachers and classmates, brainstorm every idea you have learned from reading this book about Anne Frank. Without discussion, list all ideas quickly on every corner of one blackboard until there is no space left. Now choose at least seven or eight ideas to write an essay entitled "What Anne Frank Has Taught Me."

3. Keep your own diary of this class for a two-week period. Include not only things you do but also how you feel about doing them. Be sure to date each of your daily entries.

Answers to Reading Comprehension Quiz

1. **T**; 2. **T**; 3. **F**; 4. **T**; 5. **F**; 6. **T**; 7. **F**; 8. **F**; 9. **F**; 10. **F**; 11. **F**; 12. **F**; 13. **F**; 14. **T**; 15. **F**; 16. **T**; 17. **F**; 18. **T**; 19. **F**; 20. **T**; 21. **F**; 22. **T**; 23. **F**; 24. **T**; 25. **T**.

Answers to Discussion Questions

1. She had no one else in whom to confide, so she used her diary as a "listener." By developing a personal relationship with "Kitty" she also forms a friendship bond with every diary reader. This "friend" in the "outside world" allowed her to talk freely about Nazi persecution and without Nazi restraint.

2. Two versions of the diary—the original and an edited, revised copy—and over 300 pages of diary notes were included.

3. Mr. Frank shared his edited copy with a few friends. A Dutch professor who read the diary wrote a newspaper article about it. This stirred up public interest, and soon a Dutch publisher approached Mr. Frank.

4. The Gestapo sergeant who dumped it to the floor from Mr. Frank's briefcase would never have left it behind had he known what it was.

5. He needed enough time to answer personally the thousands of letters sent to him from readers throughout the world.

6. An excess of 25 million readers, 55 languages, and 55 countries.

7. The "full diary" consists of both versions of Anne's diary, including the entries Mr. Frank had cut out in the first published edition.

8. Answers will vary.

9. The Pulitzer Prize.

10. Answers will vary. Many audiences cried. Dutch and German audiences were struck silent.

11. They cycled to Bergen-Belsen to visit and to lay flowers on Anne's gravesite.

12. Anne Frank had been an unknown girl at the time she wrote the diary.

13. Answers will vary.

14. Answers will vary.

15. She felt very protective about her private thoughts. She even refused to write in the diary in anyone's presence. Answers will vary to the second question.

16. It stirs people to respond to Anne's call to do the right thing by one another, to avoid prejudice and racism, and move toward community formation.

17. Some extremists called it a hoax. It is very much alive.

Possible Topics for Research Reports

1. **Anne Frank authenticated**

   Unfortunately, not everyone has remembered Anne Frank for what she truly was. A few Jew-haters and neo-Nazis have spread lies to discredit Anne and her book. The full diary version published in 1982 finally dispels these false charges that Anne herself did not write the diary. Prepared by the Dutch State Institute for War Documentation, the full diary gives the results of careful research concerning Anne's text. It also reports on a scientific analysis of the paper and ink Anne used to write her diary. The research and analysis prove beyond a shadow of a doubt that Anne's diary is authentic.

   a. Read the pages in the newly published full version of Anne's diary that offer proof that Anne did indeed write the text. Write a report on your findings.

   b. Read and report on the following two articles about a person who made a false charge that Anne Frank did not write the diary. Tell also about Otto Frank's reaction to these charges.
   "Anne Frank's Diary Investigated." *New York Times,* January 21, 1960, col. 4, p. 6.
   "German Teacher Apologizes." *New York Times,* October 18, 1961, col. 4, p. 28.

2. **Babi Yar**

   Give a report on the Nazi massacre of tens of thousands of Russian Jews in Babi Yar. Then ask your librarian to help you find a copy of Russian poet Yevgeny Yevtushenko's poem "Babi Yar."

3. **Anne Frank medal**

   Find out what the Anne Frank medal looks like, what the images on the medal signify, and other interesting information about it. Write:
   The Judaic Heritage Society
   P.O. Box 2022
   New York, New York 10017

4. Read the following resources about a dispute between Anne's father, Otto Frank, and an American writer/playwright named Meyer Levin, concerning a play he wrote and staged about Anne's diary. Report the details of this dispute to your class. Discuss the issues.

Newspaper and journal articles:

"Meyer Levin's Suit Over Diary Opens." *New York Times*, December 14, 1957, p. 16.

"Meyer Levin Wins $50,000 Over Play." *New York Times,* January 7, 1958, p. 40.

"Levin Suit Dismissed: Court Rules Out Action by Writer of Anne Frank." *New York Times*, January 7, 1958, p. 31.

"Award of $50,000 to Levin Voided." *New York Times,* March 1, 1958, p. 18.

"Anne Frank Play Staged in Israel." *New York Times,* November 27, 1966.

"Father Protests Anne Frank Play." *New York Times,* December 12, 1966.

"Anne Frank Play Halted in Israel—Levin's Version Withdrawn on Father's Protest." *New York Times,* January 10, 1967, p. 33.

"Betrayed by Broadway" by Rich Frank. *New York Times Book Review,* September 17, 1995, p. 9.

"Fixated on a More Jewish Anne Frank" by Richard Bernstein. *New York Times,* September 27, 1995.

Levin, Meyer. (1996, October 6). Life in the Secret Annexe. *New York Times Book Review,* pp. 70, 7.

Michaelsen, Jacob. (1997, Spring). Remembering Anne Frank. *Judaism, 46,* 220–228.

Senior, Jennifer. (1997, September 8). Beautiful Girl, Broadway Baby. *New York, 30,* 69.

Books

Graver, Lawrence. (1995). *An Obsession With Anne Frank: Meyer Levin and the Diary.* Berkeley, CA: University of California Press.

Melnick, Ralph. (1997). *The Stolen Legacy of Anne Frank: Meyer Levin, Lillian Hellman, and the Staging of the Diary.* New Haven: Yale University Press.

5. Read these articles to investigate circumstances surrounding pen-pal letters that Anne and Margot Frank exchanged with two sisters from Iowa:

"Anne Frank Letter to Iowa Pen Pal to be Sold." *New York Times,* July 22, 1988, Section A, p. 1.

"Pen Pals of Anne." *US News & World Report,* August 1, 1988, p. 9.

"Global Interest Stuns Pen Pals of Anne Frank." by Lynn O'Shaughnessy, *Los Angeles Times,* July 14, 1988, Section II, p. 1.

"Letters by Anne Frank Auctioned for $165,000." by Rita Reif, *New York Times,* October 26, 1988, Section C, p. 21.

Anne Frank Letters Purchased for $165,000 in Auction." by Paul Feldman, *Los Angeles Times,* October 27, 1988, Section II, p. 3.

6. Read this article about an acquaintance of Anne Frank who knew her at Bergen-Belsen and believes Anne would not have wanted all the excitement that has surrounded her. In reading the diary, you, too, have become Anne's "acquaintance." How do you feel about this? You may or may not agree with the opinion of Anne's friend in this article. Include your own opinion in your report.

"The Complete Anne Frank." by Anne Pons, *World Press Review,* December, 1989, Volume 36, p. 73.

7. Read this article and then write a paragraph explaining why you think (1) the judge in this case made a good decision, and (2) the boy learned a good lesson.

"A Swastika Painter, 14, Is Told To Read Frank." by Ingrid Braslow, *New York Times,* April 15, 1997, p. B 4.

A Group Discussion and Classroom Debate Issue: Family Rights Versus Public Rights to Promote Privileged Information

Step One: Gather in small discussion groups and discuss these issues, based on the information you learned from the last three reports:

- A parent's concern and opinion about the significance of his daughter's work (Otto Frank), supporting the popular version of Anne's story.

- The opinion of a person outside the Frank family who feels committed to some Jewish concerns surrounding the popular portrayal of Anne's story (Meyer Levin).

- The question of family rights versus public rights to promote privileged information, once the key players are gone. (All the key

players have died, including playwright Meyer Levin.)

- The question of how Anne Frank herself would feel about all this.

- The question of how you yourself, acting as both "Anne's acquaintance" and spokesperson, feel she would vote on this issue.

Step Two: Now, take a stand and voice Anne's vote for either family rights or public rights. Debate the pros and cons of both sides as part of a class discussion. Support your opinion on "Anne's voice" with logical arguments, based on what you have learned about her story and personality.

Activities for Chapter 8

Time For Reflection:
Anne's Message of Peace Through the
Perspective of Holocaust Experience

Vocabulary

1. **brute force**
   Brute force is savage cruelty. The Nazis used brute force on Jewish victims who were unarmed and defenseless in every other way. They stripped Jews of citizenship rights, took away their jobs and property, treated them as outcasts by passing laws against them, deported them, and then robbed them of their strength and lives through forced labor, starvation, and outright murder.

2. **catastrophe**
   A catastrophe is a widespread disaster. The Holocaust was a catastrophe beyond real definition because the full effect of the destruction it caused can never be calculated or described in words.

3. **chaos**
   Chaos is a state of utter confusion or disorder. All the action in the Holocaust produced chaos and confusion, no matter which aspect we examine.

4. **coexist**
   To coexist is to exist separately or independently but peaceably. In true community, people of different cultures accentuate their uniqueness, but also coexist peaceably and honor one another's differences.

5. **common ground**
   Common ground is a foundation of common interest or comprehension, as in a social relationship or discussion. True fellowship in community must build on common ground to assure that *all* interests, not just those of the majority, are represented.

6. **com-promise (compromise)**
   "Com" is a prefix meaning "together" plus "promise," a word meaning "a declaration that something will or will not be done." Therefore com-promise, or compromise, means declaring together that something will or will not be done. Anne's readers together form a compromise or mindset that anti-Semitism should never again destroy innocent people like her.

7. **constructive**
   Being constructive is helping to improve; promoting further development. Creativity is a constructive force that generates new ideas or methods that add growth to traditional ways of thinking or doing things.

8. **creative**
   Being creative is having the quality of being productive. Holocaust action produced only destruction to everything around it and even to its chieftains, so it can hardly be thought of in any creative sense.

9. **crime**
   A crime is an offense or wrongdoing that is

deemed injurious to the public welfare and that is legally prohibited. The Nazi plan to destroy Jews plus the growth of negative forces that nearly did wipe out this targeted group is a crime that has no parallel in history.

10. **criminal**

A criminal is guilty of causing an action deemed injurious to the public welfare or morals or to the interest of the state; serious wrongdoing or sin. Top Nazi chieftains were hateful, criminal types who orchestrated the killing of people without mercy in order to get what they wanted.

11. **cunning**

Cunning is skill employed in a sly manner, as in deceiving. Nazi cunning deceived Jewish victims into cooperating in their own destruction; for instance, they forced community leaders to form Jewish Councils that had to make decisions according to Nazi rules.

12. **cultural**

Cultural refers to the behaviors and beliefs characteristic of a particular social, ethnic, or age group. A multicultural society consists of many ethnic groups living together in harmony but continually working at it through positive interactivity.

13. **decency**

Decency is conformity to standards of taste, conduct, speech, or quality. Standards of decency were not even considered in concentration camp life where four or five people slept on each concrete slab bed, starved on diets of watery soup and bread made from sawdust, and labored hard from dawn to dusk.

14. **definition**

A definition is the formal statement of the meaning or significance of a word or phrase. Holocaust experience, as a whole, defies definition either by words or numbers, so the most effective way to grasp the meaning is to deal with one experience at a time.

15. **destructive**

Destructive refers to a cause or means to reduce to useless fragments or form. The action of the Holocaust was destructive in every direction: to the Jewish individual, to the Jewish family, to the perpetrators, to other non-Jews, to nations of Europe, to the rest of the world, and even to the Nazis themselves.

16. **documented**

Documented means that information, proof, or support of something else has been furnished. Anti-Semitic events in the Holocaust are documented by overwhelming evidence that is now public record.

17. **domain**

A domain is a realm or range of personal knowledge or responsibility. The domains and effects of Holocaust experiences are as varied as the circumstances of the victims and the perpetrators themselves because each experience had unique effects on that particular person's mind, spirit, body, actions, family, friends, and extended environment.

18. **effect**

An effect is something that is produced by a cause; a result; meaning or sense; purpose or intention. The evil effects of the Holocaust actions hit upon both the victims and the perpetrators.

19. **engage**

To engage is to act to occupy the efforts of a person. The Nazi movement grew in monumental proportions by engaging others in two evil causes that appeal to the dark side of human nature: (1) to rule over others and satisfy greed and lust for power; and (2) to shift responsibility and guilt for problems to others (a scapegoat), especially a minority group that has a history of persecution. "Get rid of Jews to solve our economic and political problems," became a Nazi slogan many people chose to believe.

20. **experience**

An experience is a particular instance of observing, encountering, and undergoing something. The human experience of the

Holocaust, for both the victims and survivors, reveals suffering and degrading treatment hard for any non-Jew to imagine.

21. **evil**

    Evil refers to that which is morally bad or wrong; harmful; characterized by suffering or misfortune. The Nazi era was so filled with an evil spirit, it devastated everything in its path: people, property, culture, rational behavior, human decency, nature, the environment, and world order.

22. **formation**

    Formation is the state of a particular condition, character, or mode in which something appears. Anne Frank's spirit has generated a desire for the formation of a human family so that no event like the Holocaust should ever hurt people like her again.

23. **fruit**

    Fruit is anything produced; an effect; a return or profit. The fruit of Anne's effort to create meaning from her meaningless life in hiding moves readers worldwide to grieve at the senselessness of her death and to take action to squelch the evil behavior that caused it.

24. **"goodness-in-action"**

    Goodness-in-action is the writer's coinage. The word good is derived from the Old English word "god." Goodness is from the Middle English and Old English word "godnes." This expression stands for the ideal for which Anne Frank is remembered. Anne Frank believed in goodness-in-action or, derivatively, "God-in-action," as the only hope for humankind's survival on earth. Anne Frank knew this, and so do the millions of people who celebrate her memory and ideal. Goodness-in-action among people of differences is synonymous to community-in-action.

25. **grief**

    Grief is keen mental suffering over loss; painful regret. Good people everywhere share in the grief of Jewish survivors of the Holocaust,

many of whom lost as many as 30 to 40 family members to Nazi brutality.

26. **growth**

    Growth is the process of growing, developing, gradual increasing.

27. **heritage**

    Heritage is something that comes or belongs to one by reason of birth. Anne Frank had no choice about being born to Jewish parents; she also had no choice about being persecuted simply because of it; but never once did she complain, for she was proud of her Jewish heritage.

28. **hope**

    Hope is the feeling that what is wanted can be had. Anne Frank's hope to live in the world and to work for humanity has materialized; her spirit of peace, which has outlasted the evil Nazis who destroyed her, is destined to urge people to higher levels of human relationships throughout time.

29. **ideology**

    The body of ideas particular to an individual, group, or culture, usually including a social plan, along with devices for putting it into operation is an ideology. Nazi ideology said the Germans were a "master race" and all other "races" such as Poles, Italians, Jews, Irish, Gypsies, were inferior. This ideology has no basis whatsoever in scientific fact.

30. **indisputable**

    Something which is indisputable is not deniable; unquestioningly valid. Even though facts about the Holocaust are indisputable, and Jewish suffering unimaginable, hatemongers in today's world still persist in torturing the Jewish spirit by calling the Holocaust a hoax.

31. **inherent**

    Inherent means existing in someone as a permanent and inseparable quality. Capacities for two kinds of action are inherent in every human being: to do good and to commit evil. Either is a matter of human choice. Anne Frank had faith that once the Nazi "phase" ended, people would elect goodness-in-action as the better choice for everyone concerned.

32. **integrity**

Adherence to moral and ethical principles is integrity. That Anne refused to judge all non-Jewish people in the world as being evil, just like the Nazis, proves her integrity remained intact, despite her own humiliating treatment.

33. **interaction**

Interaction is a reciprocal (mutual) action, effect, or influence. The interaction of Anne's voice and her readers' response is quite the opposite of the evil spirit that grew from the interaction of Hitler's raving and his followers' reply. One was love, peace, and a call for fellowship in community; the other was hate, violence, and a push to war and world domination. On the other hand, between Nazi tormentor and Jewish victim, the action was not true interaction but only action followed by helpless reaction.

34. **inter-activity**

Inter-activity derives from: "inter"—among, between, mutually; plus "activity"—a specific deed, action, function, liveliness. **Inter-activity**—a liveliness of mutual actions from all sides. Positive interactivity helps to bond in friendship people from all cultures and walks of life because they employ their talents, get to know one another through social exchange and functions, and care about one another.

35. **inter-connectedness**

Inter-connectedness derives from: "inter"— a prefix meaning between, among, mutually, together and connected—meaning united, joined, linked. "Ness" is a suffix meaning something exemplifying a state or quality. Therefore, inter-connectedness here means the state of having people, situations, talents, cultures being united and linked together as one.

36. **irrational**

Irrational is without reason, deprived of normal

or sound judgment. That innocent families like the Franks had to hide for years, only to die under guard in Nazi state prisons, just because they were Jews, shows the Nazi "government" as irrational from start to finish.

37. **justification**

Justification is a reason, fact, circumstance, or explanation that defends; according to law, justification is to show a satisfactory reason or excuse for something. If circumstances allow one individual to help another in distress, some say there is no ethical justification for ignoring the distressed person, even though the helper may be harmed himself. (What do you think?)

38. **label**

A label is a descriptive or identifying phrase. Nazis marked all concentration camp victims with cloth patches of different colors and shapes on their prison clothing, based on their "criminal classification." However, they forced Jews to wear the yellow star soon after they seized control of governments in Germany and other European countries and long before they deported them to prison camps.

39. **leadership**

Leadership is the act or instance of leading, guidance, or direction by action or opinion. Anne Frank displayed leadership qualities by her example.

40. **legal**

Legal is that which is permitted by law or lawful. An important concept about the Holocaust era was that Nazi law made punishing Jews a legal requirement and labeled anyone who helped Jews a lawbreaker.

41. **magnitude**

Magnitude is greatness in consequence or greatness of size or amount. The magnitude of the evil effects on both the victims and the perpetrators is one of three factors that make the Holocaust unique among crimes against humanity.

42. **meaning**

The end, purpose, and significance of

something is its meaning. The action of the Holocaust, which consumed Jewish life without mercy, surfaces as all meaningless, senseless, and worthless destruction.

43. **meaningful**

To be meaningful is to be full of significance, purpose, and value. Meaningful action always involves at least two or more people in a positive interactivity that benefits all participants.

44. **motivation**

Motivation is a state of desire. As a Jewish victim of anti-Semitism, Anne's expectation for good people to act in support of Jewish families has given many non-Jews a motivation to do that very thing.

45. **multifarious**

Multifarious is numerous and varied; greatly diverse. Positive interactivity should involve as much diversity in human culture as possible in order to gain the greatest possible benefits for all concerned.

46. **nature**

The particular combination of qualities belonging to an animal, person, thing, or class is nature. The nature of the crime of the Holocaust was full of deceitful action, all bent on destruction. Nazi lies promoted false racial doctrine and deceived Jewish victims about their real fate.

47. **negative**

Something negative is characterized by absence of marked qualities; involving subtraction; proceeding in a direction opposite to positive (that possesses an actual force, being, or existence). Holocaust action was largely negative and wreaked destruction on all facets of Jewish existence.

48. **network**

A network (as a noun) is an association of individuals having a common interest, formed to provide mutual assistance, helpful information, or the like, or (as a verb) to connect. Adolf Hitler showed the world how one evil spirit could network and grow into a massive force

of destruction, eventually consuming even himself. Anne's prevailing presence proves the spirit of peace networks and grows, too, has an everlasting effect, overrides evil, and produces growth in individual and group behavior.

49. **oblivion**

Oblivion is the state of being completely forgotten or unknown. The only real hope humankind has of ever having peace in the world is to push racism into oblivion.

50. **oral history**

Information of historical or sociological importance obtained usually by tape-recorded interviews with persons whose experiences and memories are representative or whose lives have been of special significance is oral history. An oral history of the Holocaust experience is available from the testimonies of Jewish victims who lived through this ordeal.

51. **order**

Order is a condition in which each thing is properly disposed with reference to other things and its purpose; methodical or harmonious arrangement. Humankind, like nature itself, comes in many sizes, shapes, colors, and cultures. The purpose? Certainly not to enforce the "new order" called for by the Nazis where the master race would rule all others. Anne Frank's call to order is the purpose intended: that good people work things out so that mutual respect and harmony in differences prevail.

52. **peace**

Peace is the normal condition of a nation, group of nations, or the world not at war; a state of mutual harmony between groups, especially in personal relations. Anne Frank proves that the spirit of peace can begin within one person and spread to millions of others throughout the world.

53. **perpetrator**

One who presents, executes, or does something in a poor or tasteless manner is a perpetrator. The perpetrators of the Holocaust included hardened criminals as well as every-day people with no former criminal records.

54. **phenomenon**

A phenomenon is a fact, occurrence, or circumstance observed or observable. The phenomenon of Jewish sabotage took place even in camps like Auschwitz and the Warsaw ghetto, right under the noses of armed Nazi guards.

55. **power**

Power is the ability to act, capability of doing or accomplishing something. Each individual has the power to affect either the well-being or ill-being of another.

56. **premeditate**

To consider or plan beforehand is to premeditate. Holocaust action, a deceitful, premeditated crime from beginning to end was explained in Adolf Hitler's book, *Mein Kampf*, long before it ever happened.

57. **progress**

Progress is movement toward a higher stage; growth or development; continuous improvement. War and domination of other people is a sign of humanity's lack of progress; on the other hand, peaceful coexistence, found in community, serves the interests of widely different heritages by focusing on (1) the legal right to cherish differences, (2) legal protection against violation of sacred beliefs and values, and (3) a continuous interactivity and interconnectedness, focused on institutionalizing common interests of all groups.

58. **progression**

Progression is the act of moving forward, onward, making progress. A progression from disorder to orderliness in human relationships took place in Anne Frank's thinking because she refused to absorb or promote the hatred assaulting her. In fact, she advocates positive interaction as a much desired alternative.

59. **promise**

A promise is a declaration that something will or will not be done. After reading Anne Frank's diary, readers register a promise to themselves to do something positive to preserve the memory of Anne's goodness.

60. **psychological**

Psychological is affecting the mind, especially as a function of awareness, feeling, or motivation. The psychological reasons explaining the motivations and harmful actions of the perpetrators of the Holocaust are as complex as each perpetrator's background and personal experiences.

61. **purpose**

A purpose is an intended or desired result. The message Anne is remembered for, that people are good at heart in spite of the bad things many of them do, acts as a pact because it motivates one's spirit away from the inhumanity of racism-in-action to the human progress gained from a comm-unity-in-action effort.

62. **racism**

Racism is a belief that inherent differences among various human races determine cultural or individual achievement, usually involving the idea that one's own race is superior and has the right to rule others. Racism is always destructive, both to the person who feels the prejudice and the one targeted for the hatred. The Holocaust, as the most salient model in history of "**racism-in-action**," clearly proves both sides of this truth.

63. **ramifications**

Ramifications are consequences. The ramifications of living through the Holocaust have left deep emotional scars in some survivors.

64. **realm**

A realm is the region, field, or domain in which anything occurs. Anne's philosophy about positive human relationships projects her readers into a realm of goodness where they feel like honoring her memory and that of other victims of the Nazi Holocaust in some way.

65. **relationship**

A relationship is a connection or involvement between people. Anne Frank's story deals with both positive and negative relationships. On one hand, are good Christian helpers who assist Jews in distress; on the other, is the NSB, probably so-called "Christians," who trample on their own countrymen just to get ahead.

66. **responsibility**

Responsibility is having a capacity for moral decisions and therefore accountable; capable of rational thought or action. The well-being and fair treatment of others, especially victims of prejudice and discrimination, is every person's responsibility.

67. **scheme**

A scheme is an underhanded plot of action to be followed. Hitler's chiefs created a criminal scheme called the "final solution to the Jewish question," calling for the total annihilation of the "Jewish race."

68. **spirit**

Spirit is an animating being or influence: Anne's promotion of fellowship, in the midst of unimaginable torture to her human spirit, has permeated the consciousness of good people in nearly every nation on earth.

69. **summons**

A summons is a request, command, or call to do something. The fact that the Holocaust actually happened is a summons for people to take action against the dark side of their natures because this massive crime shows, like no other, the nearly unlimited power evil has, if people allow it to take over their actions.

70. **survivor guilt**

Survivor guilt is those feelings of guilt for having survived a catastrophe in which others died. Survivor guilt is common among those who have lived to tell their Holocaust experiences and yet question why they escaped the fate of millions of other innocent people who were consumed in the tragedy.

71. **unity**

Unity is the state of being one; oneness. There would be no need to strive for unity if differences were not inherent. We are born as individuals, different in every way from another. Differences make us what we are, and that is good; variety does add spice to life. What is also good is for people of differences to focus on areas where they agree. Agreement is a positive business! From common agreement comes unity, and differences continue to prevail as important elements to reflect the power of choice.

72. **victim**

A victim is a person who suffers from a destructive or injurious action; a person who is deceived or cheated by personal emotions or ignorance, the dishonesty of others, or by some impersonal agency (meaning without connection to a particular person). Jewish people in the Holocaust were victims of both deceit and evil prejudice. While the Nazis did promote fake "new racial theories" to persecute Jews, they did not invent anti-Semitism. They triggered ancient religious biases against Jews and long-standing discrimination by European Christians and then used the negative feelings as the linking mechanism to fuel their modern-day hate campaign.

73. **witness**

A witness is one that gives evidence of something. Each Holocaust survivor serves as a witness to the scarring and brutal effects of racism on the quality of human life. Helpers who helped Jews to survive are witnesses, too—of heroic potential that lies not just in extraordinary individuals but in every person willing to take a risk that can pay off in a two-to-one bonus. The double reward: giving a higher quality of life to another and receiving it yourself, knowing you have made a real difference in life itself. Such interaction is the secret to finding real meaning in human existence.

Name _____ Date _____

Reading Comprehension Quiz

DIRECTIONS: This is a true and false exercise. Write a *T* if a statement is true. Write an *F* if it is false. Write your answers in the blanks next to each statement.

_____ 1. The story of Anne Frank, though tragic beyond words, also reveals how the beauty in one girl's thinking can grow into worldwide meaning.

_____ 2. At the end of the war, the Nazis destroyed most of the evidence documenting the Holocaust.

_____ 3. In terms of growth in evil action and its effects on all parties involved, the Holocaust is the most evil crime in the history of human experience.

_____ 4. A crime like the Holocaust could never be repeated in the modern world.

_____ 5. The final conclusion, drawn from Holocaust action, is that it was senseless destruction still having a ripple effect on the degree of human progress in the world.

_____ 6. An exact definition of the Holocaust: the Nazis killed six million Jewish victims.

_____ 7. Anne Frank's message of hope in the goodness of people to make the world turn out right is the only action subsequent to the Holocaust that makes any sense.

_____ 8. Evil forces can grow and cause destruction just as the power of goodness can spread for constructive purposes.

_____ 9. Because the Nazis knew their actions against Jews and others were criminal, they tried to get rid of all the evidence.

_____ 10. Nazi actions against Jews and others violated international laws of war.

_____ 11. Anti-Jewish prejudices existing in the general population of European countries made it easier for the Nazis to persecute Jews.

(continued)

Name _____ Date _____

_____ 12. Every person who learns about the Holocaust is sympathetic and wants to reverse anti-Semitism and other forms of racism in the world.

_____ 13. Hitler's agents did not really believe they could get away with their crimes against the Jewish people and other victims.

_____ 14. Right from the beginning, the Nazis orchestrated the mass murder of Jews in order to make them extinct.

_____ 15. Anne's message of hope moves reader attention away from the hateful action against her as a Jew toward the rightful claim that her people, like all minorities, deserve to be cherished as human beings just like everyone else.

_____ 16. Millions of people throughout the world have responded to Anne's message of hope.

_____ 17. Anne Frank's attitude about human relationships is a constructive mindset that can bring peace to the world.

_____ 18. Anne Frank's experience proves that a single person, even a 15-year-old girl, can affect world opinion and action.

_____ 19. Anne proves that if you look beyond yourself to achieve higher goals for others, you not only can help them but also can rise above your own problem.

_____ 20. Anne's thinking can be called creative because she strives to give new life to intergroup relationships.

Answers to Reading Comprehension Quiz

1. **T**;   2. **F**;   3. **T**;   4. **F**;   5. **T**;   6. **F**;   7. **T**;   8. **T**;   9. **T**;   10. **T**;   11. **T**;   12. **F**;   13. **F**;   14. **T**;   15. **T**; 16. **T**;   17. **T**;   18. **T**;   19. **T**;   20. **T**.

Possible Topics for Research Reports

1. **The Revisionists**
   The Revisionists are a group of "historians" who claim the Holocaust was a hoax! Give a report on their ideas, leaders, current status, and influence.

2. **The Anne Frank Center USA**
   Have students contact this center and send for information on the latest developments in Holocaust education.

Suggestions for Discussion Topics

1. Why can Holocaust experience really not be defined in words or numbers?

2. Explain how four "measuring parameters" make the Holocaust a model of "racism-in-action"?

3. Tell in your own words why chaos and confusion are appropriate descriptions for Holocaust action.

4. Look at the paragraph on Page 53 that explains the one correct response to any evil encounter. Think of any modern-day evil encounter, such as a person being involved with harmful drugs, and explain how these steps can be applied to solve the problem.

5. Explain how the diary acts as a linking mechanism from the past to promote good actions in the society of today and the future.

6. Read the last two paragraphs in this book. Discuss the meanings with your class. Tell why you agree that Anne Frank's story must be kept alive.

7. Explain what these terms mean to you:
   a. racism-in-action
   b. comm-unity-in-action
   c. Anne's message-in-action
   d. goodness-in-action

8. Tell how both goodness and evil can grow into powerful movements. Name an example of each.

9. Explain how a typical daily news report from a city called True Community of Fellowship might contrast to the daily news from your town or city.

Four Cooperative Learning Activities

The following cooperative learning activities offer exploration in the Holocaust and the life of Anne Frank. Each cooperative learning activity includes: research, reporting, summarizing, analyzing, and ideas for extending beyond the classroom. You may wish to divide the class into two groups, or assign students to the individual roles of researcher, reporter, note-taker, monitor, and time-keeper as they engage in the activities.

Cooperative Learning Activity 1: To familiarize students with an overview of Holocaust experience that provides them with background to draw parallels between Anne Frank's experience and that of other Holocaust victims.

Cooperative Learning Activity 2: To use the Holocaust as a model of "racism-in-action" against several other human crimes in history so students understand how the Holocaust crime is without true parallel.

Cooperative Learning Activity 1

Extending Research and Reflection: An Overview of Human Experiences in the Holocaust

Before starting this activity, the teacher and students should become thoroughly acquainted with: (1) **List of Research Topics for Cooperative Learning Activity One** on page 125 (underlined words are topic headings), an overview of human experiences in the Holocaust; and (2) the three-step procedure outlined below.

Classroom Procedures

Student Directions:

Step 1: Select Topics For Research Reports

1. Each group should select a section of research topics from the **List of Research Topics for Cooperative Learning Activity 1.**

2. For research, use books, mentioned in the Books About the Holocaust and Bibliography sections of this text, or any others the teacher suggests.

3. Decide on a consistent format for group/individual reports including:

   a. Number of sources required

   b. Note-taking

   c. Bibliography

   d. Written/oral presentations

   e. Visual aids

   f. Individual roles in group study/reports

   g. Criteria for evaluating oral presentations

   h. Individual assignments

   i. Group roles for study/reports

   j. Group assignments

   k. Group projects

   l. Individual projects

Step 2: Oral Reports and Note-Taking

Groups should present reports. All students should take notes. At the end of each group's reports, two good student leaders in each group should conduct an oral discussion of everyone's notes, summarize the responses in a clear group outline, and make photocopies for all group members. This serves as an excellent review activity. Furthermore, the group outline will serve two purposes at a later time:

1. As a reference tool for **Cooperative Learning Activity 2: Using the Crime of the Holocaust As a Model of Racism-in-Action**

2. As a student reference-study tool for the whole unit.

Step 3: Reflection on Anne Frank's Holocaust Experience

After all reports have been given, reflect on Anne Frank's Holocaust experiences. Consider how Anne's plight was both similar and different from experiences of other Holocaust victims. (*Note*: The idea here is not "worse" or "better" but alike and different.) Each group should present views to the whole class.

List of Research Topics for Cooperative Learning Activity 1

An Abbreviated Overview of Holocaust Experience

This is only a partial list of Holocaust topics. As you research, you may find others you wish to add. For example, the historical reasons why anti-Semitism exists in the world provide critical insight for Holocaust study. And so does the study of Nazism as a totalitarian style of government. In addition, the fate of Jewish survivors and the postwar response to the Holocaust add important summary information to this research. (Consult *Understanding the Holocaust*, 1995, by Betty Merti, for studying the roots of anti-Semitism, Hitler and Nazism, Holocaust history, and the postwar response.)

These research topics include events or concepts related to the Jews and their helpers or to events of the Holocaust.

1. Jewish businesses boycott in 1933

2. Night of Broken Glass or Kristallnacht

3. Nuremberg Laws

4. Anti-Jewish Laws of 1933

5. Nazi Master-Race Theory

6. "Legal Definition of Jew and Aryan"

7. Jewish Council (Judenrat)

8. roundups, deportation

9. transit camps, labor camps (include roll call, bathroom and sleeping facilities, starvation diets, branding of prison numbers, average life span of prisoners)

10. Warsaw ghetto/Jewish ghettos

11. medical experiments

12. Polish death camps

13. SS Einsatzgruppen

14. Hitler's Euthanasia Program

15. black market

16. underground resistance movement

17. the rescue of Jewish victims

18. German Master Race theory

19. New Order

20. concentration camps, ghettos

21. Second Solution to the Jewish Question

22. Final Solution to the Jewish Question

23. death camps in Poland

24. the Jewish refugee crisis of 1938

25. the Evian Conference of 1938

26. the role of the Red Cross in the rescue of the Jews

Cooperative Learning Activity 2

Using the Crime of the Holocaust As a Model of Racism-in-Action

Classroom Procedures

Overview of Group Work for This Entire Activity

1. Form small research teams.

2. Each team should select one or two topics from the **Research Topic List**.

3. Gather resources from a classroom library or work in the school or local library for research.

4. Describe instances of inhumanity for each topic, by answering questions from the **Suggested Format of Research Questions** on page 129 in a written report.

5. Create visual aids to explain your topic.

6. Compare similarities and differences in your topic to the Jewish Holocaust, 1933–1945. (**Step 4** under **Student Directions** explains how to do this.)

7. Give an oral report on your comparison to the class, using visual aids.

Research Topic List

1. Native American tragedy
2. American slavery
3. Armenian tragedy
4. Bosnian revolt
5. Cambodian tragedy
6. Communist rebellion in China
7. Hiroshima bombing
8. Japanese Americans during World War II
9. Stalinist Russia
10. Tribal conflict in Uganda

Student Directions

Step 1: Research your topic to answer the Suggested Format of Research Questions on page 129 for a written report.

Step 2: Prepare a written report on your topic that:

1. Follows **Suggested Format of Research Questions**

2. Includes a Bibliography section

3. Reflects work of all group members

Step 3: Create visual aids to explain your topic.

1. Use the visual aids to give an overall picture of the incident.

    Provide statistics and descriptions that portray the human tragedy (numbers/percentages of deaths, personal injuries, property destruction, loss of homes, etc.). Do the victims ever recover any of their rights/losses?

2. Make pictures, charts, diagrams, bulletin board displays to explain the conflict.

3. Create three-dimensional projects, if desired.

4. Present these visual aids during your Oral Report in Step 4.

Step 4: Give an oral report on a comparison between your topic and the crime of the Holocaust.

1. The idea here is not "better" or "worse" but similar and different.

2. Review what you have already learned: four unique features of the Holocaust make it the model for racism-in-action:

    a. Genocide, an unmatched criminal motive, seeking total death of a group

    b. The deceptive nature of the racist scheme, giving it momentum

    c. The alarming growth displayed in the evil power of racism, causing widespread destruction

    d. The magnitude of the evil effects on both sides, resulting in chaos and confusion

3. Compare similarities and differences of your topic to the Nazi persecutions of Jewish victims in the Holocaust:

    a. Apply the **Suggested Format of Research Question**s to the Jewish Holocaust first. Use the **Group Outline** you did in **Cooperative Learning Activity 1** to help you with this.

    b. Then, compare Holocaust information to your answers for the **Suggested Format of Research Questions** for your group research topic.

4. Organize an oral group presentation to give to the class, based on this comparison. Use the visual aids you made in Step 3 to explain your position.

Suggested Format of Research Questions

1. Describe the nature of the problem and the main action involved.

   a. Is the problem social, religious, economic, political, technical, financial, geographical? Is the problem new or old? If new, tell why. If old, explain.

   b. Tell how racism is a factor.

   c. Describe the actions
      (1) Is a war or civil strife involved the entire time?
      (2) Is criminal action a factor?
      (3) How is evil or deceit a part of the action?
      (4) How are destructive forces used?

   d. Give the time, place, setting of the action.

   e. Tell how long the action lasted.

2. For the persecuted group, describe how they affect the action and how the action affects them:

   a. Who is the persecuted group? Are they a minority? Describe the victims: are they civilians, military members, women, children, the aged, the infirm?

   b. What factors place them in a weakened position?

   c. Can and do they retaliate? Are they armed?

   d. Are they considered an enemy in warfare?

   e. Does the group have any government support? Who comes to their rescue?

   f. What percentage of this group are destroyed by destructive forces? Give statistics. Do the destructive forces and numbers of victims grow to huge proportions?

   g. Are the victims localized in one country, town, or city? Are they rounded up for persecution or dealt with on the spot?

   h. Do they ever recover any of their losses?

3. For the dominant group, describe how they affect the action and how the action affects them.

   a. Describe the dominant group. Are they military or government forces? Is their size at the beginning and the end of the conflict about the same? greater? smaller?

   b. What actions does the dominant group use to oppress the targeted group?

   c. Are common citizens involved in oppressing the targeted group?

   d. Is there a systematic plan for mistreatment?

   e. What is the dominant group's goal or motive?
      (1) Is genocide part of the plan?
      (2) Is the desire for power and wealth a factor?
      (3) Is widespread deception a major tactic?
      (4) Are criminal actions involved?
      (5) To what extent is the goal accomplished?
      (6) Are laws violated?
      (7) Is propaganda used as a weapon?

f. Once the dominant group has the other group in tow, does it attempt to make peace with them and set them free?

g. To what extent does the dominant group suffer from its own actions?
   (1) Do they suffer loss of life, property, power? Describe their losses.
   (2) How do their overall actions affect their country, other countries?

4. Tell how this situation has affected human progress:

   a. In the area where the conflict occurred

   b. In enhancing the ability of the groups on both sides to form true community

Extending Student Interest

Putting on a Play with a Holocaust Theme

Present one or more scenes from one of the following plays:

1. *The Diary of Anne Frank* by Frances Goodrich and Albert Hackett.

2. *The Investigation* by Peter Weiss, a play based on Nazi war crime trials held in Frankfurt, Germany. Much of the play dialogue is actual court testimony!

3. *The Man in the Glass Booth* by Robert Shaw, a play centering on the theme of the postwar response of the Holocaust survivor.

4. *Incident at Vichy* by Arthur Miller, a play set in occupied France that portrays how Jewish victims refused to believe what was really happening to them.

5. *Doctor Korczak and the Children* by Erwin Sylvannus, which concentrates on the responsibility of the German people for the Holocaust.

6. *The Deputy* by Rolf Hochhuth, which deals with the response of the Catholic Church to the Holocaust.

7. *In Holland Stands a House: A Play about the Life and Times of Anne Frank* by Sue Sanders, an adaptation of the story of Anne Frank, includes scenes from the Annexe plus dramatized events in Nazi-occupied Europe.

8. *Children of the Holocaust* by Robert Mauro. Four teenage victims' voices after their death speak of their lost hopes and dreams.

If a play cannot be presented, you could assign your students to read one or more of these dramas.

Selected Resources
for Student Research and Reports

Amdur, Richard. *Anne Frank.* New York: Chelsea House, 1993. A tracing of Anne Frank's life.

Anatoli, Kuzneton. *Babi Yar.* New York: Pocket Books, 1977. A view of the Nazi Russian massacre through the eyes of a Russian youth.

Anne Frank Stichting. *Anne Frank in the World.* Amsterdam: Uitgeverij Bert Bakker, 1985.

Appleman-Jurman, Alicia. *Alicia: My Story.* New York: Bantam, 1988. An autobiography, the author tells of her experience as a 13-year-old who escapes from the Nazi firing squad and turns to helping other Jews escape to Palestine.

Arien, Michael. *Passage to Ararat.* St. Paul, MN: Hungry Mind Publisher, 1975. Addressing many aspects of the destruction of the Armenian people in the Ottoman empire, this was the Winner of the 1975 National Book Award.

Atkinson, Linda. *In Kindling Flame: The Story of Hannah Senesh 1921–1944.* New York: Beech Tree, 1992. Executed by the Nazis and called Israel's Joan of Arc, Hannah Senesh's true story of martyrdom is supplemented by her letters and diary excerpts in this book.

Ayer, Eleanor; Helen Waterford and Alfons Heck. *Parallel Journeys.* New York: Athenium, 1995. Two true autobiographical accounts; one of a Jewish mother who gives her child for care to a non-Jewish family; the other of a young man who becomes part of the leadership for Hitler Youth.

Baruch, Miri. "Anne Frank's diary of a young girl." *Melton Journal: Issues and Themes in Jewish Education,* 23 (1990): 17–19.

Bar-Zohar, Michael. *The Avengers.* New York: Tower Publishing, 1967. Concerns the Israeli Brigade, a group of Holocaust survivors also known as "The Avengers," who set out after World War II to capture or kill Nazis.

Berenbaum, Michael. *The World Must Know: The History of the Holocaust as Told in the United States Holocaust Memorial Museum.* New York: Little, Brown, 1993. A documented chronicle of Holocaust events, complete with illustrations.

Bishop, Claire. *Twenty and Ten.* New York: Penguin Books, Inc., 1978. Non-Jewish children hide and protect ten Jewish children in occupied France.

Boas, Jacob. *We Are Witnesses: The Diaries of Five Teenagers Who Died in the Holocaust.* New York: Henry Holt, 1995. Journal entries from five youths including Anne Frank.

_____ . *Boulevard Des Miseres: The History of the Transit Camp Westerbork.* Hamden: Archon Books, 1985.

Blum, Howard. *Wanted! The Search for Nazis in America.* New York: Fawcett, 1978.

Camhi, Leslie. "The Tender Age of Innocence." *Village Voice,* 40 (1995, March 21): 17.

Chartock, Roselle K., and Jack Spenser (eds.). *Can It Happen Again? Chronicles of the Holocaust.* New York: Black Dog and Leventhal, 1995. An anthology of more than 100 eyewitness and written accounts, including excerpts from books, poems, newspapers.

Clements, Bruce. *From Ice Set Free: The Story of Otto Kiep.* New York: Farrar, Straus & Giroux, Inc., 1972. The resistance and ultimate hanging of Kiep, a Nazi-hating German.

Cohen, Elie. *Human Behavior in the Concentration Camp.* New York: Norton, 1953.

Czerniakow, Adam. *The Warsaw Diary of Chaim A. Kaplan.* Briarcliff Manor, NY: Stein & Day, 1978.

DesPres, Terrence. *The Survivor: An Anatomy of Life in the Death Camps.* New York: Oxford University Press, 1976.

Dror, Yuval. "The Anne Frank Haven in an Israeli Kibbutz." *Adolescence,* 30 (1995, Fall): 617–629.

Dwork, Deborah. *Children With a Star: Jewish Youth in Nazi Europe.* New Haven: Yale, 1991. A scholarly analysis of the lives of children under Nazi tyranny.

Elkins, Michael. *Forged in Fury.* New York: Ballantine, 1971. How a group of Jewish resistance fighters continued their hunt for Nazis after the war ended.

Epstein, Helen. *Children of the Holocaust.* New York: Bantam Books, Inc., 1980. Based on interviews with children of Holocaust survivors in the United States; reveals how they respond to the Holocaust.

Fanelow, Fania, *Playing for Time.* New York: Atheneum, 1977. Survivor of the Auschwitz camp orchestra.

Field, Herman. *Angry Harvest.* New York: Crowell, 1958. Tells how a Jewish girl hides with a Polish family.

Fisch, Robert. *Light From the Yellow Star: A Lesson of Love From the Holocaust.* Minneapolis, MN: Yellow Star Foundation, 1995. The experience of a survivor of five concentration camps tells how goodness can be learned even from the horrors of the Holocaust.

Flender, Harold. *Rescue in Denmark.* New York: Schocken Books, Inc., 1980. Account of the rescue of Denmark's Jews.

Fogelman, Eva. *Conscience and Courage: Rescuers of Jews During the Holocaust.* New York: Anchor, 1994.

Forman, James. *Ceremony of Innocence.* New York: Dell, 1970. A novel based on the true story of the White Rose, an organization of German students who opposed Hitler.

_____. *My Enemy, My Brother.* New York: Scholastic Inc., 1972. A novel of how a teenage survivor of a Nazi prison decides to find new life in Israel.

Frank, Anne. *Tales from the Secret Annex.* Translated by Ralph Manhiem and Michel Mok. New York: Doubleday & Co., Inc., 1984. Stories, fables, essays, and reminiscences.

Friedman, Ina. *Escape or Die: True Stories of Young People Who Survived the Holocaust.* Cambridge, MA: Yellow Moon Press, 1991. Personal accounts of how 12 men and women were able to survive; recalls the power of the human spirit to endure nightmarish circumstances.

Frielander, Albert, ed. *Out of the Whirlwind: A Reader of Holocaust Literature.* New York: Schocken Books, Inc., 1976.

Geis, Miep. *Anne Frank Remembered: The Woman Who Helped the Frank Family to Hide* (A. L. Gold, Trans.). New York: Simon and Schuster, 1987.

Gilbert, Martin. *Atlas of the Holocaust. Revised Edition.* New York: Marrow, 1993. A total of 316 maps, charting the course of the Holocaust.

Gladstein, Jacob. *Anthology of Holocaust Literature.* Jewish Publication Society, 1969.

Gordon, T., and H. Witts. *Voyage of the Damned.* Briarcliff Manor, NY: Stein & Day, 1974. Relates the ill-fated journey of the *St. Louis.*

Green, Gerald. *Holocaust.* Williamsport, PA: Bro-Dart Publishing Co., 1978. A novel focusing on two German families, one Jewish and one non-Jewish, under the Nazis.

Greene, Bette. *Morning Is a Long Time Coming.* New York: Archay Paperbacks, 1979.

_____. *Summer of My German Soldier.* New York: Dial Books for Young Readers, 1973.

Gutman, Israel. *Resistance: The Warsaw Ghetto Uprising.* New York: Houghton Mifflin, 1994. Written by a survivor of the uprising, this account details the event with firsthand testimony and other documentation.

Hannam, Charles. *A Boy in That Situation.* New York: Harper & Row Publishers, Inc., 1978. The autobiography of a German Jew in "that situation."

Hanser, Richard. *A Noble Treason: The Revolt of Munich Students Against Hitler.* New York: Putnam, 1979.

Hausner, Gideon. *Justice in Jerusalem.* New York: Herzl Press, 1978. Concerns the trial of Adolf Eichmann.

Hersey, John. *The Wall.* New York: Bantam Books, Inc., 1981. Historical novel about the Warsaw ghetto revolt.

Heyes, Eileen. *Children of the Swastika: The Hitler Youth.* Brookfield, CT: Millbrook, 1993. Book deals with the youth of Nazi Germany; includes personal interviews of former Hitler youth.

Hoffman Judy. *Joseph and Me: In the Days of the Holocaust.* New York: Ktav Publishing House, Inc., 1979. A true story of the author and her brother, who hid from the Nazis in occupied Holland.

Holliday, Laurel (ed.). *Children in the Holocaust and World War II: Their Secret Diaries.* New York: Simon and Schuster, 1995. An anthology of diaries written by 22 children from the ghettos, concentration camps, and occupied cities.

Hondius, Dienke, Kniesmeyer and Van der Wal, Bauco. *Anne Frank in the World.* Amsterdam: Anne Frank Stichting, 1992.

Hurwitz, Johanna. *Anne Frank: Life in Hiding.* Philadelphia: Jewish Publication Society, 1988.

Ippisch, Hanneke. *Sky: A True Story of Resistance During World War II.* New York: Simon and Schuster, 1996. The author's narrative, supplemented with photos, of her girlhood in occupied Holland and her two years with the Dutch Resistance.

Isser, Harel. *House of Garibaldi Street.* New York: Viking, 1975. Portrays Eichmann's capture and arrest.

Joff, Joseph. *A Bag of Marbles.* New York: Bantam, 1974. An autobiography that reveals how French Jews hid out in the Alps to escape Nazi capture.

Kahn, Leora, and Rachel Hager. *When They Came to Take My Father: Voices of the Holocaust.* New York: Arcade, 1996. A compilation of 50 testimonies from Holocaust survivors.

Kanfer, Stefan. *The Eighth Sin.* New York: Random House, Inc., 1978. Portrays the fate of the Gypsies under Hitler.

Katsch, Abram, and Chaim A. Kaplan, eds. *Scroll of Agony: The Warsaw Diary of Chaim A. Kaplan.* New York: Macmillan Publishing Co., Inc., 1981.

Katz, Steven. *The Holocaust in Historical Context.* New York: Oxford University Press, 1994.

Kay, Mara. *In the Face of Danger.* New York: Crown, 1977. A story of how two Hitler Youth members hide and protect two Jewish girls in an attic.

Kerr, M. E. *Gentlehands.* New York: Harper & Row Publishers, Inc., 1978.

Klarsfeld, Beate. *Wherever They May Be.* Chicago: Vanguard Press, 1975. Klarsfeld, a German Nazi hunter, writes about Nazis in hiding.

Klarsfeld, Serge. *The Holocaust—The Neo-Nazi Mythomania.* New York: Beate Klarsfeld Foundation, 1978. Written by the husband of Beate Klarsfeld, German Nazi hunter.

Klein, Gerta W. *All But My Life.* New York: Hill and Wang, 1995. An autobiography, Ms. Klein recounts her life as slave laborer for three years, life in prison, and a 1,000 mile winter death march.

Kluger, Ruth, and Peggy Mann. *The Last Escape.* New York: Doubleday, 1974. Concerns the smuggling of thousands of Jewish victims from Nazi-occupied lands into Palestine.

Kuper, Jack. *Child of the Holocaust.* New York: New American Library, 1980. Retells how a Jewish boy poses as a Christian during the Nazi era.

Landau, Elaine. *The Warsaw Ghetto Uprising.* Indianapolis: Macmillan, 1992. A narrative describing the 28-day uprising, conducted mainly by young Jews even though they knew chance of victory was slim.

Langer, Lawrence L. *Holocaust Testimonies: The Ruins of Memory.* New Haven: Yale University Press, 1991. A book that quotes and compares oral and written history from Holocaust survivors; also relates the effect of Holocaust experience on the self.

Leber, Annedore. *Conscience in Revolt: Sixty-four Stories of Resistance in Germany, 1933–45.* Boulder: Westview Press, 1994.

Leitner, Isabella. *Fragments of Isabella: A Memoir of Auschwitz.* New York: Thomas Y. Crowell Co., 1978.

Lindwer Lily. *The Last Seven Months Of Anne Frank.* New York: Anchor, 1992. Accounts of six teenagers who entered the camps with Anne, experienced all that Anne did, and tell of memories of her.

Long, Wellington. *The New Nazis of Germany.* Philadelphia: Chilton Books, 1968.

Lukas, Richard C. *Did The Children Cry? Hitler's War Against Jewish and Polish Children, 1939–45.* New York: Hippocrene, 1994. Relates how the German occupation affected youth, including those who formed armed resistance groups.

Marks, Jane. *The Hidden Children: The Secret Survivors of the Holocaust.* New York: Fawcett Columbine, 1993.

Masters, Anthony. *The Summer That Bled.* New York: St. Martins, 1972. Concerns the life and death of Hannah Senesh, Palestinian teenager.

Matas, Carol. *After the War.* New York: Simon and Schuster, 1996. A fictional tale of a Holocaust survivor who returns home to Poland.

Meltzer, Milton. *Never to Forget: The Jews of the Holocaust.* New York: Dell Publishing Co., Inc., 1977. A history of the Holocaust through survivors' testimonies.

Monckeberg, Mathilde Wollf. *On the Other Side.* New York: Mayflower Books, 1979. A diary written by a German woman who hated Hitler.

Newman, Judith. *In the Hell of Auschwitz.* New York: Exposition Press, 1963.

Noble, Iris. *Nazi Hunter: Simon Wiesenthal.* New York: Messner, 1979. Wiesenthal's biography.

Orgel, Doris. *The Devil in Vienna.* New York: Dell, 1980. A novel of a Jewish girl and her best friend, the daughter of a Nazi.

Papanek, Ernst. *Out of the Fire.* New York: Morrow, 1975. The story of a man who saved thousands of Jewish children from the Holocaust.

Primo, Levi. *Survival in Auschwitz: The Nazi Assault on Humanity.* New York: Collier, 1961. Based on the author's own experience.

Prince, Eileen. *The Story of Anne Frank.* New York: Maxwell McMillan, 1991.

Rabinowitz, Dorothy. *New Lives: Survivors of the Holocaust Living in America.* New York: Alfred A. Knopf, Inc., 1976.

Ramati, Alexander. *The Assisi Underground: The Priests Who Rescued Jews.* New York: Jove, 1978. A true story of how Italian Franciscans sheltered and protected hundreds of Jews.

Ray, Karen. *To Cross a Line.* New York: Orchard, 1994. A critically acclaimed novel set in Nazi Germany tells of Kristallnacht and a 17-year-old's brush with the Gestapo.

Reiss, Johanna. *The Journey Back: The sequel to The Upstairs Room.* New York: Harper & Row Publishers, Inc., 1976.

———. *The Upstairs Room.* New York: Harper & Row Publishers, Inc., 1972. True story of two Dutch girls in hiding from the Nazis.

Richter, Hans Peter. *Friedrich.* New York: Dell, 1973. Reveals life in Nazi Germany through a story of friendship between two German boys—one Jewish, one non-Jewish. Excellent!

———. *I Was There.* New York: Holt, Rinehart, and Winston, 1972. Reveals how two young Nazis become disillusioned with Hitlerism.

Roehn, Ilse. *Mischlinge, Second Degree: My Childhood in Nazi Germany.* New York: Greenwillow Books, 1977.

Rosenfeld, Alvin H. "Popularization and Memory: The Case of Anne Frank." In Peter Hayes (Ed.) *Lessons and Legacies: The Meaning of the Holocaust in the Changing World.* Evanston, IL, 1991.

Rubin, Arnold P. *The Evil That Men Do: The Story of the Nazis.* New York: Julian Messner, 1981. A history of the Holocaust that concentrates on the choices made by the victims, the Nazis, the collaborators, and the bystanders.

St. John, Robert. *Ben-Gurion: A Biography.* New York: Doubleday, 1971. The life of Israel's first prime minister.

Samuels, Gertrude. *Mottele.* New York: American Library, 1977. A historical novel of the Jewish partisans in Russia and Poland.

Schloss, Eva. *Eva's Story: A Survivor's Tale by the Step-Sister of Anne Frank.* New York: St. Martin's Press, 1989.

Schwartz-Bart, Andre. *The Last of the Just.* New York: Atheneum, 1973. An excellent historical novel which begins with persecution of Jews in medieval England and ends with the gas chambers of Nazi Germany.

Segal, Lore. *Other People's Houses.* New York: Harcourt Brace, 1964. A true account of how an Austrian-Jewish girl and her family took refuge in English homes to escape Nazi capture.

Senesh, Hannah. *Hannah Senesh, Her Life and Her Diary.* New York: Schocken Books, Inc., 1973. One of Israel's greatest heroines was a Jewish teenager who became a paratrooper during World War II and died trying to help Jewish victims of the Nazis.

Speer, Albert. *Inside the Third Reich.* New York: Macmillan Publishing Co., Inc., 1981. Hitler's economic coordinator of the German war effort gives a candid look at Nazi Germany.

Stadtler, Bea. *The Holocaust: A History of Courage and Resistance.* New York: Behrman House, Inc., 1975. Concentrates on many heroes and heroines who resisted the Nazis.

Stevenson, William. *The Bormann Brotherhood.* New York: Harcourt Brace, 1973. Deals with the escape and survival of Nazi war criminals.

Suhl, Yuri. *On the Other Side of the Gate.* New York: Avon, 1975. A novel based on the real-life event of smuggling an 18-month-old Jewish baby out of the Warsaw ghetto.

_____. *Uncle Mishna's Partisans.* New York: Four Winds Press, 1973. Based on the lives of a real group of Jewish resistance fighters in the Ukraine.

Switzer, Ellen. *How Democracy Failed.* New York: Athe-neum, 1975. Based on interviews with Germans who recall life under Hitler.

Ten Boom, Corrie. *A Prisoner and Yet . . .* New York: Jove Publications, 1982. Reveals how the author and her family were imprisoned and enslaved by the Nazis for helping refugees.

Trepman, Paul. *Among Men and Beasts.* San Diego: A. S. Barnes, 1978. A survivor of Bergen-Belsen reveals his experience as a Nazi prisoner.

Uris, Leon. *Exodus.* New York: Bantam Books, Inc., 1981. A novel concerning the smuggling of Holocaust survivors into Palestine before the state of Israel was declared.

Van Der Rol, Ruud, and Rian Verhoeven. *Anne Frank Beyond the Diary.* New York: Puffin Books, 1995.

von Kardorff, Ursula. *Diary of a Nightmare.* New York: John Day, 1965. The diary written during the Nazi era by a Nazi-hating young woman.

Wardi, Dina. Memorial Candles: *Children of the Holo-caust.* New York: Tavistock-Routledge, 1992.

Whiting, Charles. *The Hunt for Martin Bormann.* New York: Ballantine, 1973. Tells of the search for the missing Nazi who was Hitler's right-hand man.

Wiesel, Elie. *The Gates of the Forest.* New York: Schocken Books, Inc., 1982. A novel of how a Hungarian Jew becomes a partisan.

_____. *Night.* New York: Hill and Wang; Avon, 1972. A powerful autobiographical novel of life in Nazi prisons based on the author's own experience.

Wiesenthal, Simon. *The Murderers Among Us.* New York: McGraw-Hill, 1973. Concerns Nazi war criminals in hiding.

_____. *The Sunflower.* New York: Schocken Books, Inc., 1977. A tale of how a dying Nazi asks a Jew for forgiveness for his role in the Holocaust.

Ziemian, Joseph, *The Cigarette Sellers of Three Crosses Square.* Minneapolis: Lerner, 1975. A true story of how a group of Jewish children escape from the Warsaw ghetto and survive in the Nazi-occupied city of Warsaw.

Zuker, Liliana. *Liliana's Journal: Warsaw 1939–1945.* New York: Dial Press, 1980.

Audiovisual Materials

Below is a list of audiovisual aids that you may find useful in presenting the Holocaust to your students. Addresses are given with each aid.

"Avenue of the Just," available for rental. A 58-minute documentary which deals with questions of conscience and morality and of why some bystanders during the Holocaust reacted compassionately toward Jewish victims while others remained indifferent. Anti-Defamation League of B'nai B'rith, 823 U.N. Plaza, New York, NY 10017.

"Scenes From the Holocaust," available for rental. A 10-minute 16mm film shows sketches of life in Auschwitz, drawn by Jewish artists who were imprisoned there. Can be used not only to convey this content but also to inspire student artwork of their own impres-sions of Anne Frank and Holocaust study. Center for Holocaust Studies, Anti-Defamation League of B'nai B'rith, 823 United Nations Plaza, New York, NY 10017.

"The Legacy of Anne Frank," available for rental. An on-the-spot visit to the hiding place of Anne Frank and her family in Amsterdam, Holland. Anti-Defamation League of B'nai B'rith, 823 U.N. Plaza, New York, NY 10017.

"The Courage to Care," available for purchase. A 29-minute VHS videocassette portrays individual action of Christians who risked their lives during the Third Reich to protect Jewish families from persecution. Anti-Defamation League of B'nai B'rith, 823 United Nations Plaza, New York, NY 10017.

"Understanding Prejudice," available for purchase. A color filmstrip providing for a better understanding of scapegoating, stereotyping, and the myth of racial superiority. Anti-Defamation League of B'nai B'rith, 823 U.N. Plaza, New York, NY 10017.

"Warsaw Ghetto," available for rental. A 51-minute, black-and-white film which is an on-the-spot motion picture of ghetto life taken from SS files. Anti-Defamation League of B'nai B'rith, 823 U.N. Plaza, New York, NY 10017.

"Warsaw Ghetto: Holocaust and Resistance," available for purchase. A filmstrip and cassette that portrays the formation of and life in the Warsaw ghetto but concentrates on resistance—both passive and armed. Jewish Labor Committee, 25 East 78th Street, New York, NY 10021.

All resources below may be ordered from Social Studies School Service, 10200 Jefferson Boulevard, P.O. Box 802, Culver City, CA 90232-0802:

"The Diary of Anne Frank," available for purchase. The 170-minute 20th Century Fox movie portrayal of Anne's diary, directed by George Stevens and starring Millie Perkins and Shelley Winters. On either 2 VHS videocassettes or 2 laser discs.

"The Attic," available for purchase. This 95-minute film, based on the book *Anne Frank Remembered* by Miep Geis and starring Mary Steenburgen and Paul Scofield, portrays the Nazi occupation of Holland and the courage of both Dutch Jews and Christians under their reign.

"Anne Frank: The Diary of a Young Girl," available for purchase. On 2 audiocassettes, this reading of Anne's diary by actress Julie Harris is a good resource for slow readers as well as for general classroom use.

"Not In Our Town," available for purchase. Introduce the issue of human responsibility to students with this 21-minute VHS videocassette of how, in 1993, more than 10,000 residents in Billings, Montana, displayed strong support for Jews and other minorities who were being harassed by white supremacist groups.

"Holocaust Poster Series," available for purchase and suitable for classroom display. A 20-poster set of 18" × 24" black and white enlargements of actual photographs.

"The Master Race: History in Action," available for purchase. A 20-minute videocassette, this documentary film shows the Nazi promotion of "Big Lies" about Jews, Hitler Youth, and method of organized persecution.

"The Other Side of Faith," available for purchase. A 27-minute VHS videocassette that explores questions of individual responsibility through the portrayal of the heroic efforts of a Roman Catholic teenager who refuses to obey unjust Nazi laws and saves the lives of nearly a dozen Jews during the Holocaust.

Bibliography

Books and Journals

Altshuler, David A. *Hitler's War Against the Jews.* New York: Behrman House, 1978.

Amabile, Teresa, and Margaret Stubbs. *Psychological Research in the Classroom.* New York: Pergamon Press, 1982.

Anne Frank Stichting. *Anne Frank in the World.* Amsterdam: Uitgeverij Bert Bakker, 1985.

Arendt, Hanna. *Origins of Totalitarianism.* New York: Harcourt, Brace and World, 1966.

Aymur, Brandt. *Laws and Trials That Created History.* New York: Crown, 1974.

Bachrach, Susan. *Tell Them We Remember: The Story of the Holocaust.* Boston: Little, Brown, and Co., 1994.

Bardill, Donald. "The Making of a Person: A Psychosocial Analysis." *Social Thought,* Summer, 1976, pp. 15–25.

Barnouw, David and Van Der Stroom. *The Diary of Anne Frank: The Critical Edition.* New York: Bantam Doubleday Dell Publishing Group, Inc., 1995.

Bauer, Yehuda. *Jews for Sale.* New Haven: Yale University Press, 1994.

Berryman, John. *The Freedom of the Poet.* New York: Farrer, Straus, and Giroux, 1980.

Bertocci, Peter A., and Richard M. Millard. *Personality and the Good: Psychological and Ethical Perspectives.* New York: David McKay Company, 1963.

Block, Gay, and Makia Drucker. *Portraits of Moral Courage in the Holocaust.* New York: Holmes and Meier, 1992.

Blum, Howard. *Wanted! The Search for Nazis in America.* New York: Fawcett, 1978.

Brenner, Rachel Feldhay. "Writing Herself Against History: Anne Frank's Self-portrait as a Young Artist." *Modern Judaism, 16,* 1996, pp. 105–134.

Buber, Martin. *The Knowledge of Man: A Philosophy of the Interhuman.* Maurice Friedman (Ed.) and Ronald Gregor Smith (Trans.). New York: Harper Torschbooks, 1965.

Bullock, Alan. *Hitler: A Study in Tyranny.* New York: Harper & Row, 1962.

Charme, Stuart Z. "Sartre's Images of the Other and the Search for Authenticity." *Human Studies,* October, 1991, pp. 14, 251–264. Abstract from Silverplatter File: Sociofile Item: 92Y72621.

Ciriello, Maria. *The Principal as Spiritual Leader.* Washington, DC: United States Catholic Conference, 1994.

Collins, A., J. Brown, and A. Holum. "Cognitive Apprenticeship: Making Thinking Visible." *American Educator,* Winter, 1991, pp. 6–10, 38–41.

Cowan, Lore. *Children of the Resistance.* New York: Hawthorne, 1969.

Dawidowicz, Lucy. *Holocaust Reader.* New York: Behrman House, 1974.

_____ . *The War Against the Jews.* New York: Holt, Rinehart and Winston, 1975.

Deming, W. Edwards. *Out of the Crisis.* Cambridge: Massachusetts Institute of Technology.

Denzin, Norman K. *The Research Act: A Theoretical Introduction to Sociological Methods Second Edition.* New York: McGraw-Hill, 1978.

_____ . *Interpretive Interactionism.* Newbury, CA: Sage Publications, 1989.

Dewey, John. *Experience and Education.* New York: Collier Macmillan Publishers, 1934.

Dicks, Henry V. *Licensed Mass Murders.* New York: Basic Books, 1972.

Dressen, Willi, Ernest Klee, and Volker Reiss (Eds.). *The Good Old Days: The Holocaust as Seen by its Perpetrators.* New York: The Free Press, 1988.

Duffy, T., and D.J. Cunningham. "Constructivism: Implications for Design and Delivery of Instruction." In D.H. Jonassen (Ed.) *Handbook of Research on Educational Communications and Technology.* New York: Macmillan, 1996.

Dupuy, Trevor Nevitt. *The Military History of World War 2;* Vol. 15, *European Resistance Movements.* New York: Franklin Watts, Inc., 1965.

Eisenberg, Nancy. *Altruistic Emotion, Cognition, and Behavior.* Hillsdale, NJ: Lawrence Erlbaum Associates, Publishers, 1986.

Elliot, B. J. *Hitler and Germany.* New York: McGraw-Hill, 1968.

Evertson and Green. "Observation as Inquiry and Method." In M.C. Wittrock (Ed.) *Handbook for Research On Teaching, Third Edition.* New York: Macmillan, 1986.

Fest, Joachim. *Hitler.* New York: Harcourt, Brace, Jovanovich, 1974.

Festinger, L. *A Theory of Cognitive Dissonance.* Stanford: Stanford University Press, 1957.

Finzel, Hans W. *A Descriptive Model for Discerning Organizational Culture.* Fuller Theological Seminary, School of World Mission, 1989.

Fisher, R., and W. Ury. *Getting to Yes.* New York: Penguin Books, 1983.

Flannery, Edward. *The Anguish of the Jews.* New York: Macmillan, 1965.

Fleming, A. *Trials That Made Headlines.* New York: St. Martins, 1974.

Frank, Anne. *The Diary of a Young Girl.* New York: Doubleday, 1967.

_____ . *Tales from the Secret Annex,* translated by Ralph Manheim and Michel Mok. New York: Doubleday, 1984.

_____ . *The Works of Anne Frank.* New York: Doubleday, 1959.

Fraser, Barry J., and Herbert J. Walberg. *Educational Environments: Evaluation, Antecedents and Consequences.* New York: Pergamon Press, 1993.

Friere, Paulo. *Pedagogy of the Oppressed.* New York: Continuum, 1990.

Fulghum, Robert. *From Beginning to End: The Rituals of Our Lives.* New York: Villard Books, 1995.

Gamoran, A., and M. Berends. "The Effects of Stratification in Secondary Schools: Synthesis of Survey and Ethnographic Research." *Review of educational research, 57,* 1987, pp. 415–435.

Gangel, Kenneth. *Lessons in Leadership from the Bible.* Winona Lake, IN: BMH Books, 1980.

Geis, Miep. *Anne Frank Remembered: The Woman Who Helped the Frank Family to Hide* (A.L. Gold, Trans.). New York: Simon and Schuster, 1987.

Gervasi, Frank. *Adolf Hitler.* New York: Hawthorn, 1974.

Gilbert, Martin. *Auschwitz and the Allies.* New York: Holt, Rinehart and Winston, 1981.

_____ . *The Holocaust.* New York: Hill and Wang, 1979.

Gilford, Henry. *Reichstag Fire.* New York: Watts, 1973.

Graff, Stewart. *The Story of World War II.* New York: E. P. Dutton, 1978.

Greene, Maxine. *The Dialectic of Freedom.* New York: Teacher's College Press, 1988.

_____ . "The Occasions of Pluralism: Multiculturalism and the Expanding Community." *Educational Researcher,* 22, 1993, p. 18.

Gribble, L. *Justice?* New York: Abelard, 1971.

Grobman, A., and J. Fishman (Eds.). *Anne Frank in Historical Perspective: A Teaching Guide for Secondary Schools.* Los Angeles: Martyrs Memorial and Museum of the Holocaust.

Grosser, Paul, and Edwin Halperin. *The Causes and Effects of Anti-Semitism.* New York: Philosophical Library, 1978.

Habermas, Jurgen. *Postmetaphysical Thinking: Philosophical Essays.* William Mark Hohengarten (Trans.). Cambridge, MA: The MIT Press, 1992.

Halmos, Paul. *The Faith of the Counsellors: A Study in the Theory and Practice of Social Case Work and Psychotherapy.* New York: Schocken Books, 1966.

Hausner, Gideon. *Justice in Jerusalem.* New York: Herzl Press, 1978.

Heidegger, Martin. *Being and Time.* New York: Anchor, 1962.

Heider, J. *Tao of Leadership: Leadership Strategies for a New Age.* New York: Bantam Books, 1950.

Hilberg, Raul. *The Destruction of European Jews.* Chicago: Quadrangle, 1971.

_____ . *Perpetrators, Victims, Bystanders the Jewish Catastrophe 1933–1945.* New York: Harper-Collins, 1992.

Hondius, Dienke, Kniesmeyer, and Bauco Van der Wal. *Anne Frank in the World.* Amsterdam: Anne Frank Stichting, 1992.

Hoy, Wayne K., and Cecil G. Miskel. *Educational Administration: Theory, Research, and Practice.* New York: McGraw-Hill, 1991.

Kelley, R.E. *The Power of Followership.* New York: Bantam Doubleday Dell Publishing Group, Inc., 1992.

Kiecolt, Jill. "Stress and the Decision to Change Oneself: A Theoretical Model." *Social Psychology Quarterly,* 1994, 57, pp. 49–63. Abstract from Silverplatter File: Sociofile Item: 9409229.

Klarsfeld, Beate. *Wherever They May Be.* Chicago: Vanguard Press, 1975.

Klein, Mina C., and Arthur H. *Hitler's Hang-ups.* New York: Dutton, 1976.

Kouzes, James M., and Barry Z. Posner. *Credibility: How Leaders Gain and Lose it, Why People Demand it.* San Francisco: Jossey-Bass Publishers, 1993.

Kurzweil, Edith. "The holocaust: memory and theory." *Partisan Review,* 1996, 63, pp. 356–374.

Langer, Walter. *The Mind of Adolf Hitler.* New York: New American Library, 1978.

Leahly, Robert. "Authenticity: From Philosophic Concept to Literary Character." *Educational Theory,* 44, pp. 447–461.

Leckie, Robert. *Story of World War Two.* New York: Random House, 1964.

Leclerq, J. *The Love of Learning and the Desire for God.* New York: Fordham Press, 1977.

Levin, Nora. *The Holocaust: The Destruction of European Jewry, 1933–1945.* New York: Schocken, 1968.

Levinger, Elma. *Great Jewish Women.* New York: Behrman House, 1940.

Lorant, Stefán. *Seig Heil: An Illustrated History of Germany from Bismark to Hitler.* New York: Norton, 1974.

Lurie, Rose G. *American Jewish Heroes.* New York: Union of American Hebrew Congregations, 1960.

Marshall, H.H. (Ed.) *Redefining Student Learning: Roots of Educational Change.* Norwood, NJ: Ablex Publishing Corporation, 1992.

Mayeroff, Milton. *On Caring.* New York: Perennial, 1971.

Meltzer, Milton. *Never to Forget: The Jews of the Holocaust.* New York: Harper & Row, 1976.

Merton, Thomas. *Thoughts in Solitude.* New York: Image Books, 1958.

Misgeld, Deiter, and Graeme Nicholson (Eds. and Trans.). *Hans-Georg Gadamer on Education, Poetry, and History: Applied Hermeneutics.* Albany, NY: State University of New York Press, 1992.

Misgeld, Deiter. "Critical Theory and Hermeneutics: The Debate Between Habermas and Gadamer." In O'Neill, John (Ed.). *On Critical Theory.* New York: Seabury, 1976, pp. 164–183.

Mitscherlich, Alexander. *Doctors of Infamy.* New York: H. Schuman, 1949.

Montagu, Ashley. *Man's Most Dangerous Myth: The Fallacy of Race.* New York: Oxford University Press, 1973.

Mosse, George. *The Crisis of German Ideology.* New York: Grosset and Dunlap, 1964.

_____ . *Nazi Culture.* New York: Grosset and Dunlap, 1966.

Moustakas, Clark. *Heuristic Research: Design, Methodology, and Applications.* Newbury Park: Sage Publications, 1990.

Newman, Judith. *In the Hell of Auschwitz.* New York: Exposition Press, 1963.

Noble, Iris. *Nazi Hunter: Simon Wiesenthal.* New York: Messner, 1979.

Noddings, Nel. *Caring: A Feminine Approach to Ethics and Moral Education.* Berkeley, University of California Press, 1984.

Nyiszli, Miklos. *Eichmann's Inferno: Auschwitz.* Greenwich, CT: Fawcett, 1960.

Oakes, Jeannie, and Martin Lipton. *Making the Best of Schools: A Handbook for Parents, Teachers, and Policymakers.* New Haven: Yale University Press, 1990.

Olson, Alan. *Transcendence and Hermeneutics: An Interpretation of the Philosophy of Karl Jaspers.* Boston: Martinus Nijhoff Publishers, 1979.

O'Neill, John (Ed.). *On Critical Theory.* New York: Seabury Press, 1976.

O'Malley, John. "Style: The Integration of Action." *Human Context,* July, 1971, 3, pp. 321–338. Abstract from: Silverplatter File: Sociofile Item: 74G8698.

Palmer, Parker J. *To Know as We are Known.* San Francisco: Harper, 1993.

Parks, James. *Anti-Semitism: A Concise World History.* Chicago: Quadrangle, 1964.

Pauchant, Thierry. "Transferential Leadership: Towards a More Complex Understanding of Charisma in Organizations." *Organization Studies, 12/4,* 1991, pp. 507–527.

Paulhus, D., and R. Christie. "Spheres of Control: An Interactionist Apprach to Assessment of Perceived Control." In H.M. Lefcourt (Ed.), *Research with the locus of control construct: Assessment methods* (Volume 1). New York: Academic Press, 1981.

Peck, S. M. *The Different Drum: Community Making and Peace.* New York: Simon and Schuster, Inc., 1987.

_____ . *People of the Lie: The Hope for Healing Human Evil.* New York: Simon and Schuster, Inc., 1983.

Pinson, Koppel S. *Modern Germany: Its History and Civilization.* New York: Macmillan, 1966.

Piszkalski, Henry. *The Personality of Anne Frank in the Light of Karl Jasper's Theory of Extreme Situations.* Washington: Catholic University Press, 1980.

Poliakov, Leon. *Harvest of Hate.* Westport, CT: Greenwood Press, 1954.

_____ . *The History of Anti-Semitism,* Vol. I and II. New York: Vanguard, 1965.

Pommer. "The Legend and Art of Anne Frank." *Judaism,* 9, 1960, pp. 36–46.

Presser, Jacob. *The Destruction of Dutch Jews.* New York: E. P. Dutton, 1969.

Pritchard, John. *Reichstag Fire: Ashes of Democracy.* New York: Ballantine, 1972.

Proctor, Richard. *Nazi Germany.* New York: Holt, Rinehart and Winston, 1970.

Purpel, David E. *The Moral and Spiritual Crisis in Education.* New York: Bergin and Garvey, 1989.

Reitlinger, Gerald. *The Final Solution, 1939–1945.* New York: T. Yoseloff, 1961.

Resnick, Lauren. Introduction. In Lauren Resnick (Ed.) "Knowing, Learning, and Instruction: Essays in Honor of Robert Glasser" pp. 1–24. Hillsdale, NJ: Erlbaum Associates, 1989.

Reuther, Rosemary, and McLaughlin (Eds.). *Women of Spirit: Female Leadership in the Jewish and Christian Traditions.* New York: Simon and Schuster, 1979.

Rieff, Philip. *The Triumph of the Therapeutic: Uses of Faith After Freud.* New York: Harper and Row, 1966.

Rorty, Richard. *Contingency, Irony, and Solidarity.* Cambridge: Cambridge University Press, 1989.

Rubinoff, Lionel. "Technology and Crisis of Rationality: Reflections on the Death and Rebirth of Dialogue." *Philosophy Forum,* 15, 1977, pp. 261–287.

Sacher, Abram Leon. *A History of the Jews.* New York: Knopf, 1970.

Sapp, J.R. *Transcendent Education: A Spirit of Community.* Morgantown: University of West Virginia, 1994.

Sartre, Jean-Paul. *Being and Nothingness.* New York: Washington Square Press, 1966.

Savery, John, and Thomas Duffy. "Problem-based Learning: An Instructional Model and its Constructivist Framework." *Educational Technology,* September-October, 1995, pp. 31–37.

Schnabel, Ernst. *Anne Frank: A Portrait in Courage.* New York: Harcourt, Brace and World, 1958.

Senior, D., M.A. Getty, C. Stuhlmeuller, and J. Collins (Eds.). *The Catholic Study Bible: New American Bible.* New York: Oxford University Press, 1990.

Sergiovanni, T.J. "Leadership as Cultural Expression." In T.J. Sergiovanni and J.E. Corbally (Eds.). *Leadership and Organizational Culture,* pp. 105–114. Chicago: University of Chicago Press, 1984.

Sergiovanni, T. *Building Community in Schools.* San Francisco, Jossey-Bass, 1994.

Shapiro, William. *Trial at Nuremburg* New York: Watts, 1967.

Shelley, M., R. Doebler, P. Woods, and J. Gunden (Eds.) *The Quest Study Bible: New International Version.* Grand Rapids, MI: Zondervan Publishing House, 1995.

Shirer, William. *The Rise and Fall of the Third Reich.* New York: Simon and Schuster, 1960.

Silverman, Judith, ed. *Index to Collective Biographies for Young Readers,* 3rd ed. New York: R. R. Bowker Co., 1979.

Sixel, Friedrich W. "The Problem of Sense: Habermas v. Luhmann." In O'Neill, John (Ed.). *On Critical Theory,* pp. 184–204. New York: Seabury Press, 1976.

Smith, Gene. *Horn of the Moon.* New York: Charterhouse, 1973.

Snyder, Louis B. *Hitler and Nazism.* New York: Bantam Books, 1967.

Speer, Albert. *Infiltration: The SS and German Armament.* New York: Macmillan, 1981.

Steenmeijer, Anna, ed. *A Tribute to Anne Frank.* New York: Doubleday, 1971.

Stevenson, William. *The Bormann Brotherhood.* New York: Harcourt Brace, 1973.

Strike, Kenneth, and Jonas F. Soltis. *Ethics of Teaching.* New York: Teachers College Press, 1992.

Stubbs, Michael. *Discourse Analysis: The Socioloinguistic Analysis of Natural Language.* Chicago: The University of Chicago Press, 1983.

Suhl, Yuri. *They Fought Back: The Story of Jewish Resistance in Nazi Europe.* New York: Schocken Books, Inc., 1975.

Taylor, Charles. *The Ethics of Authenticity.* Cambridge: Harvard University Press, 1991.

Taylor, P., V. Dawson, and B. Fraser. *A Constructivist Perspective on Monitoring Classroom Learning Environments Under Transformation.* Paper presented at the annual meeting of the National Association for Research on Science Teaching (NARST), San Francisco, CA, 1995.

Todres, Leslie. "Psychological and Spiritual Freedoms: Reflections Inspired by Heidegger." *Human Studies,*

July, 1993, *16*, pp. 255–266. Abstract from Silverplatter File: Sociofile Item: 9402076.

Valentin, Hugo. *Anti-Semitism Historically and Critically Examined.* London: Gollancz, 1936.

Ury, W. *Getting Past No.* New York: Bantam Books, 1991.

Van Der Rol, Ruud, and Rian Verhoeven. *Anne Frank Beyond the Diary.* New York: Puffin Books, 1995.

Van Kaam, Adrian (Ed.) *Studies in Formative Spirituality.* Pittsburgh, PA: Institute of Formative Spirituality, Duquesne University, 1982.

Von Glasersfeld, Ernst. "Cognition, Construction of Knowledge, and Teaching." *Synthese,* 1989, 80, pp. 121–140.

Walberg, Herbert J., and Gary Anderson. "Classroom Climate and Individual Learning." *Journal of Educational Psychology,* 1968, 59, pp. 414–419.

Walling, Dana M. *Spirituality and Leadership.* San Diego, CA: University of San Diego, 1995.

Wang, M.C., G.D. Haertel, and J.W. Walberg. "Synthesis of Research: What Helps Students Learn?" *Educational Leadership,* December, 1993/January, 1994, pp. 74–79.

Wiesenthal, Simon. *The Murderers Among Us.* New York: McGraw-Hill, 1973.

Yaseen, Leonard. *The Jesus Connection: To Triumph over Anti-Semitism.* New York: Crosswood Publishing Company, 1985.

Interviews

Bauco van der Wal, Executive Director of the Anne Frank Foundation in Amsterdam, Holland, August 23, 1980.

Popular Periodicals

Brilliant, Moshe. "Anne Frank's Friend." *New York Times Magazine,* April 21, 1957. pp. 30, 32, 34.

deJong, Louis. "Girl Who Was Anne Frank." *Reader's Digest,* Vol. 71, October 1957, pp. 115–20.

Des Pres, T. "Facing Down the Gestapo." *New York Times Book Review,* May 10, 1987, p. 7.

"The Diary of Anne Frank I and II." *Commentary,* Vol. 13, May-June 1951, pp. 419–32, 529–44.

"Distressing Story." *Newsweek,* Vol 39, June 16, 1952, pp. 114–15.

Frank, Otto. "The Living Legacy of Anne Frank." *Ladies' Home Journal,* Vol. 84, No. 9, September 1967, pp. 87, 153–54.

Frank, Otto, as told to N. C. Beth. "Has Germany Forgotten Anne Frank?" *Coronet,* Vol. 47, February 1960, pp. 48–54.

Jerome, Richard. "As She Was: An Oscar-Winning Film Shows the World Anne Frank the Child, More Than Just a Symbol of Innocence Brutalized." *People Weekly,* 1996, pp. 73–76.

Jones, Gaynor. "Anne Frank's Diary: The Epilogue." *Maclean's,* Vol. 93, No. 39, September 29, 1980, pp. 8, 12–13.

Kanin, Garson. "Anne Frank at 50." *Newsweek,* Vol. 93, June 25, 1979, pp. 14–15.

"Lost Child." *Time,* Vol. 59, June 16, 1952, p. 102.

"Milestones: Died, Otto Frank, 91." *Time,* Vol. 116, September 1, 1980, p. 74.

Muhlen, Norbert. "Triumph of Anne Frank." *Commonweal,* Vol. 69, October 31, 1958, pp. 125–26.

Pick, Lies G. "I Knew Anne Frank." *McCall's,* Vol. 85, July 1958, pp. 30–31, 109–11, 114–15.

Schnabel, Ernst. "A Tragedy Revealed: Heroine's Last Days." *Life,* Vol. 45, August 18, 1958, pp. 78–80, 82–90.

Schutzer, Paul. "The Sequel to a Sandbox Snapshot." *Life,* Vol. 47, October 12, 1959, pp. 111–12, 114.

Stang, Joanne. "Stevens Relives Anne Frank's Story." *New York Times Magazine,* August 3, 1958, pp. 14, 50–51.

Waggoner, Walter H. "Anne Frank's Home." *New York Times Magazine,* September 15, 1957, pp. 96, 98.

Yerburgh, M.R. "Biography—the Diary of Anne Frank: The Critical Edition" by Anne Frank and Edited by David Barnouw. *Library Journal,* June 1, 1989, p. 114.

Newspapers

"The Openings: The Diary of Anne Frank." *New York Times*, October 2, 1955, Section 2, p. 1, col. 6.

Atkinson, Brooks. "Inspired Theater: 'Anne Frank's Legacy to the New York Stage.'" *New York Times*, October 16, 1955, Section 2, p. 1, col. 1.

"Susan Strasberg's Arrival as Stage Star to Be Heralded by Marquee Lights Today." *New York Times*, January 25, 1956, p. 25, col. 2.

Funke, Lewis. "News and Gossip Gathered on the Rialto: 'Anne Frank and France.'" *New York Times*, April 22, 1956, Section 2, p. 1, col. 3.

Gelb, Arthur. "Diary Going to Germany." *New York Times*, April 28, 1956, p. 10, col. 8.

"Drama Mailbag: Letter Writers Discuss 'The Diary of Anne Frank' and State Department." *New York Times*, May 6, 1956, Section 2, p. 3, col. 7.

Atkinson, Brooks. "Affair of State: 'Anne Frank' Regarded as Politically Dubious." *New York Times*, June 17, 1956, Section 2, p. 1, col. 1.

Hackett, Frances and Albert. "The Diary of Anne Frank." *New York Times*, September 30, 1956, Section 2, p. 1, col. 1.

"Diary Opens in Europe." *New York Times*, October 2, 1956, p. 39, col. 3.

"Germans Silent at 'Anne Frank': Audiences in Seven Cities Stunned by Play About Jewish Girl—Many Are Ashamed." New York Times, October 3, 1956, p. 30, col. 1.

"Anne Frank in Tokyo." *New York Times*, October 6, 1956, p. 18, col. 6.

"Anne's Homecoming." *New York Times*, October 7, 1956, Section 4, p. 2, col. 4.

Atkinson, Brooks. "Seasonal Blues, Three October Plays: Diary in Germany." *New York Times*, October 14, 1956, Section 2, p. 1, col. 1.

Gilroy, Harry. "Berlin's Diary: German Playgoers Strongly Affected by Recent Opening of Hackett Play." *New York Times*, October 14, 1956, Section 2, p. 3, col. 1.

Waggoner, Walter. "Diary Affects Dutch Audience." *New York Times*, November 29, 1956, p. 43, col. 1.

"'Diary' Seen in Tel Aviv." *New York Times*, January 23, 1957, p. 23, col. 5.

"Anne Frank Memorial Planned." *New York Times*, January 27, 1957, p. 17, col. 2.

Olsen, Arthur J. "Anne Frank Speaks to the Germans." *New York Times*, February 17, 1957, p 5, col. 1.

"The Diary in Israel." *New York Times*, February 17, 1957, Section 6, p. 70, col. 4.

Olsen, Arthur J. "Germans Honor Belsen Victims." *New York Times*, March 18, 1957, p. 27 col. 1.

Brilliant, Moshe. "Anne Frank's Friend." *New York Times*, April 21, 1957, Section 6, p. 30, col. 3.

Waggoner, Walter H. "Anne Frank's Home." *New York Times*, September 15, 1957, Section 6, p. 96, col. 3.

"Anne Frank a Hit in Paris." *New York Times*, October 2, 1957, p. 28, col. 1.

Fremantle, Anne. "Unwritten Pages at the End of the Diary." *New York Times*, September 28, 1958, Section 6, p. 3, col. 1.

"Nobel Winner Gets Award." *New York Times*, December 9, 1958, p. 23, col. 5.

Crowther, Bosley. "The Screen: An Eloquent 'Diary of Anne Frank.'" *New York Times*, March 19, 1959, p. 40, col. 1.

_____ . "Two Girls, Two Films, In Re Audrey Hepburn, Millie Perkins." *New York Times*, March 22, 1959, Section 2, p. 1, col. 8.

"Dutch See 'Anne Frank.'" *New York Times*, April 18, 1959, p. 19, col. 2.

Poor, Charles. "Books of the Times." *New York Times*, September 22, 1959, p. 37, col. 3.

"'Anne Frank' Film Honored." *New York Times*, October 23, 1959, p. 25, col. 2.

"Anne Frank's Diary Investigated." *New York Times*, January 21, 1960, p. 6, col. 4.

"Anne Frank House Opened." *New York Times*, May 4, 1960, p. 11, col. 4.

"Anne Frank Center Is Opened." *New York Times*, May 2, 1961, p. 22, col. 6.

"Kennedy, Praising Anne Frank, Warns of New Nazi-Like Peril." *New York Times*, September 20, 1961, p. 5, col. 4.

"German Teacher Apologizes." *New York Times*, October 18, 1961, p. 28, col. 4.

"Scarsdale Student Troupe Wins Jerusalem Ovation." *New York Times*, July 31, 1962, p. l9, col. 2.

"Pope John Receives the Father of Anne Frank in Private Audience." *New York Times*, April 20, 1963, p. 3, col. 2.

"Amsterdam Getting Anne Frank Cantata." *New York Times*, May 24, 1964, p. 92, col. 4.

"Arrestor of Anne Frank Acquitted of Hiding." *New York Times*, July 2, 1964, p. 4, col. 8.

"Dutch Honor Anne Frank on the Twentieth Anniversary of Her Arrest." *New York Times*, August 5, 1964, p. 50, col. 3.

"Anne Frank Pages Shown." *New York Times*, August 15, 1964, p. 47, col. 2.

"Austrian Court Frees Man Who Arrested Anne Frank." *New York Times*, October 16, 1964, p. 2, col. 7.

"Nazi Who Hunted Dutch Jews Held." *New York Times*, January 14, 1966, p. l0, col. 3.

"Anne Frank Play Staged in Israel." *New York Times*, November 27, 1966, p. 159, col. 3.

"A Play on Anne Frank Theme Given Premiere on French TV." *New York Times*, January 18, 1967, p. 46, col. 1.

"Ex-Nazi on Trial in Dutch Killings." *New York Times*, January 24, 1967, p. l1, col. 1.

"'The Diary of Anne Frank' Introduced at Trial of Nazis." *New York Times*, January 31, 1967, p. 14, col. 8.

"Franks' Betrayer Got Nazi Reward." *New York Times*, February 1, 1967, p. 12, col. 3.

Stang, Joanne. "Anne Frank's 'Diary' Lives Again." *New York Times*, February 12, 1967, Section 2, p. 21, col. 4.

"Three SS Sentenced in Death of Jews." *New York Times*, February 25, 1967, p. 1, col. 7.

Gent, George. "TV Review: 'Diary of Anne Frank' Well Done by ABC." *New York Times*, November 27, 1967, p. 94, col. 3.

"Dutch Get Wax Museum." *New York Times*, November 1, 1970, Section 5, p. 14, col. 6.

"Notes on People: Otto Frank." *New York Times*, March 15, 1977, p. 31, col. 3.

Godfrey, Peter. "How Anne Frank's Father Had Made Sure That the World Will Not Forget." *London Times*, April 16, 1977, p. 12, col. a.

"Man Who Hid Anne Frank Family Wins a $10,000 Ideal Award." *New York Times*, June 5, 1978, Section 2, p. 2, col. 4.

"Anne Frank's Father Backs 'Holocaust' (TV Screening)." *London Times*, February 27, 1979, p. 4, col. b.

"Anne Frank Exhibit Opens." *London Times*, March 23, 1979, p. 15, col. e.

Borders, William. "Memories of Anne Frank on Fiftieth Birthday." *New York Times*, June 13, 1979, p. 3, col. 1.

Reiter, Ed. "A Medal for Anne Frank." *New York Times*, January 27, 1980, Section 2, p. 41, col. 1.

"Otto Frank, Father of Anne Frank, Dead at 91." *New York Times*, August 21, 1980, Section 4, p. 17, col. 4.

"Full Diary of Anne Frank to Appear for First Time." *New York Times*, February 2, 1981, Section 3, p. 16, col. 2.

Montgomery, P.L. "Drafting an Epilogue to Anne Frank's Diary." *New York Times*, June 18, 1989, p. 27.

Glass, S. "Remembering Anne Frank." *New York Times*, November 6, 1994, p. D22.

"Anne Frank's Friend To Read Diary Excerpts." *New York Times*, March 7, 1995, p. C16.

Kaufman, M.T. "The Woman Who Saved the Diary of a Young Girl." *New York Times*, March 11, 1995, p. A27.

Buckvar, F. "Anne Frank's Diary Prompts a Visit." *New York Times*, March 12, 1995, p. WC11.

Petrakis, J. "'Anne Frank' Weaves a Powerful Tapestry of Facts." *Chicago Tribune*, March 22, 1996, p. D5.

Masters, K. "Anne Frank and the Reluctant Documentarian." *Washington Post*, April 7, 1996, p. G4.

Photos

1. Anne Frank at school.

2. Sign in a public park in Nazi-occupied Holland which reads "Jews Forbidden Here."

3. Yellow Star of David which Dutch Jews were forced to wear on their clothing. The lettering in the center reads "Jew."

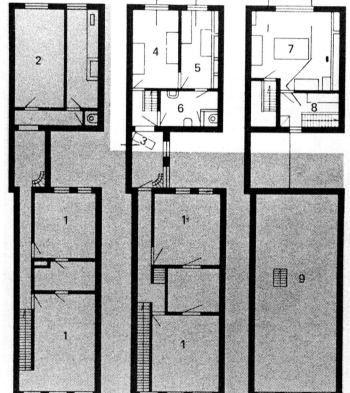

4. Floor plan of the building at Prinsengracht 263, including the Secret Annexe.

© 1984, 1998 J. Weston Walch, Publisher

The World of Anne Frank: A Complete Resource Guide

5. Bookcase door to the Secret Annexe closed, seen from the outside.

6. Bookcase door to the Secret Annexe opened, showing steps to the Annexe.

7. Mr. Frank and his main helpers. Left to right—
front: **Miep, Mr. Frank, Elli;** *back:* **Mr. Koophuis, Mr. Kraler**

8. Nazi soldiers patrolling the streets of Amsterdam.

9. Bergen-Belsen at liberation.